GOOD
—— *for* ——
BUSY PEOPLE

GOOD FOOD
for
BUSY PEOPLE

Sarah Woodward

BOXTREE

First published 1994 in hardback by Macmillan Publishers Ltd.

This paperback edition first published 1996 by Boxtree, an imprint of Macmillan Publishers Ltd, 25 Eccleston Place, London, SW1W 9NF and Basingstoke.

Associated companies throughout the world

ISBN 0 7522 0534 X

9 8 7 6 5 4 3 2 1

A CIP catalogue entry for this book is available from the British Library

Designed and typeset by TJ Graphics

Printed by

CONTENTS

INTRODUCTION

We have all experienced the tedium of preparing yet another meal – not an elaborate three courses for a dinner party, but the ordinary cooking involved in making a nutritious (and interesting) main dish for every day. What can I possibly do to this chicken breast to make it a bit more exciting? How can I grill another pork chop without going mad? Why on earth did I buy eggs? You know the feeling – what can I cook that tastes delicious but doesn't take much time?

However, the production of everyday suppers need not become a chore. Basic ingredients can be prepared in different ways without entailing extra hours in the kitchen. A willingness to draw on culinary habits outside British traditions, a judicious use of spices and herbs, above all confidence and a desire to experiment, can bring a re-awakening in the kitchen.

The aim of this book is to provide easy-to-execute and relatively rapid main course recipes centred on the basic components of today's shopping basket (or rather, supermarket trolley). The list of key ingredients is much wider than it would have been a few decades ago, reflecting the global nature of today's food supply and the change in our eating habits; and because we no longer think a main meal must involve a piece of meat or fish, the book includes plenty of recipes based on vegetables, eggs and cheese.

The cooking techniques used are not difficult, and all the recipes are graded according to the degree of skill required, from basic (which means very basic) to easy, to moderate. None of the recipes would be unapproachable after a long day at the office or looking after the family. The range of ingredients required is rarely large, although many of the dishes do call for a good selection of herbs and spices. Many of the recipes could happily take their place on the dinner party table (no puddings are included, but some of the recipes can be used as either a starter or a main course), but they are all intended just as much for everyday eating. The message is simple – good food doesn't have to take time.

A note on quantities and oven temperatures
All recipes serve 4, unless otherwise stated.

Quantities are given in imperial and metric measures. Try not to mix the two. For each recipe you should use either imperial or metric measures, not a combination of the two. A wineglass, in my recipes, holds 6 fluid ounces (175ml). Teaspoons should be level, not heaped.

Oven temperatures are given in Centigrade, Farenheit and Gas Mark. Ovens vary enormously in their efficiency – you know your oven best and may like to make adjustments accordingly.

Shopping

In the perfect culinary world we would all shop little and often, popping round daily to our local shops to pick from the freshest ingredients (which would of course be readily available, with plenty of seasonal and regional produce). Instead we find ourselves loading up the trolley on the weekly or even monthly journey to the supermarket, to fill the fridge and the freezer back home.

There is a balance between these two extremes which many of us try to achieve. Relying on supermarkets for both basics and exotica, we can still support specialist retailers and visit local markets from time to time to stay in touch with seasonality and obtain local produce. In particular, I buy my fish from the fishmonger. The supermarkets, which have achieved so much in broadening the range of foods available to us, still have some work to do in this department.

But wherever and whenever you shop, it is important to be able to choose the best. Do not be frightened to sniff, poke and squeeze to assess the ripeness of fruit and vegetables – this can be especially important at your local greengrocer, who may tolerate longer shelf-lives than the supermarkets. Avoid retailers who object to such behaviour – they have something to hide. Look at packing dates to get the freshest eggs, check that your pasta is labelled 100% durum wheat, examine the ingredients before choosing that ready-prepared meal. Above all, be fussy.

Be adventurous, too. As a child when travelling I was always told to pick from the menu something that I hadn't eaten before and now I apply the same rule when I go shopping. The supermarkets offer an ever-expanding range of ingredients from around the world, some of which will be new to you. Take them home and try them out rather than sticking to old favourites. You will be rewarded with new taste experiences, some of which will become new favourites.

However well you shop, there will be times when you have nothing but odds and ends and store-cupboard ingredients in the house. Many of the recipes in this book are intended for just those moments.

Store-cupboard Ingredients

The store-cupboard is the key to good food for busy people. First and most important are the spices, which allow you to give a variety of tastes to the same piece of meat or fish: think of the difference between a salmon steak poached with star anise and the same piece of salmon grilled with a spicy coating of coriander and cardamom, strips of steak sprinkled with sesame seeds or coated in crushed black peppercorns, chicken breasts braised with saffron or chargrilled and sprinkled with toasted cumin seeds.

Pasta and rice ensure that you can always produce a meal when you haven't been shopping, especially if you have a tin or two of Italian plum tomatoes to supply a sweet sauce, or a stock cube and a pinch of saffron for a risotto. Olive oil provides a cooking medium, a flavouring agent, an irreplaceable gloss. Cans of beans and petits pois are instantly acceptable vegetables while jars of artichoke hearts, olives and sun-dried tomatoes provide pre-dinner nibbles. For piquancy and flavour look for vinegars, Worcestershire or soy sauce, or the kick of Tabasco.

It is worth investing time in making sure your store-cupboard is well stocked if you want to have choice when you are under pressure – or simply when you are bored with your normal repertoire. By definition stores keep, so wastage is not a problem – except in the case of spices, which will turn stale if not kept tightly sealed.

ANCHOVIES The nicest anchovies are those preserved in salt rather than olive oil. They require thorough rinsing, or even soaking, before use and are good enough to be eaten all on their own. The contents of a small tin or jar of anchovies has all sorts of uses: to liven up a pizza, to make anchovy butter for fish or steak, perhaps to add substance and flavour to a salad, to fill quarters of baked red peppers, or simply to form a part of a little dish of antipasti.

ARTICHOKE HEARTS Artichoke hearts preserved in olive oil are excellent as antipasti, for salads, even in cooking. I prefer those in glass jars to those in tins. Once opened, they should be kept in the fridge and used relatively rapidly.

BAMBOO SHOOTS Tinned bamboo shoots are a useful store-cupboard vegetable to add to a stir-fry. They have a particular affinity with chicken and pork.

BEANS Tinned beans provide easily accessible bulk for soups and salads, cassoulets and casseroles. White haricot beans are good with sausages and pork, while green flageolets are the ideal side dish for lamb; cannellini and borlotti beans both feature large in Italian cooking, whether it be for Tuscan bean soup or as an antipasto with tuna fish; red kidney beans are a feature of many Caribbean and Central American dishes, from the simple beans and rice to the elaborate chile con carne. The only bean I am not fond of is the butter bean, but that is purely personal. Although dried beans tend to have a better texture when cooked, obviously their use is impractical when you are in a hurry.

BURGHUL Burghul or cracked wheat needs only brief soaking before use and is a useful way of supplying bulk with minimum effort. It is most familiar in the Middle Eastern salad, tabbouleh, where it should be interspersed with a large quantity of fresh herbs, but it can also be used in hot dishes such as pilavs.

CAPERS Like anchovies, capers are nicest when preserved in salt, in which case they need 10 minutes soaking before use. Those pickled in vinegar have a tendency to taste of little else. Capers are useful for adding a piquant flavour to a sauce or stuffing.

CHICKPEAS Cans of chickpeas allow you to make hommos and couscous in a hurry, and that is not the end of their use in the culinary repertoire. Dishes from Provence to India, Spain to Turkey make wide use of the seeds of this native plant of Asia and Southern Europe and you should not be without a tin or two. As with beans, dried chickpeas have a better texture when cooked, as well as providing you with useful chickpea water. The lengthy soaking they need; though; is not always practical.

CHILLI SAUCE There are many different kinds of chilli sauce available. Some blow your head off, others add just a touch of warmth on the tongue. I generally find the West Indian hot pepper sauces too fierce, preferring Chinese sweet and hot chilli sauce, but you must experiment to find the one you prefer. The chilli sauce fanatic might like to keep both types, varying their use according to the provenance of the dish.

COCONUT MILK A tin of coconut milk is a useful item to have in the store-cupboard, to be used in South Indian curries, Caribbean dishes or even puddings – try whipping together sweetened chestnut purée and coconut milk.

COUSCOUS Quick-cook couscous, which can require as little as 10 minutes steaming, is now widely available. Although the vegetable stews traditionally· served with couscous are time-consuming affairs to prepare, steamed couscous liberally coated in butter or olive oil makes a good side dish for a wide variety of meats. It is especially popular with spicy sausages.

DRIED FRUITS Dried fruits are useful in many savoury dishes as well as sweet ones. Those I use most often in cooking are apricots (buy the presoaked variety to save time), dates and raisins.

DRIED MUSHROOMS Less than 1oz (30g) of dried mushrooms will be sufficient to flavour a risotto for 2 people, making this one of the most rewarding of store-cupboard ingredients in terms of the ratio of space to results. Dried wild mushrooms are the nicest – ceps, horn of plenty, chanterelles and morels all dry well, although they are expensive. Dried wild mushrooms rehydrate surprisingly quickly – do not soak them for more than 15 minutes or so or they will lose their flavour, and always be sure to use the soaking water in the recipe. Dried Chinese mushrooms are useful for stir-fries.

FLOURS Cornflour is commonly used as a thickening agent in Chinese cooking and it is useful to have a small packet in the cupboard when it comes to stir-fries. Strong plain white flour is a wise buy for making flat bread and pizzas, which need only 30 minutes or so to rise before cooking. Wholemeal flour is good for bread, but it is a mistake to substitute it for white flour in thickening casseroles or for a coating prior to frying. Personally I find wholemeal pastry leaden, and dread being presented with a wholemeal quiche.

HARISSA A small tin of the red hot North African chilli paste is useful for flavouring couscous and other spicy stews.

HERBS (DRIED) Of course we all prefer to use fresh herbs, and for those without gardens or green fingers this is a great deal easier today due to the year-round availability of packaged herbs from the supermarket. Some herbs dry reasonably well however, and are useful out of season. Dried bay leaves and rosemary can be excellent; freeze-dried chives, oregano, tarragon and thyme are useful. Many Turkish dishes require the use of dried rather than fresh mint for authenticity. Sage is less successful when dried, tending to be rather musty, and basil, chervil, coriander and parsley should only be used fresh.

HONEY Clear honey provides an impromptu glaze for a piece of lamb, pork or duck and a sweetening agent for sauces. The nicest honeys are those with a distinctive flower flavour, reflecting the feeding grounds of the bees.

LENTILS Shaking off their dowdy image, lentils cooked in stock and wine and finished with butter and parsley or a slick of oil have now become an acceptable restaurant side dish, particularly for fish, game or poultry. They also make a good base for soups and winter salads – try tossing crispy lardons of bacon into warm lentils cooked with garlic and a few carrots and dressing the whole with a mustard vinaigrette. Lentils cook in 30 minutes provided they are fresh but older ones can take much longer to become al dente, so buy in small quantities. The best lentils are the grey-green ones from Puy in France.

MUSTARDS There is a significant difference in flavour and fierceness between English and French (i.e. Dijon) mustard. In dishes calling for plenty of mustard I usually use the Dijon variety, but I also keep a small tin of English mustard powder so that I can add a pinch to salad dressings. The mild grainy mustard known as *moutarde de Meaux* is useful for adding sharpness to creamy sauces (try it with kidneys or in a white sauce for boiled ham), and German and Scandinavian mustards have a distinctively sweet character which is difficult to replace when preparing dishes originating in those countries – gravadlax sauce, for example, needs a sweet mustard.

NOODLES Chinese egg noodles are useful for soups, and to stir-fry with vegetables. For stir-frying, they must of course be first boiled or steamed. I am also fond of shrimp-flavoured noodles and rice vermicelli.

NUTS Nuts make a difference to many savoury dishes, especially when combined with dried fruits. My store-cupboard contains almonds (both whole blanched ones and flaked almonds), cashew nuts, hazelnuts, pinenuts, pistachios and whole walnuts. The pinenuts, unfortunately one of the most expensive, are my favourite, especially when lightly toasted and sprinkled over salad leaves.

OILS *Olive oil* is the one I most use most frequently, not just for dressings but as a cooking medium. It is a mistake to think that you can substitute sunflower for olive oil when frying certain dishes where the oily juices from the pan form the basis for the sauce. You should use an inexpensive 'plain' oil for cooking, keeping the extra virgin oil for salad dressings and for dishes which are finished with a dribble of olive oil. Fanatics like me may choose to keep two (or more) grades of extra virgin oil: one supermarket brand for everyday use and one estate-bottled cold-pressed oil for treats.

Sunflower oil has a neutral taste and is good combined half and half with olive oil in salad dressings and mayonnaise, when olive oil alone can have too powerful a flavour.

Groundnut oil is the best for stir-frying and deep-frying (except when cooking vegetable fritters or fish for an Italian *fritto misto*, in which case olive oil is necessary).

Mustard oil gives an authentic flavour to Bengali-style curries.

Nut oils, hazelnut and walnut, make special salad dressings. They are expensive but a small amount packs plenty of flavour. Roasted red peppers with a dribble of walnut oil and a squeeze of lemon are particularly good.

Sesame oil is important in many stir-fried dishes, when a little is added towards the end of cooking to give a distinctive flavour. It is particularly widely used in Korean cookery.

OLIVES Olives are good not just to nibble before the meal but as an ingredient in their own right. In Provence, a few olives are often a last-minute addition to a pasta sauce, a rabbit casserole or a roast fillet of lamb, where they provide texture, flavour and visual appeal. The best olives are preserved in their own oil rather than brine; I find the unpitted ones tend to have more flavour, and certainly keep their shape better during cooking. Wrinkly black olives and firm green ones, tinned or bottled, are both useful in the store-cupboard. I am less than convinced by olive paste, which tends to taste rather sour. If you want paste, it is a matter of moments to process pitted black olives with olive oil, adding your own seasoning at the same time.

PASTA Pasta is the friend of the cook who has not had time to do the shopping. With a packet of dried pasta and one or two simple store-cupboard ingredients such as tinned tomatoes, eggs and bacon, or even just garlic, chilli and olive oil, you can always produce a meal.

Dried pasta should be made from 100% durum wheat. It is now available in myriad shapes and sizes, designed not just for visual appeal but to suit different kinds of sauces. Slippery spaghetti offsets the crisp bits of bacon and lightly scrambled egg of carbonara; quill-shaped penne is perfect for a chilli-hot tomato sauce, which will insinuate itself into the hollows of the pasta; lady-like farfalle, with its egg-timer waist, suits smoked salmon. Creamy sauces in general go well with tagliatelle, shellfish with spaghetti. Thick flat pappardelle is classically combined with hare sauce. Stuffed pasta like tortelloni, agnolotti, cappelletti and ravioli generally needs little sauce, just a touch of butter and herbs, a swirl of cream or a dollop of fresh tomato.

The shape of pasta also affects the way it is cooked. You would not bake long thin pasta but you can put boiled macaroni or rigatoni in the oven. Small solid pastas like the 'tiny ears' of orecchiette or the squares of quadrucci are good in soups.

I prefer to use good quality dried pasta to the 'fresh' chilled pasta, which is hardly ever seen in Italy. True fresh pasta, either made yourself or bought from an Italian delicatessen, is quite another matter and needs only the briefest cooking, preferably on the day it is made or at least bought. Fresh pasta can be flavoured with spinach (pasta verde), tomato for a red colour, even with squid ink for sinister black. Dried flavoured pasta is less successful, relying more on colour than on extra taste.

As a general rule, allow 3–4oz (85–115g) of pasta per head for a generous main course serving. Always cook the pasta in plenty of water, 5¼ – 8 pints (3–4 litres) to cook sufficient pasta for 4 people. The water should be well salted, but the addition of oil is unnecessary. Make sure the water is boiling fiercely before you add the pasta and stir the pasta well once you have put it in the pan, to prevent it sticking.

Cooking times for dried pasta are impossible to give. The time taken will depend on the shape, the manufacturer and the freshness. Look at the instructions on the packet and start tasting several minutes before the recommended cooking time is reached. If you are using 'fresh' chilled pasta, you may find you need to cook it longer than the instructions on the packet. Freshly-made pasta rarely requires more than a few minutes. Whatever the variety, the pasta should, we all know, be al dente or firm to the tooth, but the definition of when this state is reached is highly personal.

When you drain the pasta, do not try to get rid of every drop of water – it should remain slightly moist. Stir in a knob of butter or a swirl of olive oil before adding the sauce.

PETITS POIS Petits pois are the only tinned vegetables apart from tomatoes and beans which find their way into my store-cupboard. They make an excellent quick vegetable dish when heated with a sliver or two of garlic, a tablespoon of crème fraîche and plenty of freshly ground black pepper. You can also try stirring a few shreds of lettuce into the pan just before serving.

POLENTA This staple of Northern Italy has become fashionable in recent years, and is often served at outrageous prices in trendy eateries. In fact it is cheap and simple to make, provided you have the rapid cooking variety. I have found, however, that the proportions of polenta to water given in the instructions on some brands tend to be over-generous towards the polenta, resulting in too stodgy a consistency, so err on the light side. Any left-over polenta can be cut into slabs, brushed with oil and grilled until crispy on the surface – in fact, I prefer my polenta this way to the hot, gloopy mixture with lashings of butter.

RICE Just as you wouldn't want only one type of pasta in the store-cupboard, nor should you have only one type of rice. The different varieties of rice vary enormously in their shape, size and cooking properties. Try making risotto without using Arborio, Carnaroli or Vialone rice and you will be in trouble, for the grains will not swell sufficiently to absorb the liquid; but if you try to boil Arborio rice like the long-grain type you will end up with a sticky mess.

The rice I use most often is the small-grained Basmati rice, whose use need not be restricted to curries and Middle Eastern dishes. One of the nicest ways of cooking it is Persian fashion: the rice is briefly boiled and then put in a heavy casserole with plenty of butter, a teatowel below the lid, the rice left for 30 minutes or so over the lowest possible heat to steam in its own liquid, the butter forming a crispy base. Another good way to cook Basmati is to measure three times the quantity of water to rice, boil it for a minute and then cover the pan and leave it over a low heat until all the water is absorbed. It is very important if using either of these cooking methods to make sure the rice is very thoroughly washed beforehand, to rid it of excess starch.

A small packet of wild rice is useful for exotic stuffings. Brown rice may be healthy, but personally I don't like the flavour, so there is none in my cupboard.

SALT I prefer to use coarse sea salt which has been naturally dried, and keep a large jar by the hob so that I can throw in a pinch or a handful as necessary. This salt can also be put in a grinder to allow diners to add more if necessary when the meal is served (after they have taken their first bite – nothing is more irritating to the cook than to see food being salted before being tasted). Bay salt is useful for some dishes, such as prawns grilled whole in their shells – pop a few fresh bay leaves in the jar and leave for a week or two for the flavour to permeate the salt.

SOY SAUCES The plethora of choice in the supermarkets means that you can now choose whether you want Japanese or Chinese soy sauce, Indonesian or Thai. Although each does have a distinctive style, it would be ridiculous to expect the casual cook to keep all in stock. I settle for light and dark soy sauces, a distinction which is useful – the dark version, which is more fermented, is sweeter and more powerful (the Japanese Kikkoman brand is especially good).

SPICES Vital for variety, spices are the key to many of the recipes in this book. Those I consider essential in the store-cupboard are allspice berries, cumin seeds, cayenne pepper, cinnamon (ground and in sticks), cloves, coriander (seeds and ground), nutmeg, ground ginger, paprika, saffron, turmeric and of course black peppercorns. Also very useful are caraway, cardamom, juniper berries, fennel, fenugreek, mustard seeds, sesame seeds and mace. In general I keep spices in their whole form, roasting and grinding them as needed in a coffee grinder kept especially for this purpose. The berries and seeds stay fresh for much longer than the ready ground variety, and the process takes little time.

STOCK (CUBES AND HOME-MADE) Stock cubes are perfectly good in many dishes, although they are no substitute for the real home-made variety. If you do have a spare moment in the kitchen and some bones, a carcass or vegetables to hand, it is worth making a few batches of stock for the freezer, so you can turn out, say, a sensational risotto at short notice. The ready-made stocks known as *fonds de cuisine* now available in some supermarkets are good for enriching sauces, but too expensive for use in large quantities. The reality is that four times out of five you will use a stock cube, and shouldn't feel guilty about it. Do, however, remember to moderate the amount of added salt when cooking with stock cubes.

SUGAR A pinch of sugar is useful in salad dressings, to bring out the flavour of a tomato sauce, combined with vinegar in sweet and sour dishes, in marinades. In most savoury dishes I use granulated white sugar, although I prefer demerara sugar for puddings.

TABASCO Tabasco is named after the Mexican state which provided the hot pepper which Mr McIlhenny of Louisiana used in the 1860s as a basis for his now world-famous sauce. Tabasco should be used in cooking along the Bloody Mary principle – a few drops of Tabasco to give the final kick.

TINNED TOMATOES, PASSATA, TOMATO PASTE, SUN-DRIED TOMATOES Canned Italian plum tomatoes would be the very first thing I would buy for my store-cupboard if I was forced to build it up from scratch. With a tin of tomatoes you can make a sauce for pasta, meat, fish or vegetables with the minimum of fuss and extra ingredients. I am not however a fan of tinned tomatoes with added flavourings such as garlic or herbs – better to add your own, which is not exactly time-consuming and will make the taste far fresher. The same goes for passata (sieved tomato purée).

Tomato paste is useful for adding to fresh tomato sauces to back up the flavour. A teaspoon whipped into plain yoghurt or stock gives colour as well as extra taste. I prefer to buy paste in tubes so that you can use it little and often.

Sun-dried tomatoes are rarely used in cooking in Italy, being preferred as an antipasto, but elsewhere in the world they have become part of many modish recipes. I usually buy them preserved in oil to allow me to use them straight away when I need them.

TINNED TUNA Small tins of high-quality tuna, preferably preserved in oil, are an important addition to the store-cupboard, providing the base for pasta sauces, salads, or a classic sauce for veal.

VINEGARS Vinegar is not just for salad dressings – it can be added in small quantities at the end of cooking to give bite to a sauce, and can even be a cooking medium. There is a huge choice of vinegars on offer, which can be confusing to the uninitiated. I regard red and white wine vinegars, Spanish sherry vinegar and balsamic vinegar from Modena as essentials; useful extras are cider, raspberry, rice wine, shallot and tarragon vinegars. You may like to flavour your own white wine vinegar – stick a branch of tarragon or a shallot or two in the bottle and leave for a few weeks for the flavour to infuse.

WINE (RED, WHITE, SHERRY, VERMOUTH, CHINESE AND JAPANESE WINES) The idea of 'cooking wine' is anathema. There is only one type of wine, and that is for drinking. If you can't drink it, don't cook with it, because it won't add anything to the food and is more likely to have a negative effect. If you are buying wine specially for a recipe, then by all means choose one from the region in which the dish originated, but there is no need to be slavish about this – simply use something drinkable and you won't go far wrong.

Fortified wines like sherry and vermouth are sensible additions to the store-cupboard; just a small quantity will add its distinctive flavour to a dish. It is no use trying to cook scallops au Noilly with white wine and herbs – the flavour of the classic vermouth Noilly Prat is difficult to imitate. I also keep the bone-dry fino and the dry but full oloroso sherries for cooking with as well as drinking. Do remember that sherry does not keep indefinitely once opened, as many people seem to believe. A week in the fridge is its absolute maximum of life, so it is sensible to buy sherry in half bottles, as the Spaniards do (and they should know).

Chinese rice wine and *Japanese sake* are again hard to replace for flavour and are worth acquiring in small bottles from specialist shops if you plan to cook many dishes from these countries.

WORCESTERSHIRE SAUCE The exact recipe for Worcestershire sauce may be a secret, but labelling requirements mean we now know the ingredients – two vinegars, molasses, well-matured anchovies, tamarind, shallots and garlic all contribute to the unmistakable flavour. A dribble of Worcestershire sauce can lift a casserole or a tomato sauce; it also makes a good base for dipping sauces.

Perishable Essentials

As well as store-cupboard ingredients, there are those foodstuffs which do not keep forever but which are used so widely that you should try always to have them in your fridge. In the ideal culinary world, I would never be without the following:

BACON Traditionally cured bacon is quite different in flavour, texture and behaviour in the pan from the processed bacon produced from intensively reared pigs. Good bacon should have plenty of fat, which provides the flavour; it should be dark in colour rather than too pink; it will have a firm, meaty texture rather than a flaccid feel; and most important of all, it will give off fat rather than water in the pan. I prefer to buy bacon in one large slice – say 12oz (350g) – and cut it to the required thickness; I find this useful as I prefer in general to use oblong cubes of bacon (lardons) rather than thin slices.

Some supermarkets now offer the Italian pancetta in this form, as well as selling ready-prepared lardons. Look out also for their 'traditional cure' bacon. A well-cured piece of bacon will keep in the fridge for several weeks. Bacon is so useful in enlivening a wide variety of ingredients that I regard it as an essential item in the kitchen.

BREAD One of the foodie features of the last ten years is the number of fancy breads which have become available, not just in smart delicatessens but in supermarkets across the country. No longer do you simply have to make a choice between white or brown, stick or loaf, you can choose between olive oil breads from the south of Europe and rye breads from the north, breads flavoured with sun-dried tomato or studded with olives, fruit and nut breads, part or fully baked baguettes (sometimes even distinguished between French and 'English' style depending on the flour and salt used), *pugliese* bread from Italy or *pain de campagne* from France, or flat breads, from focaccia to nan. Although few of these breads closely resemble those available in their purported country of origin, their appearance is to be welcomed, as in any widening of choice.

Many breads can be successfully frozen and reheated, making them useful back-ups. A slice of two of ciabatta, a few antipasti, and you have a smart starter. Nut breads are very good served with cheese. And the country breads are excellent for cooking – you can't make an Italian bread and tomato soup with your typical British white loaf.

BUTTER I keep only unsalted butter, preferring to add my own salt as needed. It can be useful to prepare clarified butter for cooking. Simply melt the butter and skim off the scum, or, better still, strain the melted fat through muslin.

Clarified butter will keep for some time in the fridge. If you have no clarified butter, add a little oil to the butter in the pan to prevent it from burning.

For curry fans, it is a good idea to keep a jar of ghee, Indian clarified butter. Its nutty flavour is unmistakable and it keeps longer in the fridge than ordinary butter.

CHILLIES Chillies vary in size and shape, colour and flavour and above all in degree of heat; and there is a huge range. It is important to match the right chilli to the right dish – small, dried red chillies for a pasta sauce from southern Italy, very hot round red bell pepper chillies for Caribbean dishes, small fierce green chillies for some curries and large, mild ones for others. Whether you leave the seeds of the chilli in or not will also have a significant effect on how hot the eventual dish is. One word of caution – when preparing chillies always make sure you wash your hands well afterwards, as chilli juice is extremely painful if it gets in your eyes.

The ones I use most regularly are both small and large dried red chillies (which keep for months) and small fresh green chillies which will keep for a week or two in the fridge. I also make chilli oil, which can be very useful for stir-frying. Heat ½ pint (300ml) of groundnut oil, add 20 or so small dried red chillies and leave to steep. Chilli oil is available in supermarkets, as are various kinds of chilli sauce.

CITRUS FRUITS I always have lemons, limes and oranges available, as their juice can make all the difference to a sauce, a marinade or a salad dressing. Orange juice is good with pork and some fish such as tuna and salmon; a piece of the rind makes a big difference to a beef casserole. Lemons are especially important when cooking fish, whether as a few slices popped in the cavity of a whole fish to go under the grill, or as the key constituent of a marinade to 'cook' raw fish. I often use lemon juice for a touch of sharpness to cut through a lamb or chicken casserole. Limes are important in many ethnic dishes, and again go well with fish. The juice of each can be used with olive oil to dress salads: orange for watercress and root vegetables, lemon for artichokes, asparagus and spinach, lime with beetroot and broccoli. If you are planning to use the zest of the fruit, try to buy the unwaxed variety.

FRESH GINGER Fresh ginger is very different from the dry powdered spice and there is no substitute for its lemony, mildly hot flavour. A small piece of fresh ginger root will keep for several weeks in the fridge, and I make sure there is always some there. To prepare ginger, remove the skin with a sharp knife and chop the flesh very finely; alternatively, grate the peeled ginger on the finest holes of the grater, to release the juice but leave behind the fibrous strands of the root.

As with garlic, the length of time you cook ginger affects the degree of flavour. Chopped ginger in stir-frying or a marinade, or a touch of ginger juice added at the end of cooking will give a more prominent taste of the root than that added at the beginning of preparing a slow-cooking casserole or curry.

GARLIC I use garlic a lot and always have plenty in the kitchen. The drier heads keep well (think of all those strings of garlic hanging from kitchen walls), but the fat and juicy new season's garlic should be used relatively rapidly. You should discard any garlic which has started to shoot.

ONIONS (RED AND WHITE) and SHALLOTS Onions are essential to so many dishes that my kitchen is never without them. They keep well but you should discard any which have started to sprout. I generally use the large mild Spanish onions rather than the fiercer smaller varieties. The fascinating thing about onions is the gradation of their flavour depending on how long they have been cooked: briefly fried onions, which have barely turned translucent, add a completely different taste to a dish than the sweetness of those which have been slowly stewed until they are meltingly tender and lightly browned.

I am fond of red onions, which are particularly good in salads: a tomato and onion salad made with the traditional British white onion simply doesn't work, as the onion overpowers rather than complements the tomato, whereas a red onion, as would be used in Italy, is the perfect foil.

I find raw spring onions too harsh but cooking brings out their sweetness. Try chargrilling whole spring onions to serve alongside a piece of duck or chicken. Of course spring onions are vital to many stir-fried dishes.

Shallots should not be allowed to brown during cooking or they will turn bitter. They are expensive but not many are needed as they add a distinctive flavour. A few chopped shallots briefly fried, the pan deglazed with vinegar, make a rapid sauce for meat; whole shallots roasted in their skins are a good side dish for lamb. Shallot butter and vinegar are both excellent.

PARMESAN CHEESE If it is not marked Parmigiano Reggiano it's not the real thing and your tastebuds will suffer accordingly. Real Parmesan is expensive, but you don't need a great quantity to make a difference to a dish. I prefer to buy a hunk of Parmesan and grate off a little as I need it – Parmesan will keep for weeks wrapped up in greaseproof paper in the fridge. Make sure, if you have the choice, that you buy the more mature, harder cheese designed for cooking rather than softer cheese meant for eating straight.

POULTRY
AND
GAME

CHICKEN

There is a tendency among food writers to harp on about the taste advantages of corn-fed, free-range chicken, so to save you the tedium I shall note only that it is worth the considerable extra expense. Of course, the more people who buy well-reared birds, the cheaper they will become. So please, be selective in your chicken – your choice will benefit all of us who care not just about animal welfare but about the availability and price of real food.

BREAST

Chicken breast is the most popular choice for a simple supper, but it is actually rather difficult to cook well. There is a fine balance between undercooked chicken breast, which is emphatically to be avoided due to the risk of salmonella, and dry, overcooked meat. Chicken breast grilled without its skin is good for you but it can be woolly and tasteless. For improved results, protect the surface of the meat with a smear of powerfully flavoured sauce, for example mustard or hoisin, or stuff the centre with a flavoured butter so that the fat drips through, keeping the meat juicy. When cooking in a frying-pan or wok, briefly sear the meat and then simmer it in a little flavoured liquid, or fry it as briefly as possible in very hot oil. Better still, marinate the breast first. And for kebabs choose boneless chicken thighs rather than breast meat.

Grilled Chicken Breasts with a Dijon Mustard and Tarragon Sauce

The pale Dijon mustard of France has a light touch of tarragon, which makes it ideal for combining with that herb in a cream sauce for chicken. If you can't get *crème fraîche*, the slightly sour flavour of which is good with mustard, make sure you use double cream or the sauce will curdle when you boil it. For added piquancy, the chicken breasts themselves are rubbed with a little mustard before grilling. If you have some available, throw a few halved and seeded white grapes into the sauce just before serving.

Preparation time: 10 minutes
Cooking time: 15 minutes
Grade: basic

Suggested accompaniment: boiled long-grain rice, to which strips of green pepper are added a couple of minutes before draining

4 teaspoons plus ½ tablespoon Dijon mustard (do not substitute English mustard as it is too hot)	salt and freshly ground black pepper
4 skinless chicken breasts	1 tablespoon chopped fresh tarragon or 1 teaspoon dried tarragon
8fl oz (250ml) *crème fraîche*	
1 glass dry white wine	

● Smear a teaspoon of mustard all over each chicken breast and leave to stand for 10 minutes. Pre-heat the grill to maximum.

● Grill the chicken breasts for 5 minutes on either side and leave to rest for a minute or two before serving. While the chicken is grilling, make the sauce: mix together the *crème fraîche*, the wine and the remaining mustard, bring to the boil, stirring, then turn down to a simmer for 10 minutes. Season to taste and stir in the chopped tarragon just before serving.

Chicken Breasts with Herb Butter on Ciabatta

America has always had a passion for meat on bread, and in recent years the West Coast in particular has embraced Italian breads to make their own Cal-Ital sandwiches. This recipe comes from that innovation, livening up grilled chicken breasts with butter and fresh herbs and serving them on a wedge of toasted ciabatta. Ordinary toast simply won't work, but you can play around with the herbs, using just basil, or all tarragon or replacing them with flat-leaved parsley, even with lovage if you have some.

Preparation time: 10 minutes
Cooking time: 10–15 minutes
Grade: easy

Suggested accompaniment: a selection of bitter salad leaves such as radicchio, rocket, frisée, lamb's lettuce and escarole, dressed with olive oil and lemon juice

a handful each of fresh basil and tarragon	4 skinless chicken breasts
2oz (55g) unsalted butter	1 ciabatta loaf
salt and freshly ground black pepper	4 large or 8 small tomatoes, the most flavourful available

● Finely chop the herbs. Give the butter, herbs and plenty of seasoning a quick whizz together in the processor, or alternatively pound together. Divide the herb butter into 4. Pre-heat the grill to maximum.

● Insert a sharp knife horizontally into the middle of each chicken breast 1in (2.5cm) from one end. Slide it along to make a cavity, until the knife is 1in (2.5cm) from the other end. Spread a knob of herb butter into each cavity.

● Cut 4 boat-shaped pieces of foil (this will catch the buttery juices as they run) and place a chicken breast in each, leaving the top surface open. Grill for 5–7 minutes on either side according to the thickness of the chicken breasts. Cut the ciabatta in half horizontally and then vertically, so you have 4 pieces. Toast these under the grill with the chicken until they are lightly browned on both sides. Meanwhile finely dice the tomatoes.

● To serve, put the chicken breasts on top of the toasted ciabatta and dribble over the buttery juices from the foil parcels. Top with diced tomato and freshly ground black pepper, pile some dressed salad leaves alongside and serve immediately, before the toast becomes soggy.

Chicken Breasts with Mushrooms and Sun-dried Tomatoes

In Italy sun-dried tomatoes are generally used only as antipasti, not as ingredients in the actual cooking. However, Californian cuisine adopted the sun-dried tomato as its own and it soon found its way into all manner of dishes. I find sun-dried tomatoes useful in adding flavour and colour to chicken – here cooked with mushrooms as well, to make a one-pan dish.

Preparation time: 10 minutes
Cooking time: 25–30 minutes
Grade: easy

Suggested accompaniments: buttered long-grain rice and a tomato and onion salad

4oz (115g) shallots or 1 red onion	4 skinless chicken breasts
8oz (225g) brown cap mushrooms	2 glasses dry white wine
8 sun-dried tomatoes in oil	salt and freshly ground black pepper
1 tablespoon olive oil	

● Chop the shallots or onion finely. Wash the mushrooms thoroughly and slice across into 2 or 3 pieces. Drain the tomatoes and chop coarsely.

● Heat the oil in a large lidded frying-pan over a gentle flame and sweat the shallots for 5 minutes. Now add the mushrooms and cook for another 5 minutes. Turn the heat up and fry the chicken breasts for 1 minute on either side to seal. Pour over the white wine and allow to bubble for a minute. Now add the chopped sun-dried tomatoes and seasoning to taste, turn down the heat to low and cover. Allow to simmer for 15 minutes until the chicken is cooked through, and serve.

Kung-po Chicken

This classic Sichuan dish features that Chinese province's favourite ingredient, dried red chilli peppers. This particular recipe was given to me by an accomplished cook wasting away in the obscure outpost of Golmud, in Qinghai province, which adjoins Sichuan. Golmud is a dusty, miserable town whose only claim to fame is that it marks the end (or the beginning) of the highest road in the world, from Lhasa. After several weeks of yak butter tea and tsampa porridge, culminating in 48 hours on a rickety bus with nothing but biscuits to eat, anything would have tasted delicious, but the Four Star restaurant's Kung-po Chicken was just as good when I got home. I did, however, reduce the number of chillies from 8 to just 2 – it's up to you, but the original burns the roof of your mouth off.

Preparation time: 10 minutes
Cooking time: 5 minutes
Grade: easy if you are used to stir-frying

Suggested accompaniments: plenty of boiled rice and a stir-fried vegetable dish

2 skinless chicken breasts, approx 12oz (350g)	1 tablespoon rice or white wine vinegar
3 teaspoons cornflour	1 teaspoon white sugar
1/2 teaspoon coarse salt	2 tablespoons cold water
1 large onion	1 1/2 tablespoons vegetable oil
2 dried red chillies	1 teaspoon Chinese chilli sauce
3 tablespoons chicken stock	(or more to taste)
1 tablespoon tomato paste	

● Chop the chicken into small pieces, about the size of a grape. Roll the chicken in 1 teaspoon of the cornflour and the salt. Chop the onion roughly and the chillies finely. Mix together the remaining cornflour, the stock, tomato paste, vinegar, sugar and water and stir well to ensure there are no lumps.

● In a wok or large frying-pan, heat the oil over a fierce heat. When it is very hot, add the onions and chillies and stir-fry for 2 minutes. Now add the chicken pieces and cook for another 2 minutes. Pour in the sauce mixture and bubble until the mixture thickens. Turn down to a simmer for 1 minute, then add the chilli sauce to taste (be careful – taste before you add) and serve.

Chicken with Butter Tomato Sauce

Another recipe from my travels – this time plundered from the cook of the guesthouse in which I stayed in New Delhi. This is a dish designed to suit Western palates, with its mild spice and buttery, creamy sauce. Cooks who can adapt to supposedly English cooking are much in demand in India, resulting in a peculiar kind of 1930s nursery food with added spice. This particular Anglo-Indian dish, however, is an unqualified success. If you have ghee, do use it rather than European butter – it adds an unmistakable nutty flavour to the dish.

Preparation time: 10 minutes
Cooking time: 15 minutes
Grade: moderate

Suggested accompaniment: plain boiled Basmati rice is all you need

3 skinless chicken breasts, 1–1¼ lb (450–550g)	2fl oz (50ml) tomato paste
	1 teaspoon white sugar
2 teaspoons ground cumin	¼ teaspoon cayenne pepper
½ teaspoon coarse salt	¼ teaspoon black pepper
2 small fresh green chillies	6fl oz (175ml) double cream
4 large tomatoes	1 tablespoon chopped fresh
2½ oz (75g) ghee or butter	coriander
1 teaspoon grated fresh ginger	

● Dice the chicken into bite-sized pieces and roll them in the cumin and salt. Deseed the chillies and dice them finely. Slice the tomatoes thinly.
● Melt 2oz (55g) of the butter in a large frying-pan over gentle heat (if you are using ghee, which has been clarified and therefore will not burn, you can heat it more fiercely). Skim off the scum from the butter and turn up the heat to medium. Add the ginger and chillies and fry for 1 minute; now add the spiced chicken and cook, stirring, for another 3 minutes.
● Add the tomato paste, sugar, cayenne pepper and black pepper to the pan and stir well. Turn down the heat to low and pour in the cream. Stir to amalgamate the sauce and allow to just simmer for 5 minutes. Now add the sliced tomatoes and the coriander, reserving a few leaves

to sprinkle on top of the finished dish. Cook gently for another 5 minutes, check the seasoning, stir in the remaining nugget of ghee or butter, sprinkle with the reserved coriander and serve.

'Moroccan' Chicken Salad

There are endless variations for warm chicken salad, many with a North American flavour. Tex-Mex restaurants serve a 'Mexican' salad of chargrilled strips of chicken with chopped avocado, tomato, chilli and lime juice; New Yorkers enjoy grilled chicken breast with croûtons and crispy bacon on iceberg lettuce with a mayonnaise dressing; Californian chicken salads are likely to go heavy on the sun-dried tomatoes and fresh herbs, with perhaps a few grilled vegetables or a shaving of Parmesan thrown in, and certainly some balsamic vinegar and extra virgin olive oil.

The origins of my own favourite chicken salad are not clear – I call it Moroccan because I first ate it in Taroudannt, beneath the High Atlas, but it is not a dish you would find in a traditional North African cookery book. It is best made with green cracked olives flavoured with herbs and garlic.

Preparation time: 10 minutes
Cooking time: 5 minutes
Grade: basic

Suggested accompaniment: pitta bread

2 skinless chicken breasts	4oz (115g) pitted green olives
2 cloves of garlic	4 tablespoons olive oil
2 large tomatoes	2 tablespoons flaked almonds
¼ cucumber	1 teaspoon paprika
1 crisp lettuce (I use Webb's or Cos)	juice of 1 lemon

● Chop the chicken into bite-sized pieces. Finely chop the garlic. Wash the tomatoes and cucumber and dice. Chop the lettuce into fine shreds.
● Combine the lettuce, tomato and cucumber in a salad bowl and sprinkle in the olives. Heat the oil in a frying-pan, add the chicken and fry over fierce heat for 3 minutes, until it is cooked through. Remove with a slotted spoon and sprinkle over the salad. Now add the garlic and almonds to the oil and fry briefly, stirring, until both are lightly coloured. Add the paprika to the contents of the pan, stir in well, and pour the lot over the salad. Add lemon juice to taste and serve.

Chinese Barbecue Chicken

The Chinese love barbecues, although they tend to have them indoors in winter. Given the general behaviour of the British summer, perhaps we should adopt this approach. This very simple marinade is highly effective. You may be surprised by the amount of sugar – watch it caramelize as the little kebabs cook.

Preparation time: 10 minutes, at least 20 minutes before cooking
Cooking time: 6–8 minutes
Grade: basic

Suggested accompaniments: boiled rice and shredded spring onions

4 skinless chicken breasts (you could also use 6 boneless thigh fillets)	4fl oz (100ml) dark soy sauce 2 dessertspoons white sugar
4fl oz (100ml) dry sherry	cocktail or kebab sticks

- Chop the chicken into bite-sized pieces and thread a couple of pieces on to each cocktail or kebab stick.
- Mix together the remaining ingredients in a small saucepan. Put over a gentle heat and bring slowly to the boil, stirring all the time, so that the sugar melts. Now turn up the heat and boil hard, uncovered, for 5 minutes, stirring occasionally. The mixture will reduce and thicken slightly. Take off the heat and allow to cool for a few minutes.
- Pour the liquid over the chicken kebabs and leave to stand for at least 20 minutes, turning them once. Cook over glowing coals on the barbecue for 3–4 minutes on each side, basting with the marinade when you turn the kebabs over. Serve with the remaining marinade as a dipping sauce.

LEG AND THIGH

The roast chicken is brought gleaming brown to the table, the carver picks up his or her favourite knife, the first cut is made, and then comes the familiar call to those around the table – breast or leg? In some households the breast is considered the more ladylike meat, but personally I always go for leg. Not just because it tends to be the juiciest part of a roast chicken, but because I find the darker meat has more flavour than the sometimes insipid white breast. My instincts are the same when choosing jointed cuts of chicken. Chicken thighs and drumsticks cooked on the bone take a little longer, but are actually easier to cook than breast, for the balance between over- and under-cooking is less fine, with consequently less risk of dryness.

Breaded Drumsticks with Pesto

Pesto, the classic mixture from Genoa of pinenuts, pecorino and Parmesan cheeses, basil and olive oil pounded together to form a chunky sauce, was one of the marketing success stories of the 1980s. Gone is the time when you had to track pesto down in Italian delicatessens in Soho, or make it yourself (although in the height of summer the home-made variety is still worth the effort).

With this proliferation of the product has come a correspondent widening of its use. Traditionally served with linguine, pesto can now be found dribbled over chargrilled vegetables and squid or spread into the slashes in the flesh of a baked red mullet. Not all of these innovations are entirely successful, but I have found pesto marries well with chicken. Spread between the skin and flesh of a chicken drumstick, it adds plenty of interest when you bite through the crisp breadcrumbs.

Preparation time: 15 minutes
Cooking time: 20 minutes
Grade: easy

Suggested accompaniments: new potatoes, grilled tomatoes

8 chicken drumsticks	½ a French stick, preferably
1 jar pesto sauce	slightly stale (crusts removed)
salt and freshly ground pepper	olive oil
	2 lemons

● Pre-heat the grill to medium hot.
● Roll the chicken skin down to the bottom of the leg. Rub pesto all over the flesh, then roll the skin back up the leg to seal in the sauce.

- Use a food processor or grater to make breadcrumbs from the French stick. Season the breadcrumbs well and sprinkle them over a plate.
- Roll the chicken drumsticks in the breadcrumbs. Lay them on a grill tray and sprinkle more breadcrumbs over the uppermost surface. Dribble over some olive oil.
- Cook the drumsticks under the grill, not too close to the heat, so that the breadcrumbs don't burn. After 10 minutes, by which time the surface should be nicely browned, turn them over, sprinkling more breadcrumbs over the uppermost surface and dribbling over more oil. After another 8–10 minutes they will be ready – watch carefully to make sure the breadcrumbs don't burn. Serve with quarters of lemon.

Chicken Thighs with Beans, Cabbage and Rice

This dish combines everything necessary for a substantial supper in one frying-pan. Chicken thighs are cooked with the traditional peasant trio of cabbage, beans and rice, flavoured with juniper berries. The finished dish is topped with cheese and breadcrumbs and crisped under the grill, giving it an enticing appearance and a contrast of textures.

Preparation time: 5 minutes
Cooking time: 30 minutes
Grade: moderate

Suggested accompaniment: nothing extra is necessary

1 large onion	8 juniper berries
1 clove of garlic (*optional*)	salt and freshly ground black pepper
½ a Savoy cabbage	4oz (115g) long-grain rice
1 tablespoon vegetable oil	4oz (115g) hard cheese, grated e.g. Emmenthal, Gruyère
8 skinless chicken thighs, with bone	2 tablespoons stale breadcrumbs
2 x 14oz (400g) tins flageolet beans	1oz (30g) butter

- Coarsely chop the onion and garlic. Shred the cabbage, discarding the central core. In a lidded frying-pan large enough to take all the ingredients, heat the oil and fry the onion and garlic over medium high heat for 5 minutes, until softened. Now add the chicken thighs and cook for 1 minute on either side, to seal. Add the shredded cabbage and turn to coat in the fat. Add the beans and their liquid, 2 tablespoons of cold water, the juniper berries and seasoning to taste. Bring to a simmer and

leave to cook, uncovered, over a medium heat for 15 minutes.
- Meanwhile bring a pan of salted water to the boil and cook the rice for 10 minutes, until just al dente.
- After the chicken has cooked for 15 minutes, stir in the drained rice and continue to cook for another 5 minutes. Meanwhile, pre-heat the grill to maximum.
- Turn up the heat to boil off any liquid remaining in the frying-pan and check the seasoning. Pick out the juniper berries if you like. Scatter the grated cheese and the breadcrumbs over the surface and dot with the butter. Put the pan close under the grill until the surface is browned and serve.

Chicken Thighs with Vinegar and Paprika

In southern Spain, chicken is prepared with seasonal vegetables, flavoured with sherry vinegar and plenty of paprika. The resulting dish is gaily coloured by the spice and the red pepper and has plenty of underlying bite from the vinegar. If you don't have the exact combination of vegetables, don't be put off – simply use whatever you have available.

Preparation time: 10 minutes
Cooking time: 30 minutes
Grade: moderate

Suggested accompaniment: plain boiled rice, sprinkled with parsley

1 large onion
1 red pepper
4 sticks celery, leaves attached
1 fennel bulb, feathery fronds attached
2 cloves of garlic
2 tablespoons olive oil
8 chicken thighs with bone (*I prefer to leave the skin on for flavour, but you can also use skinless thighs, in which case reduce the cooking time by 5 minutes*)
1 tablespoon paprika
salt and freshly ground black pepper
2 tablespoons sherry vinegar or, failing that, red wine vinegar

- Coarsely chop all the vegetables, including the leaves of the celery and fennel. Finely chop the garlic. In a lidded frying-pan large enough to take all the chicken thighs, heat the oil over a medium high heat. Fry all the vegetables together, stirring, for 5 minutes. Add the garlic and fry for another 5 minutes. Now add the chicken thighs and cook for a couple of minutes on each side, to seal. Sprinkle in the paprika and plenty of seasoning and stir well. Stand back and pour in the vinegar. When it starts to splutter, add 6 tablespoons of cold water. Cover the pan and cook for 20 minutes over a medium low heat, until the chicken is cooked through. Check the seasoning and serve.

Korean Chicken Kebabs

This dish is characteristic of Korean cooking, featuring a marinade with sesame in both oil and seed form, garlic, ginger, soy sauce and sugar, and spring onions interspersed between the pieces of meat on the kebab. Typically the kebabs would be cooked over charcoal but a hot grill does as well. If you don't have spring onions don't be put off – although they add texture, flavour and colour, they are by no means indispensable.

Preparation time: 20 minutes, at least 30 minutes before you want to cook
Cooking time: 15 minutes
Grade: easy

Suggested accompaniment: boiled noodles tossed with fried garlic, ginger and the green of the spring onion and dressed with soy sauce, sesame oil and vinegar

8 boneless, skinless chicken thighs	2 teaspoons white sugar
24 small spring onions	2 tablespoons sesame oil
1 tablespoon sesame seeds	4 tablespoons dark soy sauce
3 fat cloves of garlic	
½ in (1cm) piece of fresh ginger	8 long wooden kebab sticks

● Cut each chicken thigh across into 3 pieces. Trim the green from the spring onions (I keep it to add to the noodles which I serve with the dish). Thread a piece of chicken on to a kebab stick, then pierce a spring onion through the narrow side so that it sticks out. Put another 2 pieces of chicken, alternated with another couple of spring onions, on to each kebab stick.
● To make the marinade, first toast the sesame seeds in a dry frying-pan over a high heat until they start to pop – a matter of a minute. Stir to make sure they do not burn. Peel the garlic and ginger and chop finely; add the toasted sesame seeds and sugar. Stir the sesame oil and soy sauce into this mixture.
● Lay the kebabs on a grill pan and pour over the marinade. Turn a couple of times to coat. Leave for 30 minutes, longer if possible.
● To cook, pre-heat the grill to maximum. Cook the kebabs close to the grill for 6–7 minutes on either side; baste with the marinade when you turn them over. Serve immediately.

Spiced Chicken Kebabs with Green Pepper

A typically Middle Eastern combination of cumin, coriander and turmeric is used to spice these little chicken kebabs, which are topped and tailed with a slice of green pepper. Instead of grilling the kebabs I prefer to roast them, which results in juicier peppers. You could also use chicken breast for this recipe.

Preparation time: 20 minutes
Cooking time: 15 minutes
Grade: basic

Suggested accompaniments: pitta bread and a cucumber salad

6 boneless chicken thighs	pepper
2 large green peppers	½ teaspoon coarse sea salt
2 teaspoons whole cumin seeds	2 tablespoons olive oil
1 teaspoon ground coriander	fresh coriander (*optional*)
½ teaspoon turmeric	
½ teaspoon freshly ground black	cocktail sticks

- Chop each chicken thigh in half across and then cut each half into 3 pieces. Remove the core of the peppers and cut into 1/2in (1cm) strips; cut each strip in half across. Put a strip of pepper, a piece of chicken and then another strip of pepper on to each cocktail stick. Continue until all the chicken and pepper are used up. Place the kebabs on an oven tray.
- Briefly roast the whole cumin seeds in a dry frying-pan over a high heat, stirring constantly to make sure that they do not burn. Mix together all the spices and the salt with the olive oil and pour this mixture over the kebabs. If you can leave them to stand for 30 minutes, their flavour will be improved.
- Pre-heat the oven to 180°C/350°F/Gas Mark 4. Roast the kebabs for 15 minutes, and just before serving sprinkle with the chopped coriander if you have it. They are just as good cold as they are hot.

Chicken Thighs Braised in Soy Sauce

This highly-flavoured dish is a good way of enhancing the slightly tasteless meat of a battery-reared chicken. I usually make it with chicken thighs, but the technique also works well with a whole chicken jointed into small pieces.

The result is tender pieces of meat with a slightly burnished colour, smothered in a thick dark sauce concealing little pieces of ginger and garlic. The aroma as you serve the dish is very powerful.

Preparation time: 10 minutes
Cooking time: 25–30 minutes
Grade: moderate

Suggested accompaniments: I serve the chicken on a bed of crisp shredded lettuce (Webb's or Cos), accompanied by plain boiled rice

---

1 tablespoon vegetable oil	½ teaspoon freshly ground black pepper
8 chicken thighs on the bone, with skin	4 tablespoons dark soy sauce
3 cloves of garlic	1 tablespoon sesame oil
1in (2.5cm) piece of fresh ginger	1 teaspoon white wine vinegar
2 teaspoons sugar	

- Heat the vegetable oil over a high heat in a frying-pan large enough to take all the chicken pieces. When the oil is hot add the chicken, skin side down, and fry for 3 minutes, until the skin is lightly browned. Turn over and fry for another 2 minutes. Remove the chicken with a slotted spoon, pat dry with a piece of kitchen paper and discard the oil.
- Peel the garlic and ginger and chop finely. Put the chicken thighs in a casserole or deep frying-pan in which they will all lie flat. Sprinkle over the ginger, garlic sugar and pepper and pour in the soy sauce and sesame oil. Add sufficient water to come half-way up the chicken.
- Bring to the boil, turn down to a rapid simmer, cover and cook for 20–25 minutes, until the chicken pieces are cooked through. Remove the chicken and put to keep warm. Turn the heat up and boil the sauce rapidly for 3 or 4 minutes, until it is reduced to a syrupy consistency. Add the vinegar, spoon over the chicken and serve.

WHOLE BIRD

Cooks in a hurry are put off whole chickens – nobody wants to joint them, and they take far too long to roast. The result has been a boost to the supermarkets, who now sell us chicken thighs, with or without bones, breasts, with or without skin, even drumsticks off the bone. Thank goodness, because they can be very useful. But not at the expense of a whole bird.

So why buy a whole chicken, unless you are cooking Sunday lunch? Well, first, roasting isn't the only option. A steamed chicken cooks in 30 minutes; a pot-roasted one in 45. Second, even if a roast chicken does take over an hour in the oven, the cook is not exactly under pressure. When you get home, season the chicken to your taste, with butter and tarragon, yoghurt and paprika or cumin and olive oil slipped between skin and breast. Then slam the bird in the oven and forget about it at least for the next hour and a quarter.

The result will feed 4 and is difficult to ruin (unlike chicken breasts, which although quick to cook demand attention from the cook and can easily end up dry and tasteless). Finally, it is far cheaper to buy whole chickens rather than those ready-butchered, especially if you value the flavour as well as the quality of life of corn-fed, free-range birds. And you have the added benefit of the chicken carcass – freeze it until you have the time to make stock.

Steamed Whole Chicken with Saffron Butter

Steaming is a popular way of cooking both chickens and small joints of lamb in Morocco. It is also very quick. The bird is basted with plenty of saffron and butter, and when cooked is finished in the oven with more of the same plus coarse salt and cumin seeds, obviating the danger of the pallid complexion which can result from steaming. In a cross-cultural move, I find a wok complete with lid and tray for holding the bird is the best utensil for this dish; if you use a traditional steamer, the cooking time will be a little longer.

Preparation time: 10 minutes
Cooking time: 30–35 minutes
Grade: easy, provided you have a wok with a lid and a tray to put inside it to hold a plate above the steaming water

Suggested accompaniments: the nicest way to eat this chicken is with your fingers, with a hunk of bread; follow up with a salad

1 teaspoon saffron strands	1 heaped teaspoon whole cumin
3oz (85g) unsalted butter	seeds
1 small whole chicken, preferably	½ teaspoon coarse sea salt
corn-fed, approx 3lb (1.3kg)	

● Pound together half the saffron and 2oz (55g) of the butter. With your fingers, carefully separate the skin of the chicken from the breast, on either side of the breastbone. Working from each end, push the butter and saffron mixture between the flesh and the skin.

● Fill the wok with water to the level of the metal tray that holds dishes for steaming. Over a medium flame, bring the water to a steady simmer. Put the chicken breast side uppermost on a metal plate which will fit inside the wok. Put the plate on the tray, cover the wok, and steam the chicken for 25–30 minutes. Half-way through cooking, you should top up the water level.

● While the chicken is steaming, pre-heat the oven to 220°C/425°F/Gas Mark 7. Mix together the cumin seeds, salt, remaining saffron and remaining butter. When the bird is ready (the flesh should have retracted on the legs, which should fall easily away from the body), remove from the wok and discard any liquid on the plate. Spread the butter mixture all over the surface of the bird. Cook in the pre-heated oven for 5 minutes, until the surface is lightly browned, and serve.

Spanish Pot-roasted Chicken

As this dish cooks it gives off the scent of the Mediterranean, a powerful combination of garlic, olive oil, the scrub herbs rosemary, bay and thyme, and of course wine. This aroma infuses the chicken, which will remain wonderfully juicy and tender. Although it takes a little time, this dish requires minimum effort and is ideal for a summer supper in the garden.

Preparation time: 10 minutes
Cooking time: 45–50 minutes
Grade: easy

Suggested accompaniments:
potatoes sautéed in olive oil; fresh peas or broad beans stirred into the pan contents are very good

1 corn-fed, free-range chicken, approx 3½ lb (1.6kg)	4 fresh bay leaves
salt and freshly ground black pepper	1 large sprig of rosemary
	several sprigs of fresh thyme
2 whole heads of garlic (*preferably new season*)	2 tablespoons olive oil
	6fl oz (175ml) dry sherry
	1 tablespoon sherry vinegar

- Remove any excess fat from inside the chicken and wipe it clean. Season well inside and out. Break the heads of garlic into individual cloves but do not peel them. With string tie the herbs into a bunch, leaving sufficient string to hang out over the edge of the casserole.
- Heat the oil in a casserole in which the chicken will just fit, and briefly fry the whole chicken on all sides, so that it is lightly browned. When it is fully browned, lay the chicken so that it is resting on its side. Turn the heat down to medium and add the garlic cloves, the bunch of herbs, the sherry and the sherry vinegar. Cover and leave to cook for 25 minutes.
- Now turn the chicken over on to the other side. Check the liquid – if it has nearly all gone, add a little water. Cover and cook for a further 20 minutes. The chicken should be done by this time (check by poking a skewer between leg and breast, the juices should run clear). If not, cook a little longer – but be careful or it will go dry. Similarly, if you are cooking a smaller chicken reduce the times slightly.
- Remove the herbs and garlic, carve the chicken and pour over the contents of the pan.

POUSSIN OR SPRING CHICKEN

In past years the poussin or spring chicken has found few friends amongst food writers. A roast poussin certainly can be a miserable, shrivelled thing. But there are other ways of cooking the baby birds, such as pot-roasting, grilling or barbecuing them, which have good results. And precisely because of their size poussins are a boon to cooks in a hurry, because quite obviously they will cook more quickly than an older bird.

Pot-roasted Poussin with Celery

You can add a wide variety of flavourings to the pot in which you are to cook the poussin, but it is important that there should be some vegetable which will give off liquid.

My favourite is celery, especially if you have the leaves as well as the stalks. (It is a mystery to me why retailers remove the very useful leaves of celery.)

Preparation time: 10 minutes
Cooking time: 30–35 minutes
Grade: easy

Suggested accompaniment: lentils with butter and parsley
Serves: 2

1 head of celery, preferably with leaves attached	juice of 1 lemon
1 large onion	2fl oz (50ml) water
2 tablespoons olive oil	salt and freshly ground black pepper
2 poussins	

- Wash the celery well and chop the stalks across at ½in (1cm) intervals. If you have the leaves, chop them coarsely. Peel the onion and chop finely.
- In a heavy casserole large enough to take both poussins, heat the oil over a medium high flame. Fry the onion and celery stalks and leaves for 5 minutes, stirring regularly. Now add the poussins and allow to take on a little colour – this should take a minute or two on each side. Leave the poussins breast side down. Pour in the lemon juice and the water, add plenty of seasoning, and as soon as the liquid starts to bubble turn the heat down to medium low. Cover and cook for 10 minutes. Now take off the lid, turn the poussins breast side up, and if the bottom of the pan is dry add a little more water. Cover and cook for a further 10 minutes. A small poussin will be done by this time – it is ready when the leg falls easily away from the body and the juices run clear. Larger poussins may need another 5 minutes.

Grilled Poussin with Cumin

I was once taken by an Egyptian taxi driver to his favourite restaurant in Cairo, down a back street near the Pyramids. There was no menu because there was no choice – the only thing on offer was grilled baby chicken. The chicken were served perfectly plain, with nothing more than a sprinkling of coarse salt, cumin seeds and a wedge of lemon. They were so delicious that we ate two each, burning our fingers as we tore them apart.

The Cairene grill was an open wood fire above which long racks of the little birds were turned. Poussins grilled more conventionally lack the smoky flavour but are still very good. Spatchcock the birds by splitting them down the backbone, so that they cook more quickly.

Preparation time: 5 minutes
Cooking time: 25 minutes
Grade: easy

Suggested accompaniments: halved tomatoes spiked with herbs and/or garlic and grilled alongside the birds; pitta bread
Serves: 2

2 poussins, about 12oz (350g) each, spatchcocked	2 teaspoons coarse sea salt
	1 tablespoon cumin seeds
2 tablespoons olive oil	1 lemon

● Pre-heat the grill to maximum. Rub the birds all over, inside and out, with the olive oil and salt. Grill breast side down for 10 minutes then turn breast side up, putting the bird close to the heat. Grill for a further 10 minutes. Check that the birds are nearly done by piercing the flesh between the breast and leg – the juices should run clear. If they don't, cook for another 5 minutes – but be careful not to overdo it or the flesh will be dry. When the poussins are cooked, sprinkle the cumin seeds over them and return the birds to the grill for 3 or 4 minutes until the cumin is nicely browned. Watch carefully to make sure the seeds do not burn. Serve immediately with quarters of lemon.

DUCK

The traditional British duck, purportedly from Aylesbury, has been joined in the shops by his French cousin, the Barbary duck. Better still, both are now available jointed. This allows you to choose the best of each – the substantial legs of the British duck and the meaty breast of the Barbary are my preferences. When roasting a whole bird, both have their advantages, but require different treatments. The British duck, not surprisingly, responds well to the traditional method of long, slow cooking, producing brown flavourful meat and plenty of fat in which to roast the potatoes. The Barbary on the other hand, needs a relatively short blast in a hot oven and a brief period of respite before the carving process, which should reveal still pink meat.

Duck Breasts with Honey and Ginger

Duck coated in salty, gingery honey and roasted rare produces a lacquered meat with a pleasing sweetness and a backbone of spice.

Preparation time: 5 minutes, 15 minutes before you want to cook
Cooking time: 12–15 minutes
Grade: easy

Suggested accompaniment: Chinese egg noodles

1 heaped teaspoon powdered ginger	1 teaspoon salt
2 tablespoons clear honey	4 duck breasts

- Mix together the ginger, honey and salt. Make a few shallow cuts on the flesh side of each duck breast. Smear the honey mixture all over the meat and leave to stand for 15 minutes.
- Pre-heat the oven to 200°C/400°F/Gas Mark 6. Roast the duck breasts for 12–15 minutes (slightly longer if you don't like them pink through). Allow the meat to rest for 5 minutes, then slice thickly and serve.

Duck Breasts with a
Sweet and Sour Mint Sauce

Not Chinese but Italian sweet and sour, relying on red wine, sugar, balsamic vinegar, lemon juice and shallots to give the balance, with the unusual addition of chopped mint to lift the sauce at the end. If you don't have shallots don't worry, although they do add texture as well as sweetness to the sauce, which is also good with lamb.

Preparation time: 5 minutes,
Cooking time: 15 minutes
Grade: moderate

Suggested accompaniments: cubes of potatoes briefly boiled and then fried with whole, unpeeled cloves of garlic in olive oil or the fat from the duck; a salad of bitter leaves

4oz (115g) shallots	juice of ½ a lemon
1 tablespoon olive oil	salt and freshly ground black
1 tablespoon brown sugar	pepper
6fl oz (175ml) red wine	1 tablespoon chopped fresh mint
2 whole cloves	or ½ teaspoon dried mint
2 tablespoons balsamic vinegar	4 duck breasts

● Pre-heat the oven to 200°C/400°F/Gas Mark 6. Peel the shallots and chop finely. Heat the oil over a low heat in a frying-pan and allow the shallots to sweat gently for 10 minutes. They should not brown or they will become bitter.

● Meanwhile gently heat the sugar in a separate saucepan over a low heat, stirring continuously. Just as the sugar starts to turn liquid, pour in the wine (stand well back, it will spit). Stir well together and add the cloves. Turn up the heat, bring to the boil and allow to boil uncovered until the quantity is reduced by half – about 5 minutes. Now add the balsamic vinegar, lemon juice and seasoning. Bring just back to the boil, then take off the heat. Add the sweated shallots and the mint, check the balance of sweet and sour and the sauce is ready.

● You can make the sauce in advance or while the duck breasts are roasting. Depending on thickness and how pink you like them, they take between 12–15 minutes in the pre-heated oven. Make sure you allow them to stand for 5 minutes before carving into slices, and add the juices to the sauce.

Grilled Duck Breasts with Pears

Pears go well with many birds, goose, duck and partridge being my favourite matches. There are all sorts of complicated recipes for duck with pears, but I find the dish very successful in its simplest form: grilled duck breasts partnered with lightly grilled pears topped with a little sugar. Although it is so basic, this dish always receives a warm welcome, probably because in Britain it is a little-known combination (although it is very popular in Spain).

Preparation time: 10 minutes
Cooking time: 15–20 minutes
Grade: easy

Suggested accompaniment: I like to serve this dish all on its own, but you may want to add some potatoes

4 ripe pears	salt and freshly ground black
4 duck breasts	pepper
	2 teaspoons brown sugar

● Pre-heat the grill to maximum. Peel the pears, leaving the stalks on, cut them in half vertically and remove the core. With a sharp knife, make 4 or 5 equally spaced shallow cuts down the rounded side from the stalk to the base, being careful not to cut right through to the other side. Press lightly on the rounded surface so that the pear fans out slightly. Season the pears with salt.

● Make a few slashes in the skin side of the duck breasts and season well on both sides. Cook the meat breast side up for 5 minutes close to the grill. Now turn skin side up and cook for another 5–10 minutes, depending on how thick the breasts are and on whether you like your meat pink. When it is cooked to your satisfaction (cut into a piece to make sure), remove to rest for 5 minutes, draining off the fat. Meanwhile put the pears, rounded side up and sprinkled with the sugar, under the grill for 5 minutes, until the sugar melts and caramelizes slightly. Serve 2 halves of pear per breast.

Spiced Duck Legs

The important thing when cooking the traditional British duck is to make sure as much of the fat as possible is released. Cooking duck legs in a frying-pan may seem an unlikely way of achieving this aim, but in fact, provided the meat cooks slowly and the skin is well scored, the method works well. There is no need to add fat to the pan before you start, but you should use a heavy-based non-stick pan to make sure the duck does not stick before some fat has seeped out. The skin is finally crisped with a mixture of ginger and cinnamon, my favourite spices with duck.

Preparation time: 5 minutes
Cooking time: 25 minutes
Grade: easy

Suggested accompaniment: a purée of potatoes with celeriac or parsnip

4 duck legs	2 teaspoons ground ginger
1 teaspoon coarse salt	½ teaspoon freshly ground black
2 teaspoons cinnamon	pepper

- With a sharp knife, score each leg 3 or 4 times on the skin side – the aim is to cut through the skin but not the flesh.
- Over a gentle flame, heat a heavy-based frying-pan in which all the duck legs will fit. Lay the duck legs in it skin side down; there is no need to add fat, as this will be released from the duck. Cook gently for 10 minutes, then drain off almost all the fat and turn the legs over. Cook for a further 10 minutes. Meanwhile mix together the salt and all the spices; spread this mixture over the skin side of the duck. Drain off excess fat, turn up the heat and turn the duck over again so that the spiced skin is against the frying-pan. Cook for 3–4 minutes, until the skin is crisp, and serve.

GUINEA-FOWL

Named after the Guinea coast of Africa from whence it originated, the guinea-fowl was first raised in Britain in the fifteenth century. Today it is widely farmed in Europe, especially in France, where slow-braised guinea-fowl with cabbage is a classic dish. The French, as usual, understand how to treat their ingredient, for the guinea-fowl is a lean bird, best braised or pot-roasted. Cooked in the oven it has a tendency to dryness unless very well larded. One matter of intrigue – whatever happens to guinea-fowl eggs?

Pot-roasted Guinea-fowl with Lemon and Garlic

Don't be put off by the amount of garlic in this recipe; the whole cloves cooked in their skins acquire a sweet creaminess which is not at all pungent. Traditionally the garlic is spread on thick slices of bread served alongside the bird. The lemon is, I suspect, a more recent addition to this Spanish peasant dish, which can be prepared equally well with pheasant. It adds a welcome touch of sharpness to the rich sauce.

This is an excellent dish for a dinner party, as it needs virtually no attention from the time the birds are put in the pot. If you think your guests are sensitive souls, reduce the amount of garlic, and correspondingly the lemon, which needs the sweetness of the garlic to balance it.

Preparation time: 15 minutes
Cooking time: 50 minutes, needing little attention
Grade: moderate

Suggested accompaniment: little bowls of green pepper dressed with vinegar and tomatoes with olive oil, to sprinkle over the bread

1 onion	6fl oz (175ml) dry white wine
1 head of garlic	2fl oz (50ml) water
1 lemon, preferably unwaxed	salt and freshly ground black
6 rashers unsmoked streaky bacon	pepper
2 tablespoons olive oil	½ teaspoon paprika
2 small guinea-fowl, approx 2lb	4 slices of thick white country
(900g) each	bread

● Coarsely chop the onion. Break the head of garlic into cloves, leaving them unpeeled. Grate the zest of the lemon and squeeze out the juice. Cut the bacon into thin strips, removing the rind.

- Choose a large heavy-based casserole into which both birds will fit snugly. Heat the oil over a high heat and quickly brown each of the birds (about 1 minute on either side). Remove the birds and put to one side.
- Now add the chopped onion, unpeeled garlic cloves and bacon to the pan. Fry, stirring regularly, over a medium heat for 5 minutes, until the onion is lightly coloured. Add the lemon zest and juice, the wine and water and bring to the boil. Season to taste (not too much salt because of the bacon) and stir in the paprika. Turn down to a simmer and put in both birds on their sides. Cover and leave to cook over a moderate heat for 20 minutes. Turn the birds on to their other sides, cover and cook for a further 15–20 minutes, depending on size.
- Put a piece of bread on each plate. Remove the birds from the pan and put them on a carving dish. Fish out the whole garlic cloves from the sauce and spread a few on to each slice of bread. Top with bacon and onion. Put a portion of guinea-fowl beside each piece of bread and pour over the remaining pan juices.

QUAIL

These little birds are delicious provided they remain moist during the cooking, which is why I prefer to grill, fry or steam rather than roast them.

Steamed Quail with Chinese Leaf

This simple recipe, loosely borrowed from Chinese tradition, produces succulent white birds scented with garlic and ginger, coloured with a splash of soy sauce and sesame and served on a bed of wilted greens.

Preparation time: 10 minutes
Cooking time: 15 minutes
Grade: easy, provided you have a steamer or a wok with a lid and steaming tray

Suggested accompaniment: stir-fried rice with vegetables

8 quail (*2 per person*)	1 large head of Chinese leaf
1 teaspoon salt	dark soy sauce
4 fat cloves of garlic	sesame oil
2in (5cm) piece of fresh ginger	

- Wipe the quail clean inside and out with a dry cloth and rub the salt into the surface of their breasts. Peel the garlic and ginger and chop together finely. Stuff each quail with some of the garlic and ginger mix.
- Separate the Chinese leaves and wash. Line the steamer with half of the leaves and pile the quail on top. Lay the remaining leaves over the birds.
- Steam the quail for 15 minutes over a medium heat. Pile the wilted leaves on a plate, topped with the birds. Dribble a little soy sauce and sesame oil over the dish, to give colour and flavour, and serve immediately. The quail are best eaten with the fingers.

Quail with Sherry and Raisins

Quail are very popular in Southern Spain, where they are found in the wild. The traditional way of cooking them is to brown the birds in fat, flambé them in brandy and finally braise them in white wine, montilla or fino sherry. A handful of raisins is sometimes added to the sauce for sweetness.

Preparation time: 5 minutes
Cooking time: 30 minutes
Grade: moderate – if you lack confidence, leave out the brandy, as the flames shooting out of the pan can be quite frightening

Suggested accompaniments: long-grain rice into which you have stirred a little saffron water or, failing that, turmeric; roast or grilled halved tomatoes

1 teaspoon cumin	2 tablespoons brandy
½ teaspoon coarse salt	6fl oz (175 ml) dry sherry or dry white wine
½ teaspoon freshly ground black pepper	2fl oz (50ml) water
8 quail (2 per person)	2oz (55g) raisins
2 tablespoons olive oil	

- For this recipe you need a deep, lidded, long-handled frying-pan large enough to take all the birds.
- Mix together the cumin, salt and pepper and rub the mixture all over the quail, inside and out (if you can do this 15 minutes or so before cooking, so much the better). Heat the oil over a high heat. When it is almost spitting, put in the birds and fry them for 3 minutes on either side, until they are well browned. Stand well back, add the brandy and if necessary set light to it – if the pan is sufficiently hot, it may self-ignite, so be very careful. Shake the pan until the flames die down then add the sherry or wine. Allow to bubble for 1 minute then add the water and the raisins. Make sure all the birds are lying on one side, turn the heat down so the mixture simmers, and cover.
- Cook for 10 minutes, then turn the quail over on to the other side. Cover and cook for a further 10 minutes. Remove the quail and boil the sauce a little to reduce. Check the seasoning, spoon the raisins and juice over the quail and serve.

Grilled Skewered Quail

The Italians adore *uccelli* or small song birds, skewered on wooden sticks and cooked over an open fire with the addition of nothing more than salt and pepper, olive oil and lemon juice. We British may turn our nose up at sparrows, but quail prepared in the same manner find a warm reception, rarely coloured by sentimentality. Whether it is hypocritical to console ourselves that the quail are farmed rather than caught from the wild in nets is open to question. There is, however, no doubting that the taste of these little birds is delicious, whether you are using the barbecue or the grill.

Preparation time: 15 minutes
Cooking time: 15 minutes
Grade: easy

Suggested accompaniments: bread and a salad

---

8 quail (*2 per person*)
2 tablespoons extra virgin olive oil
coarse sea salt and freshly ground black pepper

4 lemons

8 long kebab sticks
string or cotton

- Pre-heat the grill to maximum. Make sure all the feathers have been removed from the quail and skewer them: push a kebab stick through the body cavity so that it emerges at the neck end and pierce the wings at their tips through a little flesh, so that they are stretched out along the stick. Now stretch out the legs in front of the body and tie them together around the stick with string or cotton. The result is a long thin bird stretched out along the kebab stick, looking not unlike a miniature hare. Cut the lemons into quarters and put a piece on each end of each kebab stick.
- Rub olive oil all over the flesh of the birds and season well. Grill close to the heat for 7 minutes on each side. Eat with your fingers as soon as they are cool enough to handle, squeezing over the juice from the cooked lemons and adding more coarse salt as necessary.

TURKEY

If you think the chicken has been abused by mass-producers, take a look at the turkey. I am talking not about humane rearing conditions (although we should all be concerned with the way our food is produced) but about the simple matter of taste. Frankly, most of the turkey available today tastes of absolutely nothing at all. If you doubt this, try a naturally fed free-range bronze-wing turkey (on offer in selected supermarkets during the pre-Christmas glut) to rediscover the flavour. I am sorry to say I rarely cook with the turkey breasts currently available; as for the turkey mince, it is so execrable that I never buy it. However, I include two recipes for turkey in the hope that the quality of the meat we buy will improve.

Turkey Fillets with Bacon, Chicory and Ricotta

Prime fillets of turkey are prized in Bologna, so much so that they are cooked with those precious ingredients, Parma ham, Parmesan and white truffles. It is unlikely that you have fresh white truffles sitting in your cupboard. Even without the truffles, the combination of turkey, cheese and ham or bacon is a good one. I serve turkey fillets stuffed with basil and ricotta, surrounded by bacon and topped off with a couple of leaves of chicory to add a touch of bitterness. But don't worry if you don't have any chicory or basil; the turkey, bacon and cheese combination stands well alone.

Preparation time: 15 minutes
Cooking time: 20 minutes
Grade: moderate

Suggested accompaniments: boiled new potatoes; a chicory salad or a green vegetable

4 small thin turkey fillets	freshly ground black pepper
4 rashers smoked streaky bacon	2oz (55g) ricotta
1 head of chicory	8 large leaves of basil
½ oz (15g) butter	
½ tablespoon olive oil	4 cocktail sticks

● Pre-heat the oven to medium hot, 180°C/350°F/Gas Mark 4. With a flat object lightly beat the turkey fillets to flatten them. Remove any rind or bone from the bacon. Separate 8 leaves from the head of chicory. Heat the butter and oil together in a frying-pan over a medium heat, and when they are sizzling add the turkey fillets. Fry for just 30 seconds on each side, to seal the meat.

● Remove the turkey fillets from the pan, retaining the pan juices, and pat dry with kitchen paper. Season well with freshly ground black pepper. Lay each fillet on a rasher of bacon. Spread the ricotta over the upper surface of the turkey and lay a couple of basil leaves on top of each fillet. Roll up the fillets and bacon together so that each fillet is surrounded by the bacon, and secure each roll with a cocktail stick. Now spear a leaf of chicory on the cocktail stick on either side of the turkey and bacon roll. Place the rolls on their side in an open earthenware dish, dribble over the pan juices and bake uncovered in the pre-heated oven for 20 minutes.

Turkey with Dried Apricots

This recipe from Eastern Europe was traditionally made with fresh apricots, but dried ones also work well and are more practical. If, however, you have fresh apricots available, add them towards the end of the cooking time.

Preparation time: 10 minutes
Cooking time: 25 minutes
Grade: moderate

Suggested accompaniments: boiled long-grain rice or crusty bread; a green salad

2 onions	1 teaspoon cinnamon
2 cloves of garlic	¼ teaspoon cayenne pepper
1¼ lb (550g) skinless turkey breast	1 tablespoon white wine vinegar
4oz (115g) ready-soaked dried apricots	1 tablespoon tomato paste
1oz (30g) butter	salt and freshly ground black pepper
1 tablespoon olive oil	6fl oz (175ml) water
2 teaspoons sugar	1 tablespoon chopped fresh dill

● Peel and chop the onions and garlic. Cut the turkey breast into 1½in (4cm) pieces. Dice the dried apricots.

● In a lidded heavy-based pan, melt the butter with the oil over a gentle heat. Add the onions and garlic and fry gently for 5 minutes, until the onions turn translucent. Now turn up the heat to medium hot and add the turkey pieces. Fry briefly, stirring, for 2 minutes, until lightly browned.

● Now add the apricots, sugar, cinnamon, cayenne, vinegar, tomato paste and salt and pepper to taste, and stir well to make sure the meat is thoroughly coated. Add the water and stir again. Bring to the boil, turn the heat down as low as it will go, cover, and leave barely to simmer for 15 minutes.

● At the end of this time stir again, check the seasoning, stir in the dill, and serve.

GAME

Always a seasonal extra for country dwellers, game has now also become easily available to townies through the efforts of the supermarkets. The smaller game birds such as partridge and grouse can be used for a rapid luxury supper, needing only a knob of butter, a few strips of bacon and a quick blast in a very hot oven. Some 'game', venison being the prime example, is now also farmed, so that it is for sale all year round.

HARE

Hare may not be something you expect to find in a collection of recipes for everyday cooking, but many supermarkets now stock it in season and not all recipes for hare require long slow casseroling. Admittedly, you are unlikely to buy hare on a regular basis, but don't avoid it altogether.

Roast Leg of Hare with Paprika

Provided they are well larded with bacon and are cooked rapidly at a high heat, the back legs of the hare roast very well, producing tender, juicy meat. For best results, the meat should still be slightly rare near the bone.

Preparation time: 5 minutes
Cooking time: 30 minutes
Grade: basic

Suggested accompaniments: grilled polenta; braised Savoy cabbage

2 teaspoons sweet paprika	4 joints of back leg of hare, total
½ teaspoon freshly ground black	weight 1½–2lb (675–900g)
pepper	16 rashers smoked streaky bacon
1 tablespoon olive oil	

- Pre-heat the oven to 220°C/425°F/Gas Mark 7. Mix the paprika and pepper with the olive oil and smear this mixture all over the surface of the meat. Wrap 4 rashers of bacon around each joint, so that the surface of the meat is completely covered.
- Roast in the pre-heated oven for 25–30 minutes, depending on the size of the joints. Allow to rest for 5 minutes before serving, so that the juices distribute themselves through the meat.

Pasta with Hare Sauce

This recipe from Northern Italy can be prepared using fresh hare or remnants left over from a casserole. If starting from scratch, it is best to use saddle meat, which is the most tender. Traditionally the *sugo* would simmer for hours, but a quick version is quite possible. The chocolate adds depth to the sauce and the finishing swirl of balsamic vinegar and olive oil gives a sweet-sharp touch and a little gloss.

Preparation time: 15 minutes
Cooking time: 40 minutes
Grade: easy

Suggested accompaniment: hare sauce is served in Italy with pappardelle, thick strips of pasta; you could also use tagliatelle or fettucine

---

1 large Spanish onion
2 large carrots
2 sticks of celery, preferably with leaves attached
2 cloves of garlic
4 rashers smoked streaky bacon or, better still, 4oz (115g) pancetta cut in one thick slice
2 tablespoons olive oil
8oz (225g) saddle of hare

1 glass red wine
14oz (400g) tin plum tomatoes
2 squares dark chocolate (*it must be dark – milk chocolate will not do*)
salt and freshly ground black pepper
balsamic vinegar
extra virgin olive oil

- Finely chop the onion, carrots, celery (including the leaves) and garlic. Chop the bacon or pancetta coarsely, removing the rind.
- Heat the oil in a heavy-based pan over a medium heat. Add the bacon, and when the fat starts to run put the chopped vegetables in the pan. Cook for 10 minutes, stirring occasionally, until the vegetables are soft and lightly browned. Meanwhile remove the saddle meat from the bone and cut it into thin strips. When the vegetables are ready, turn up the heat, add the hare meat and fry for 1 minute, stirring. Now pour in the red wine and allow to bubble before adding the contents of the tin of tomatoes and the squares of chocolate. Stir until the chocolate has dissolved, season to taste with freshly ground black pepper and a little salt, turn down the heat so that the sauce is just simmering, cover and leave to cook for 25 minutes.
- Meanwhile cook the pasta. Just before serving, add a few drops of balsamic vinegar and extra virgin olive oil to the sauce, check the seasoning, and pile a good ladle of sauce on to each plate of pasta.

PHEASANT

Pheasant has been a part of our diet and our countryside for so long that it is easy to forget the bird came originally from the East – although its vibrant plumage should give a clue, for the British Isles are unlikely to have produced so extravagant a creature. In recent years a glut of pheasants has made them very affordable, especially if you live in the country, where in season a pheasant can often be cheaper than a chicken.

For townies, pheasant is now sold in many supermarkets as well as butcher's shops, not just as a whole bird but jointed. Pheasant makes a change from chicken and in fact can often be substituted for it – try stir-fried pheasant with cashew nuts.

Spiced Roast Leg of Pheasant

Spices were in regular use in the British kitchen from early in the days of the spice trade, and their pungent aroma and flavour were often used to mask the ripeness of overly hung game. The pheasant you buy today may not need disguising but will still take well to an outer coating of mixed spice, roasted to a crisp in the oven. Rather than using a ready-prepared mixture, I prefer to mix my own spices, ensuring greater flavour and improved texture. It is a good idea to keep a separate coffee grinder specifically for spices.

Preparation time: 5 minutes, provided you are using a grinder
Cooking time: 25 minutes
Grade: basic

Suggested accompaniments: mashed potatoes and a green vegetable

2 teaspoons ground cinnamon	peppercorns
1 teaspoon mace	1 teaspoon coarse salt
1 teaspoon ground ginger	2 tablespoons extra virgin olive oil
4 whole cloves	4 pheasant legs
1½ teaspoons whole black	

- Pre-heat the oven to 200°C/400°F/Gas Mark 6. Grind all the spices and the salt together or use a pestle and mortar. The result should be a coarsely ground mixture rather than a smooth powder. Mix in the olive oil and smear the spice mixture all over the pheasant legs.
- Roast in the pre-heated oven for 25 minutes, basting occasionally.

Stir-fried Pheasant Breast with Cashew Nuts

Breast of pheasant stir-fries even better than chicken. The meat absorbs the Chinese flavours of garlic, ginger, soy sauce, spring onion and five-spice powder but unlike the tasteless, woolly chicken often found in a stir-fry the gaminess of the pheasant also comes through. This is especially important here in Britain, where a stir-fried dish tends to have a higher proportion of meat to other ingredients than would be usual in China, due to the fact that the dish often stands alone rather than being one among many. If there is plenty of meat, it is an added bonus if it tastes of something other than the flavourings. For a special dish, add cashew nuts to your stir-fried pheasant.

Preparation time: 5 minutes
Cooking time: 15 minutes
Grade: moderate

Suggested accompaniments: boiled rice and stir-fried vegetables or plain peas

4 small or 2 large skinless pheasant breasts	½ teaspoon Chinese five-spice powder
2 fat cloves of garlic	2 tablespoons dry sherry
1in (2.5cm) piece of fresh ginger	2 tablespoons dark soy sauce
8 spring onions	1 dessertspoon sesame oil
2 tablespoons vegetable oil	2fl oz (50ml) chicken stock (*or, better still, pheasant stock if you have any available*)
2oz (55g) unsalted cashew nuts	

- Chop the pheasant breasts into bite-sized pieces. Chop the peeled garlic and ginger very finely. Chop the spring onions into ¼in (0.6cm) pieces, including the green ends.

- In a wok or large frying-pan over a high heat, heat the vegetable oil. Add the garlic and ginger and stir-fry for 1 minute, until they take on a little colour. Add the spring onions and stir-fry for another minute. Now add the pieces of pheasant and the cashew nuts and continue to stir-fry for a further 2 minutes, making sure the meat is sealed all over. Add the five-spice powder, stir well, and pour in the sherry. As soon as the sherry bubbles, add the soy sauce, the sesame oil and the stock. Turn down the heat to medium, cover, and cook for 10 minutes, until the pheasant is cooked through.

Pheasant Breast with Apples and Cream Sauce

Whole pheasant pot-roasted with butter and apples, the sauce finished with lashings of thick cream, is much enjoyed in Normandy. A similar effect is easily created using just the breasts of the bird, retaining the richness but reducing the cooking time. For further Norman authenticity and to enhance the apple flavour, you can pour a couple of tablespoons of Calvados into the pan before adding the cream.

Preparation time: 10 minutes
Cooking time: 20–25 minutes
Grade: easy

Suggested accompaniments: it may not be very Norman, but I like egg tagliatelle with this dish; you could also have plain boiled potatoes or new potatoes and peas

4 Cox's or other sweet eating apples (*avoid the more watery varieties such as Golden Delicious, which do not brown as well*) 1½oz (45g) unsalted butter	4 skinless pheasant breasts, 4fl oz (100ml) double cream or *crème fraîche* salt and freshly ground black pepper

- Peel the apples and slice thinly into half-moons, discarding the cores. Pre-heat the oven to low, just enough to warm plates.
- Melt the butter in a frying-pan and fry the whole pheasant breasts over a gentle heat for 6–7 minutes on either side, until cooked through. Put in the oven to keep warm.
- Turn the heat under the frying-pan up to medium and add the apple slices to the fat in the pan. Season well with plenty of salt and cook for a couple of minutes on each side, until lightly browned. Now add the cream to the pan and bring to the boil. Simmer for a couple of minutes, add black pepper to taste, pour over the pheasant breasts and serve.

Spanish Sweet and Sour Pheasant

This dish is usually make with partridge in Spain, but pheasant is an excellent and more available substitute. I prefer to use a whole jointed pheasant, which is certainly more economical, but if you have no butcher to joint the pheasant and are not sure how to approach it yourself, you can also use pheasant breasts. Despite the amount of vinegar used, the result is only slightly sharp – the carrot and onion have as much to do with adding the sweetness as the sugar. The vegetables absorb almost all the liquid, leaving a thick purée which coats the meat.

Preparation time: 10 minutes (longer if you have to joint the pheasant yourself)
Cooking time: 25 minutes for breasts, 35 for a jointed whole bird
Grade: moderate

Suggested accompaniment: potatoes mashed with olive oil

---

2 large carrots
2 large onions
2 sprigs of parsley
2 tablespoons olive oil
1 fat pheasant, jointed (*you could also 4 whole pheasant breasts*)

2 teaspoons brown sugar
salt and freshly ground black pepper
6fl oz (175ml) good-quality red wine vinegar

- Peel the carrots and onions and grate them coarsely (you can either use a food processor or the coarse blade of a grater). Chop the parsley finely, stalks and all.
- In a pan large enough to take all the pieces flat, heat the olive oil over a fierce heat and brown the pheasant for 1 minute on each side. Remove the pheasant and add the grated carrots and onions and chopped parsley to the pan. Turn the heat down to medium and fry for 10 minutes, until very soft.
- Put the pheasant back into the pan, stir in the sugar and salt and black pepper to taste, and pour in the vinegar. Bring to the boil, turn down to a simmer, cover, and cook for 15 minutes for breasts, 25 minutes for a whole jointed bird.

RABBIT

Rabbit has made a comeback in recent years, with an increase in its farming, and is now widely available in supermarkets. It deserves its regained popularity, being a lean white meat which makes a pleasant change from chicken. Rabbit on the bone can be sautéed and casseroled, but if it is to be roasted it must be well larded with fat to counteract dryness; boneless rabbit needs only brief cooking in the frying-pan.

Sautéed Rabbit

Sautéed rabbit dishes are common throughout the Mediterranean, where rabbit, whether wild or reared, has long been an important element of the peasant diet. The usual additions to the meat are olive oil, onions, garlic, bacon or the local ham, and tomatoes, with perhaps a glass of the local white wine and a sprig or two of the herbs of the scrub, thyme, oregano and rosemary. If you like, you can also add a handful of small black olives towards the end of the cooking time.

Preparation time: 10 minutes
Cooking time: 30 minutes
Grade: moderate

Suggested accompaniment: buttered egg tagliatelle

2 onions	1 glass white wine
2 cloves of garlic	14oz (400g) tin tomatoes
6 rashers smoked streaky bacon	salt and freshly ground black
4 tablespoons olive oil	pepper
1 whole rabbit, jointed, or 4 legs	a sprig each of thyme, oregano
of rabbit	and rosemary

● Peel the onions and chop them coarsely. Finely chop the peeled garlic. Dice the bacon, removing the rind.

● Heat the oil over a high heat in a frying-pan large enough to take all the pieces of rabbit. Add the rabbit and fry for 5 minutes, turning once, until nicely browned. Now add the onions, garlic and bacon dice and turn the heat down to medium. Continue to fry for another 10 minutes, again turning the rabbit once.

● Pour in the wine and allow to bubble. Add the tomatoes, broken up with the back of a wooden spoon, and their juice, season well, and tuck in the herbs. Allow to bubble merrily for 10–15 minutes, until the rabbit is cooked through (cut into a piece to check) and the sauce nicely reduced. The exact cooking time of the rabbit will depend on the size of the joints and the age of the animal. When it is ready, check the seasoning and serve.

Rabbit with Sherry Vinegar

Boneless rabbit makes a pleasant change from chicken breasts. For a soothing supper, cook it as a blanquette, in a thick creamy white sauce flavoured with a little mustard. For a sharper dish, try it Spanish-style, cooked with garlic and spices in sherry vinegar.

Preparation time: 5 minutes
Cooking time: 10 minutes
Grade: easy

Suggested accompaniments: sauté potatoes and green beans with lemon juice

1¼lb (550g) boneless rabbit	½ teaspoon freshly ground black pepper
2 fat cloves of garlic	
2 tablespoons olive oil	salt
2 teaspoons paprika	4 tablespoons sherry vinegar
1 teaspoon ground coriander	

● Chop the rabbit into bite-sized pieces and finely chop the garlic.
● In a large heavy-based frying-pan, heat the olive oil over a medium heat. When it is nearly spitting, add the rabbit pieces and the garlic and stir-fry for 2 minutes. Sprinkle over the spices, season with a little salt, pour in the vinegar, and cover immediately or the vinegar will evaporate. Turn the heat down to low and cook for 7 minutes, shaking the pan half-way through, then serve.

WOOD PIGEON

Wild wood pigeon are not as tender as the farm-reared squabs and need careful treatment to be appreciated at their best. This means either very brief or fairly lengthy cooking. A roast wood pigeon tends to be chewy and dry – either braise the bird whole in a little highly-flavoured liquid or remove the breasts and roast, grill or fry them for the shortest of time before laying the thick pink slices over salad leaves.

Braised Wood Pigeon Chinese-style

The Chinese are frequent eaters of pigeon, which they generally serve either deep-fried or braised. Be prepared to eat the pigeons with your fingers.

Preparation time: 10 minutes
Cooking time: 35 minutes
Grade: moderate

Suggested accompaniments: the pigeon would be served as one dish among many in a Chinese meal; as a main course, serve it with rice and stir-fried vegetables

4 wood pigeons	2 tablespoons gin
1 teaspoon coarse salt	½ pint (300ml) light chicken stock
3 tablespoons dark soy sauce	2 whole star anise
1in (2.5cm) piece of fresh ginger	juice of 1 lemon
2 tablespoons vegetable oil	1 teaspoon white sugar

- Wash the wood pigeons inside and out and rub in the salt and half the soy sauce. Leave to stand for 10 minutes. Peel the ginger and chop finely.
- Heat the oil until spitting and quickly fry the wood pigeons to brown – 1 minute on each side. Discard the oil.
- In a casserole large enough to take all the pigeons, mix the remaining ingredients and bring to a simmer. Add the pigeons on their side, cover and simmer for 15 minutes. Now turn the birds over to their other side and simmer for a further 15 minutes. Remove the pigeons from the casserole and put to keep warm – traditionally the Chinese chop them into small pieces with a cleaver, but you can also serve them whole. Strain the sauce and if necessary reduce a little. Pour over the pigeons and serve.

Warm Pigeon Salad with Sesame Dressing

Pigeon breasts briefly roasted until brown on the outside but still a tender pink on the inside make a substantial topping for a warm winter salad. You will have to remove the pigeon breasts yourself, but this is easily done with a sharp knife; freeze the legs and carcasses until you have time to make stock or soup. This version of the salad is marginally oriental, with a sesame and soy dressing; you could also try whole walnuts with walnut oil, or toss in a few wild mushrooms and dress the salad with olive oil and lemon juice.

Preparation time: 5 minutes
Cooking time: 15 minutes
Grade: moderate

Suggested accompaniment: bread

2 pigeons
2 tablespoons sesame seeds
4 tablespoons sesame oil
1/2 teaspoon sugar
1 tablespoon white wine vinegar

1 tablespoon dark soy sauce
mixed bitter salad leaves, such as raddichio, lamb's lettuce, frisée, rocket and chicory

● Pre-heat the oven to 220°C/425°F/Gas Mark 7. With a sharp knife, remove the breasts from the pigeons and roast them for 8 minutes. Set them aside for 5 minutes to rest.
● To make the dressing, put a dry frying-pan over a high heat and toast the sesame seeds, stirring continuously. This will take a minute or two – the seeds are ready when they start to colour and pop. Pour in the sesame oil, followed by the sugar, vinegar and soy sauce. Bubble together for 1 minute, stirring continuously, and take off the heat.
● Wash the salad leaves and put into a serving bowl. Slice the pigeon breasts thickly and scatter over the salad. Pour over the hot dressing, making sure you scrape out all the sesame seeds, and serve.

VENISON

Although farmed venison may lack the depth of flavour of meat from a wild animal, it is both tender and lean, with a not too pronounced gaminess, making it popular even with those who declare that game is too rich for their palate. A venison casserole is a winter favourite, but does take a long time, since the meat needs to be first marinated and then cooked very slowly. Venison steaks, on the other hand, need the quickest of cooking, although they too benefit from at least a short dip in a marinade. Welcome new sights for quick cooks are minced venison, which makes excellent meatballs, and venison sausages.

Marinated Venison Steaks

Although farmed venison steaks can be cooked without prior marinating, they are even better for an hour or so in olive oil scented with herbs, juniper berries and a dash of balsamic vinegar. As with all steaks, the cooking is especially successful if you have a ridged cast-iron griddle, which leaves the meat still pink in the centre and scarred across the flesh with deep dark sear marks.

Preparation time: 10 minutes, 1 hour before cooking
Cooking time: 10 minutes
Grade: easy

Suggested accompaniment: potato and celeriac mash, in a ratio of $2/3$ potato to $1/3$ celeriac

1 teaspoon juniper berries	1 teaspoon balsamic vinegar
½ teaspoon black peppercorns	2 tablespoons extra virgin olive
2 large sprigs of fresh thyme	oil
1 sprig of fresh rosemary	4 venison steaks

● Crush together the juniper berries and the peppercorns. Strip the leaves from the thyme and rosemary and chop finely. In an earthenware dish large enough to take all 4 steaks flat, mix the crushed juniper, pepper and chopped herbs together, add the vinegar and then stir in the olive oil. Lay the steaks in the dish, turning over once or twice to coat in the marinade mixture, and leave covered in a cool place for at least 1 hour, (but not the fridge, which is too cold and will not allow the flavours to mingle), turning the steaks over half-way through.
● To cook, heat a skillet over a high heat, or heat the grill to maximum. Take the steaks out of the marinade and cook for 3 minutes on one

side if using a skillet, or 5 minutes close to the grill. Turn over, baste with the remaining marinade and cook for another 2–3 minutes on the skillet or 4–6 minutes under the grill, depending on how thick the steaks are and whether you like your venison rare or not. Allow the steaks to rest for a couple of minutes before serving, so that the juices can spread through the meat.

Venison Meatballs with Flageolet Beans

Venison makes excellent meatballs and hamburgers, provided the mince has plenty of seasoning. For a substantial winter supper, I bake peppery venison meatballs with flageolet beans. The dish is finished with breadcrumbs drenched in olive oil and flavoured with garlic, giving a pungent aroma and a crispy top. If you also have some venison sausages, you can use half sausages and half meatballs, creating a sort of venison cassoulet.

Preparation time: 10 minutes
Cooking time: 30 minutes
Grade: easy

Suggested accompaniment: French bread

1¼ lb (550g) venison mince	2 x 14oz (400g) tins ready-
½ teaspoon salt	cooked flageolet beans
2 teaspoons freshly ground black	4 tablespoons beef stock
pepper	2 tablespoons dry breadcrumbs
1 tablespoon olive oil	2 cloves of garlic (*optional*)

● Pre-heat the oven to 180°C/350°F/Gas Mark 4. Season the mince with the salt and pepper and with your hands form it into balls approximately 1in (2.5cm) across. Heat the oil in a frying-pan over a high heat and fry the meatballs for 2 minutes on either side.

● Place the fried meatballs in a large earthenware dish in which they will all fit. Drain the beans and pour over the meatballs. Add the stock and cook, uncovered, in the pre-heated oven for 15 minutes.

● Now sprinkle with the breadcrumbs and the crushed chopped garlic if you are using it. Cook for another 5–10 minutes, until the breadcrumbs are lightly browned and the beans are bubbling. Serve immediately.

MEAT

LAMB

Lamb is still a seasonal meat, and British lamb bought in the winter and early spring will often be from a more mature lamb, traditionally known as hoggett. This meat needs slower treatment than the later spring lamb, and is better cooked more thoroughly rather than served pink. The inverse of the seasons 'down under' means that young lamb is available all year round, but the British spring lamb of late spring and early summer is worth waiting for; some of the best meat of all comes from lambs reared on the hills of Wales. Look for firm, light pink meat, avoiding cuts that appear flabby or too dark a red. Frozen lamb is not as flavoursome as the fresh meat and tends to shrink more during cooking, so it is best cooked on the bone.

CHOPS

Lamb chops range from delicate little nuggets of meat attached to the long thin curving bones of the best end to the thick chunks of meat encircled by creamy fat of the chump chop. The skill of the butcher shows especially in the preparation of a well-trimmed rack of lamb, one of my favourite cuts of meat for a quick dinner party dish.

Grilled Lamb Chops with Quick Pinenut and Sultana 'Jam'

A small pile of sweet nuts and fruit beside a plain grilled lamb chop makes all the difference to the dish, transforming it from a work day meal to something mildly exotic. Using redcurrant jelly as the base of the 'jam' means that it is very quick to put together – in fact it takes less time than the chops do to grill. I am fond of the combination of pinenuts and sultanas with lamb, but you could also use blanched almonds and dried apricots, using white instead of red wine. For a similar effect with pork, cook skinned walnuts in plum jam with red wine and a couple of cloves.

Preparation time: nil
Cooking time: 15 minutes
Grade: basic

Suggested accompaniments: new potatoes, glazed carrots and turnips

4 lamb chops (*I particularly like loin chops for this dish*)	1 glass red wine
1½ tablespoons redcurrant jelly	juice of ½ a lemon
2 tablespoons pinenuts	salt and freshly ground black pepper
2 tablespoons sultanas	

● Grill the lamb chops to taste 5–7 minutes on each side under a hot grill. Allow to rest for a few minutes before serving.

● Meanwhile make the 'jam'. In a small heavy pan, gently melt the redcurrant jelly over a gentle heat. Add the pinenuts, sultanas and red wine and turn up the heat so that the wine bubbles. Allow to simmer uncovered for 5 minutes, until there is little liquid left. Add a squeeze of lemon juice and seasoning to taste, and serve with the lamb chops.

Chump Chops Roasted on a Bed of Leeks

The classic Welsh combination of lamb and leeks is here given a marginally oriental touch with the addition of powdered ginger and soy sauce. The juice from the roasting chump chops drips down into the leeks, which are braising in stock, soy sauce and vinegar. The end result is rosy lamb lightly flavoured with ginger and tender shreds of leek in a thin but powerful gravy.

Preparation time: 10 minutes
Cooking time: 25–30 minutes
Grade: basic

Suggested accompaniment: a purée of ⅔ potato to ⅓ celeriac, made with chicken stock and seasoned with celery salt

1½lb (675g) leeks	4fl oz (125ml) chicken stock
4 large lamb chump chops	1 tablespoon dark soy sauce
½ teaspoon ground ginger	1 tablespoon sherry vinegar (*failing that, you could use red wine vinegar*)
¼ teaspoon freshly ground black pepper	

● Pre-heat the oven to 180°C/350°F/Gas Mark 4. Trim the leeks of their green ends and slice the white parts into very fine shreds. Wash well. Trim the chops of any excess fat and rub the ginger and pepper into the meat.

● Pile the leeks into a shallow ovenproof tray just large enough to take all the chops and which you can take straight to the table, and pour over the stock, soy sauce and vinegar. Lay the chump chops on top, so that the shredded leeks are covered. Roast for 25–30 minutes, depending on the size of the chops and how pink you like the meat. Stand for 5 minutes before serving.

Rack of Lamb with a Mustard and Polenta Crust

A rack of lamb, the row of small best end of neck cutlets left joined together, is one of the most useful (if expensive) cuts for dinner party cooks in a hurry. Properly trimmed of fat, the bones left bare, it needs only a brief blast in a hot oven and looks very attractive to serve. Your guests will be especially impressed if you coat it with mustard and polenta to produce a crisp crust.

Preparation time: 5 minutes
Cooking time: 25–30 minutes
Grade: moderate

Suggested accompaniments: cubes of potato fried in olive oil with whole cloves of garlic; a green salad

2 trimmed racks of lamb, approx. 10–12oz (280–350g) each 2 dessertspoons Dijon mustard	2 tablespoons polenta 1 tablespoon olive oil

- Pre-heat the oven to 220°C/425°F/Gas Mark 7.
- Trim almost all the fat off the back of the lamb. Lay the racks trimmed side up on a roasting dish. Smear the mustard all over the surface; sprinkle the polenta evenly over the mustard. Dribble a little olive oil over the polenta.
- Roast the racks in the oven for 20–25 minutes, depending on how large they are and how pink you like the meat. Heat the grill up to maximum. When the racks are cooked to your satisfaction (if you are not sure, cut between the two central bones to check) put them under the grill for 3 or 4 minutes to crisp up the crust – watch carefully to make sure it doesn't burn.

Lamb Chops with Flageolet Beans

Lamb and flageolet beans is a classic combination in France. Typically the cut known as *gigot* is used (if you are roasting a leg of lamb, try putting some drained flageolets in the roasting pan for the last 30 minutes of cooking), but lamb chops also do well. The key is to ensure that the beans are flavoured with the meat juices, by cooking the two together.

Preparation time: 5 minutes
Cooking time: 25 minutes
Grade: easy

Suggested accompaniment: bread

4 tomatoes	salt and freshly ground black
½ clove of garlic	pepper
2 x 14oz (400g) tins ready-cooked flageolet beans	1 sprig of fresh rosemary
1oz (30g) butter	4 lamb chops

- Pre-heat the oven to 180°C/350°F/Gas Mark 4 and heat the grill to maximum. Skin the tomatoes by dipping them in boiling water, and dice the flesh. Rub the cut side of the garlic around a shallow cooking dish, earthenware if possible.
- Drain the flageolets and mix them with the chopped tomatoes. Put them in the earthenware dish with the butter and plenty of salt and pepper. Tuck in the sprig of rosemary.
- Season the chops and cook them fat side up under the grill for 5 minutes, until the fat is nicely browned. Now put the chops in the oven on top of the beans. Cook for 20 minutes then allow to stand for 5 minutes before serving – the beans will be deliciously flavoured with the cooking juices from the meat.

FILLET

It is from the fillet of lamb that those delicate little rounds of meat known as *noisettes* are cut. They need little cooking and can be served at their simplest with a flavoured butter, which I prefer to the highly reduced meat stock and red wine sauce typical of bourgeois restaurants. The fillet can also be roasted whole with a few aromatic agents.

Noisettes of Lamb with Rosemary and Olive Butter

The affinity of rosemary and lamb is well known, although the marriage must be handled delicately – too much of the herb can swamp the delicacy of the meat.

Preparation time: 10 minutes
Cooking time: 15 minutes
Grade: basic

Suggested accompaniments: boiled new potatoes; grilled halved tomatoes topped with thyme and breadcrumbs

1¼ lb (550g) fillet of lamb 1 heaped tablespoon stoned green olives	1 small sprig of fresh rosemary 2oz (55g) unsalted butter freshly ground black pepper

- Cut the lamb across at 1½in (4cm) intervals into thick rounds. Pre-heat the grill to maximum or, better still, warm an oiled cast-iron skillet. Beat together the olives, the needles of the rosemary and butter with pepper to taste, until you have a smooth paste.
- Cook the lamb for 4-5 minutes on either side, and leave to rest for 5 minutes before serving with a little nugget of the butter on top of each noisette.

Gingered Fillet of Lamb

The lemony flavour of fresh ginger complements lamb, making a light dish for summer. This sauce goes as well with leg steaks as with the tender fillet.

Preparation time: 5 minutes
Cooking time: 15 minutes
Grade: easy

Suggested accompaniments: cubed potatoes fried in olive oil with garlic; a green salad

1¼lb (550g) neck fillet of lamb salt and freshly ground black pepper 2in (5cm) piece of fresh ginger 2 tablespoons extra virgin olive oil	pinch of brown sugar 1 teaspoon light soy sauce juice of ½ a lemon

- Pre-heat the oven to 140°C/275°F/Gas Mark 1. Cut the fillet across at 1in (2.5cm) intervals, so that you have thick mini-rounds. Season well. Peel the piece of ginger and grate it finely, making sure you keep the juice.
- Heat the oil in a heavy-based frying-pan over a medium high heat, and when it is spitting add the lamb pieces. Fry for 4 minutes on each side and transfer to the warm oven.
- Turn the heat under the pan to low and add the grated ginger to the oily juices. Cook, stirring, for 2 minutes, then add the sugar and soy sauce, and cook for another minute. Take off the heat and stir in the lemon juice well. Return the pieces of lamb to the pan, turning them to coat them with the sauce, and serve.

Roast Fillet of Lamb with Tomatoes and Olives

Whole neck fillet of lamb is an excellent cut to roast quickly and serve simply with its juices. In Provence these juices are enhanced with orange juice, tomato, garlic, local herbs and, of course, olive oil. The execution is basic in the extreme, the end result impressive. It is important for the flavour that you use an earthenware dish.

Preparation time: 10 minutes
Cooking time: 20–25 minutes
Grade: basic

Suggested accompaniments: buttered tagliatelle; green beans, steamed and dressed with garlic and lemon juice

---

4 very ripe tomatoes
2 or 3 sprigs of fresh thyme
4 or 5 large leaves of basil
2 tablespoons small black pitted olives
2 neck fillets of lamb, total weight approx. 1¼–1½lb (550–675g)

2 fat cloves of garlic
salt and freshly ground black pepper
juice of 2 oranges
2 tablespoons extra virgin olive oil

● Pre-heat the oven to 230°C/450°F/Gas Mark 8. Dice the tomatoes. Strip the leaves from the sprigs of thyme and shred the basil leaves. Rinse the olives well under the cold tap. Finely chop the garlic.

● Mix together the diced tomatoes, chopped garlic, herbs and olives, and lay them in an earthenware dish large enough to take both fillets whole. Lay the fillets on top and season with plenty of freshly ground black pepper and a little salt. Pour over the orange juice and olive oil.

● Roast uncovered for 20–25 minutes, depending on how rare you like your lamb. Allow to rest for 10 minutes before carving into thick slices, surrounded by the tomatoes and olives and the juices.

LEG
–

A small leg of spring lamb is one of the quickest of joints to roast, needing a relatively brief blast in a very hot oven and a short rest before carving to reveal the juicy pink meat beneath the browned exterior. For extra flavour, make slits in the meat with a sharp knife, poke in slivers of garlic, and lay the leg on a couple of sprigs of rosemary or lavender. A boned leg of lamb, or *gigot*, makes an even quicker roast, whilst leg steaks are the most rapid of all to prepare – especially if the meat is cut into strips and stir-fried.

Leg Steaks with Lemon and Cumin Butter

Flavoured butters are immensely helpful to the cook under pressure. Taking only a few minutes to prepare, they lift a grilled cut of meat or fish to a higher plane – provided, that is, you use best-quality butter, which for me means French unsalted, preferably from the Isigny region of Normandy. I particularly like the combination of citrus fruit with butter: orange butter with fish, for example, and this sharp lemon butter, gently flavoured with cumin, to melt over grilled lamb. I have suggested leg steaks, but you could just as easily use lamb chops.

Preparation time: 5 minutes, 15 minutes before serving so you can chill the butter
Cooking time: 10 minutes
Grade: basic

Suggested accompaniments: new potatoes; carrots

1 lemon, preferably unwaxed	1 teaspoon ground cumin
2oz (55g) best-quality unsalted butter	4 leg of lamb steaks

● Grate the lemon rind finely. Squeeze the juice from ½ the lemon. Mix together the butter, lemon zest, lemon juice and cumin; this is most easily achieved using a food processor, but you could also use a pestle and mortar. Chill the butter in the freezer while you cook the lamb (if making the butter in advance, simply keep in the fridge).
● Grill the lamb under a very hot grill for 5 minutes on either side. Allow the steaks to stand for 5 minutes before serving with a good chunk of the butter on top of each.

Leg Steaks with Caper Sauce

Capers have been a traditional English accompaniment to boiled mutton since the sixteenth century, when the barrels of vinegar containing the pickled flower buds were first imported from the Mediterranean. An old-fashioned caper sauce is still a good one to serve with lamb – it will go well with chops as well as with leg steaks. More mature lamb, which your butcher will know as hoggett, has a more powerful flavour to stand up to the piquancy of the sauce than the delicate new season's lamb of spring and summer.

Preparation time: minimal
Cooking time: 30 minutes
Grade: moderate

Suggested accompaniment: mashed potatoes, made in traditional style with lashings of milk and butter and plenty of freshly ground black pepper

---

4 leg of lamb steaks	³/₄ pint (450ml) lamb or chicken stock
salt and freshly ground black pepper	1 heaped tablespoon capers, drained
1oz (30g) unsalted butter	1–2 tablespoons of white wine vinegar, to taste
½ tablespoon vegetable oil	1 tablespoon chopped parsley, if available
1 level tablespoon plain flour	

- Trim the leg steaks of any fat and season.
- Melt the butter and oil together in a frying-pan large enough to take all 4 steaks, over a gentle heat. Add the lamb steaks and fry gently, turning once or twice, for 10–15 minutes according to thickness. Although I normally like my lamb pink, for this traditional recipe it should be cooked just to the point where the juice runs brown rather than pink when you pierce the flesh.
- Transfer the lamb to a just-warm oven. Keep the fat in the pan over a low heat and stir in the flour. When it has absorbed all the fat, add a tablespoon or two of the stock. Stir this well in, then add the remaining stock in a steady trickle, stirring all the time to avoid lumps. When you have added all the stock, turn up the heat and, still stirring, allow the sauce to boil for a couple of minutes, until it thickens and becomes slightly creamy.
- Pour the sauce through a fine sieve to remove any lumps. Then add the capers and vinegar to taste (the amount of vinegar depends on the saltiness of the stock). Bring back to a simmer, check the seasoning, put the cooked steaks in the sauce and turn over once or twice to coat.
- Finally, sprinkle with the parsley and serve.

Stir-fried Lamb with Black Bean Sauce

In Indonesia, the world's largest Muslim country, lamb replaces pork in stir-fry dishes, for obvious reasons. The result is especially successful with black bean sauce.

For particular authenticity you could use the Indonesian version of soy sauce, *keçap manis*, which is thick, dark and sweet and available in many supermarkets.

Preparation time: 15 minutes
Cooking time: 8 minutes
Grade: easy

Suggested accompaniment: boiled rice

1¼ lb (550g) leg of lamb steak	2 tablespoons groundnut oil
2 cloves of garlic	1 teaspoon sugar
4 shallots	4 tablespoons black bean sauce
½ in (1cm) piece of fresh ginger	2 teaspoons rice or white wine
2 fresh green chillies (*or more to*	vinegar
taste)	1 tablespoon dark soy sauce

- Trim the meat of any fat and slice into long thin strips. Peel the garlic, shallots and ginger and chop them all finely. Deseed the chillies and cut into long thin strips.
- Heat the oil in a wok or frying-pan. Add the garlic, ginger, shallots and chillies and stir-fry for 1 minute. Now add the strips of meat and stir-fry for a further 2 minutes. Sprinkle over the sugar, cook for 30 seconds then add the black bean sauce. Finally add the vinegar and soy sauce. Allow to bubble for 4 minutes then serve.

MINCED LAMB

Not so long ago, you had to rely on your butcher if you wanted minced lamb, but now almost every supermarket stocks it. By all means use it to make lamb burgers, but don't neglect the wide range of Middle Eastern dishes which rely on minced lamb, from stuffed vegetables to kebabs and köfta, small highly spiced meatballs.

Red Lamb Burgers

These take their name from the colour of the ingredients, the paprika, tomato and carrot combining with the minced lamb to produce a colourful burger. These ingredients are not there purely for effect, however: the finely grated carrot melts into the meat as it cooks to add sweetness as well as bulk, which is further enhanced by the paprika and the tomato. These burgers are excellent for the barbecue.

Preparation time: 5 minutes, provided you have a food processor
Cooking time: 15–20 minutes
Grade: easy

Suggested accompaniments: shredded lettuce and bread

Makes 4 large burgers:	
2 large carrots	1 tablespoon tomato paste
1 large onion	1 tablespoon Worcestershire sauce
1¼ lb (550g) minced lamb	Tabasco
1 teaspoon paprika	salt and freshly ground black pepper

- Scrub the carrots or peel them if they are old. Finely grate the peeled onion and carrot (this is easiest in a food processor). Squeeze the grated vegetables well to remove any excess moisture and mix them with all the remaining ingredients. The amount of Tabasco is up to you (you may wish to leave it out altogether if you are feeding children), but make sure you add plenty of seasoning.
- Shape the mix into 4 thick, equal-sized burgers. You can grill them, fry them or, best of all, cook them on a cast-iron griddle over a flame. Cook slowly at first, turning up the heat towards the end to char the outsides. The cooking time will vary between 15–20 minutes, depending on the cooking method, the thickness of the burgers and whether you like your lamb slightly pink.

Kurdish Lamb Kebabs

Traditionally these long thin sausage-shaped kebabs were made by the Kurds with their local meat, goat, but minced lamb is a more tender option which is easier to find in the supermarket. The kebabs are at their very best when grilled on the barbecue, replicating the charcoal braziers over which they are cooked by shepherds and in the markets of south-eastern Turkey, but they are also good cooked under the grill.

Preparation time: 20 minutes
Cooking time: 8–10 minutes
Grade: basic but messy

Suggested accompaniment: as part of a barbecue; with a burghul wheat salad with plenty of fresh herbs (tabbouleh)

---

2 small red onions	½ teaspoon freshly ground black
3 cloves of garlic	pepper
1oz (30g) fresh flat-leaved parsley	1½ lb (675g) minced lamb
4 small dried red chilli peppers	1 lemon
(*or more if you like your food hot*)	16 long wooden kebab skewers,
1 teaspoon coarse salt	approx. 10in (25cm) long

- Pre-heat the grill to hot or get the charcoal glowing on the barbecue.
- Finely chop the onions and garlic. Remove the stalks from the parsley and chop the leaves finely. Remove the seeds from the chillies if you don't want the kebabs hot, and chop the dried chillies finely.
- Mix together all the ingredients except the lemon and knead with your hands for 3 or 4 minutes. Dampen your hands with warm water and pull off a lump of the lamb mixture the size of a small egg. Mould this evenly down the length of one of the skewers, leaving 1in (2.5cm) at either end. Repeat for each skewer – you should have sufficient meat mixture for all 16.
- Cook over the barbecue or on an oiled tray close to the grill for 4–5 minutes on either side, until the surface is lightly browned. Serve with quarters of lemon.

Lamb Meatballs with Chickpeas in an Onion and Lemon Sauce

A clever trick in Middle Eastern cooking is to caramelize onions before adding lemon juice to the sauce, to give a slightly sweet and sour taste. Traditional recipes require the onions to sweat slowly for 45 minutes or more, but the cheating cook can achieve a similar result by quick-frying the onions until brown and then adding a little sugar. The sweetness of the chickpeas and the sharpness of fresh coriander enhance the effect in a one-pot supper of lamb meatballs, which is equally good in summer or winter.

Preparation time: 15 minutes
Cooking time: 35 minutes
Grade: easy

Suggested accompaniments: plain boiled rice or warm pitta bread, and a salad of finely chopped tomato, onion and cucumber, sprinkled with salt and

1lb (450g) white onions	½ teaspoon freshly ground black
2 cloves of garlic	pepper
2 small fresh green chillies	1¼ lb (550g) minced lamb
2 tablespoons olive oil (*you can also use sunflower oil*)	1 teaspoon white sugar
1 teaspoon ground cinnamon	14oz (400g) tin chickpeas
1 teaspoon ground cumin	juice of 2 lemons
½ teaspoon salt	2 tablespoons chopped fresh coriander

- Peel the onions and chop them coarsely. Peel the garlic and deseed the chillies; chop both finely. In a large heavy-based pan, heat the oil and fry the onions over a medium high heat for 10 minutes, stirring regularly, until they are browned all over. While the onion is cooking, make the meatballs: add the cinnamon, cumin, salt and pepper to the minced lamb and mix together well. Form into balls the size of a walnut.
- When the onion has been frying for 10 minutes, add the chopped garlic and chillies and the sugar. Continue to fry over a medium high heat for 2 minutes, stirring continuously, then add the meatballs. Gently turn them until they are browned on all sides (which will take no more than a minute or two), and then pour in the contents of the tin of chickpeas, the lemon juice and if necessary a little water to cover. Bring to the boil, turn down to a simmer, cover and leave to cook over a low flame for 20 minutes.
- One minute before serving, stir in the chopped coriander. Taste the sauce for balance – you may like to add more lemon juice or sugar.

Persian Rice with Lamb and Almonds

The Persian way of cooking rice is very simple, with deeply satisfying results. The briefly boiled rice is steamed in its own water on a base of melted butter, creating a crisp topping and perfectly separate grains of rice. For added effect the Persians used to put a layer of dried fruits and nuts in the rice, and sometimes on feast days minced lamb was part of the filling. There is no need to serve this dish as part of a banquet, as it is very good on its own.

Preparation time: 15 minutes
Cooking time: 30 minutes, requiring no attention
Grade: easy

Suggested accompaniments: thick plain yoghurt to spoon over the rice; a green salad

12oz (350g) Basmati rice (*the variety is important*)	2 tablespoons flaked almonds (*a mixture of pinenuts and almonds is also good*)
2oz (55g) ready-soaked dried apricots or sultanas (or *a mixture of the two*)	1 teaspoon allspice
8oz (225g) minced lamb	salt and freshly ground black pepper
	3oz (85g) butter

- Rinse the rice for 3 or 4 minutes under cold running water to remove the starch. Bring a large pan of salted water to the boil and cook the rice for 4 minutes, then drain.
- Roughly chop the dried fruit. Mix together the minced lamb, nuts, fruit and allspice. Add plenty of seasoning.
- In a heavy-based casserole dish melt 2oz (55g) of the butter. Lay half the drained rice in the base of the dish, then spread over the rice the meat, nut and fruit mixture. Cover with the remaining rice and dot with the remaining butter. Lay a clean teatowel over the dish then put on the lid; turn up the corners of the teatowel over the lid.
- Cook over a low heat for 25 minutes then turn out the contents of the dish, making sure you scrape out the crispy base.

Shoulder of Lamb

Shoulder of lamb appears to me seriously underpriced in the supermarkets, for it is an excellent cut. It is the very best meat to use for lamb casseroles; so-called 'stewing lamb' is generally fatty offcuts. However, the meat from a shoulder of lamb, whether on or off the bone, does usually require long, slow cooking – unless, that is, you slice it very finely for the barbecue.

Mongolian-style Barbecued Lamb

Barbecuing food at the table is a popular way of eating in northern China in the winter months, having the advantage of keeping you warm as well as well fed. For the nation which developed the wok as the most fuel-efficient way of cooking, this is an important consideration.

Vast quantities of meat can be consumed at one sitting – one book of mine recommends allowing 1¹/₂lb (675g) of meat per diner – and as a result the meals tend to become long drawn-out affairs, with plenty of merrymaking.

Preparation time: 15 minutes, 30 minutes before cooking
Cooking time: 5 minutes
Grade: basic

Suggested accompaniment: shredded spring onion

1¹/₂lb (675g) boned shoulder of lamb (*you could also use a more expensive cut such as fillet or boned leg*) 2in (5cm) piece of fresh ginger	3 tablespoons dark soy sauce 2 tablespoons dry sherry 1 tablespoon sesame oil 1 heaped dessertspoon white sugar

- Cut the lamb into thin slices (traditionally the meat should be paper thin but I like it a little chunkier). Grate the ginger. Mix together all the ingredients and leave to marinate for 30 minutes.
- When the barbecue coals are really glowing, put on the lamb a few slices at a time. It is traditional to let each diner cook his or her own meat. It needs no more than a couple of minutes on each side, and you can also sprinkle on a few shreds of spring onion at a time.

BEEF

Our general enthusiasm for red meat has waned, particularly in the light of the BSE scare, but the occasional roast joint of beef is still for me, at least, a welcome treat, provided the beef comes from a grass-fed herd. I particularly like forerib of beef cooked on the bone, a cut which is cheaper than the traditional sirloin. Provided you like your beef rare, a roast ample for 4 people will take under an hour to cook in a very hot oven. The most important part of the cooking process is to allow the meat to rest for at least 15 minutes before carving, to allow the juices to spread evenly, giving that wonderful rosy hue.

The cheaper cuts of beef, such as shin and flank, need long slow cooking to be appreciated at their best. As a result, they have become less popular and represent a bargain buy for those with the time to prepare them. Meat designated as stewing or braising beef similarly requires an hour in the oven or on the stove at the very minimum, and preferably 2 or 3. So for those with little time, therefore, the most popular cuts of beef are likely to be steaks and the cheaper mince.

Whatever cut of beef you choose, it should come from a well-hung carcass (good butchers recommend a minimum of 2 weeks). Look for meat which is a deep rich red, well marbled with slightly yellow fat, with little or no gristle between the fat and the lean. When you push your thumb into a cut of beef, the surface should rise up again immediately; avoid flaccid meat.

STEAK

Steak can be grilled, fried, braised or stir-fried, cooked whole or first cut into cubes or strips, even minced, stretching the steak further so that it no longer represents an extravagance. The price and the thickness of the cut may help you to decide how to cook it. It would be a criminal act to slice up a substantial piece of bank-breaking fillet for the wok, but this can be a sensible approach to a small thin slice of rump or even sirloin steak. I would avoid the 'quick-fry' steaks, which tend to be tough.

Steak on Toast with Yoghurt

In Greece and Turkey cubes of meat are often marinaded in yoghurt before cooking, to break down the fibres and therefore increase the tenderness. Tough pieces of lamb may need as much as 24 hours of this treatment, but rump steak will benefit from just 30 minutes in a marinade – although if you have time to leave it longer, so much the better. The meat can then be grilled or fried, as here. I serve the steak on toast piled with a crisp salad of cucumber and onion, the yoghurt marinade warmed through and poured over the lot.

Preparation time: 5 minutes, at least 30 minutes before cooking
Cooking time: 5 minutes
Grade: basic

Suggested accompaniment: none needed

1¼ lb (550g) rump steak	pepper
6fl oz (175ml) thick Greek yoghurt	½ teaspoon coarse salt
juice of ½ a lemon	½ a cucumber
good pinch of sugar	2 red onions or 1 Spanish onion
1 tablespoon tomato paste	1 fat clove of garlic
2 teaspoons paprika	4 thick slices of white country bread
1 teaspoon cumin	1 tablespoon olive oil
1 teaspoon freshly ground black	

- Trim any fat from the steak and cut into 1in (2.5cm) cubes. Mix together the yoghurt, lemon juice, sugar, tomato paste, spices and salt and put in the steak to marinate. Leave for at least 30 minutes.
- Peel the cucumber and onions and chop coarsely. Peel the clove of garlic and cut in half. Toast the bread and rub with the cut side of the clove of garlic. Pile the cucumber and onion on top of the toast.
- When you are ready to cook, heat the oil in a frying-pan over a high heat. Pick the cubes of steak out of the marinade and briefly fry, stirring, until they are cooked to your satisfaction – I, liking my steak rare, cook them for no more than 2 minutes. Pile the steak on top of the salad and stir the marinade into the pan off the heat – it should just warm through from the heat of the pan, otherwise it will curdle. Pour the warm, spicy yoghurt over the toast, salad and meat and serve.

Rump Steak with a Red Wine, Chilli and Caper Sauce

A plain rump steak can be a little dull – after the first few mouthfuls I find myself looking for a contrast to the straight taste of meat. For this reason I like to serve my steaks with a small amount of highly-flavoured sauce. This recipe from southern Italy is a favourite: the pan juices from the cooked steak are finished with a splash of red wine, a touch of chopped garlic, a sprinkling of red chillies and a handful of capers to produce a fiery contrast to the steak.

Preparation time: 5 minutes
Cooking time: 10 minutes, depending on how you like your steak done
Grade: moderate

Suggested accompaniments: fried potatoes or potatoes baked in their jackets; steamed broccoli, or a roasted red pepper salad dressed with extra virgin olive oil and balsamic vinegar

---

4 thick cut rump steaks
2 fat cloves of garlic
½ teaspoon chopped dried red chilli (*small Italian dried chillies are best*)

½ tablespoon tomato paste
1 tablespoon capers, rinsed
2 tablespoons olive oil
1 large glass full bodied red wine
freshly ground black pepper

- Pre-heat the oven to 140°C/275°F/Gas Mark 1, so that you can keep the steaks warm while you make the sauce. Peel the garlic and chop very finely. Crush the chillies. Dilute the tomato paste in 1 tablespoon of water.
- In a heavy-based frying-pan in which all the steaks will fit, heat the oil over a high heat until it is just spitting. Stand well back and add the steaks. Fry for 2–4 minutes on each side, depending on how thick the steaks are and how rare, or well done, you like them. Put the steaks in the oven to keep warm.
- Keep the pan over a high heat, stand well back and add the wine. Allow to bubble fiercely for 1 minute then add the garlic. Cook for a further minute, stirring, then add the diluted tomato paste and crushed chillies. Cook over a fierce heat for a further minute or two, by which time the sauce will have reduced to a slightly syrupy consistency. Now reduce the heat, stir in the capers to heat through and season the sauce to taste (I use plenty of freshly ground black pepper). Put the steaks back in the pan and turn them over in the sauce so that they are just coated. Serve immediately.

Steak with Mustard, Cream and Whisky Sauce

A very different sauce for steak from the one before, this uses expensive ingredients simply cooked to produce a rich, old-fashioned result. The mustard, which must be the mild grainy variety, adds sharpness and texture; the whisky flavour comes through powerfully whilst the harsh spirit is bubbled off; and the cream combines the mixture into a smooth sauce which will make a steak feel truly luxurious. If you were a chef you might use an Islay whisky for its smoky contribution to the sauce but personally I prefer to drink the Islay and use the cheapest blended whisky for cooking.

Preparation time: none
Cooking time: 10 minutes for the sauce; the steak will vary depending on how rare you like it
Grade: easy

Suggested accompaniments: boiled new potatoes and a green vegetable or salad

---

1oz (30g) unsalted butter
1 tablespoon mild, grainy French mustard (*moutarde de Meaux*)
2 tablespoons whisky
4fl oz (100ml) double cream (*it is important that it should be double cream or it will curdle − you could*

also use crème fraîche)
salt and freshly ground black pepper
4 steaks (*you can use rump, sirloin or fillet, but the latter is my favourite with this sauce*)

● You can make the sauce in advance if you like and reheat it.
● Melt the butter over a gentle heat and cook the mustard for 1 minute. Now turn up the heat and add the whisky. Stir well together and allow the whisky to bubble for 3 minutes. Now stir in the cream and allow to simmer for 5 minutes. Check seasoning and serve the sauce with the steak of your choice, which can be grilled, fried or, best of all, cooked on an iron skillet.

Tagliatelle with Strips of Beef, Olives and Anchovies

This makes a very easy, piquant sauce for pasta. I sometimes add red chillies as well for extra bite. If you use a shaped pasta such as penne, you could also serve this as a salad.

Preparation time: 10 minutes
Cooking time: 3 minutes for the sauce, 10 minutes for the pasta
Grade: easy

Suggested accompaniment: a green salad to follow

12oz (350g) sirloin or rump steak	*(85–115g) per person)*
2 cloves of garlic	3 tablespoons extra virgin olive oil
4oz (115g) stoned black olives	
2oz (55g) tin anchovies in olive oil	freshly ground black pepper
tagliatelle *(allow 3–4oz*	2 tablespoons chopped flat-leaved parsley

- Trim any fat from the steak. Cut the meat into strips about $\frac{1}{4}$in (5mm) thick and $1\frac{1}{2}$in (4cm) long, trying to cut with the grain. Finely chop the garlic. Coarsely chop the olives and anchovies, reserving the latter's oil (this can be done with a quick whizz in a processor – but be careful not to reduce them to a paste).

- Put a large pan of salted water on for the pasta. It is easiest to cook the pasta first and then cook the sauce, which only takes a few minutes.

- To make the sauce, heat the oil over a fierce flame. When the oil is very hot, add the steak and fry for 1 minute. Now add all the remaining ingredients except the parsley, but including the anchovy oil. Cook, stirring, for another minute, season well with freshly ground black pepper, stir in the parsley so that it just wilts and pour the whole lot over the pasta.

Japanese-style Sesame Steak

In Japan strips of steak are marinaded in toasted sesame seeds, soy sauce and the local sake before being grilled over a charcoal barbecue and served with a dipping sauce. I serve a similar dish, after making a few concessions on behalf of the British kitchen. Dry sherry replaces sake in the marinade, the grill rather than the barbecue does the cooking (though by all means barbecue the steak in summer) and there is even a drop of Worcestershire sauce in the dipping sauce. The result may not be authentically Japanese, but it is highly delicious.

Preparation time: 10 minutes, plus 30 minutes marinating
Cooking time: 5 minutes
Grade: easy

Suggested accompaniments: boiled rice (preferably Japanese sticky rice); strips of peeled cucumber dressed with salt, sugar and white wine vinegar (or, better still, rice vinegar)

For 1¼ lb (550g) rump steak	
Marinade:	*Dipping sauce:*
2 tablespoons sesame seeds	6 thin spring onions
2 tablespoons light soy sauce (*if you have Japanese soy sauce, so much the better*)	1in (2.5cm) piece of fresh ginger
	2 tablespoons light soy sauce
	juice of ½ a lemon
2 tablespoons dry sherry	1 teaspoon white sugar
1 teaspoon white sugar	a few drops of Worcestershire sauce

● Trim any fat from the steak and cut the meat into strips ½in (1cm) across by 2in (5cm) long. In a dry frying-pan over a high heat toast the sesame seeds for a minute or two, stirring them constantly, until they start to pop. Watch very carefully to make sure they don't burn. Crush the toasted seeds and mix with the remaining marinade ingredients, add the steak and leave for 30 minutes.

● To make the dipping sauce, chop the white part of the spring onions very finely. Peel the ginger root and grate finely, making sure you catch the juices. Mix the spring onion and grated ginger with the remaining ingredients.

● To cook the steak, turn the grill up to maximum and place a metal baking tray under it to heat up. When the baking tray is very hot, add the strips of steak, and grill for 2 minutes on one side. Turn over, baste with the remaining marinade and cook for another minute or two, depending on how well cooked you like your steak. Alternatively cook briefly over the glowing coals of the barbecue. Serve the steak immediately, with a little bowl of dipping sauce for each diner.

Fried Steak with Green Chillies

Obviously, you will only try this Chinese dish if you like chillies. But to the wary, it is worth pointing out that once the seeds have been removed and the chillies fiercely browned in oil, their heat is much reduced, although by no means eliminated. Just as much bite comes through from the peppercorns.

Preparation time: 10 minutes, at least 30 minutes before you want to cook
Cooking time: 5 minutes
Grade: easy

Suggested accompaniment: rice

1¼ lb (550g) rump steak	2 tablespoons dry sherry
4 fat cloves of garlic	2 teaspoons white sugar
1 teaspoon black peppercorns	20 small fresh green chillies
2 tablespoons dark soy sauce	1 tablespoon vegetable oil

● Trim any fat from the steak and cut the meat into strips ½in (1cm) wide and 2in (5cm) long. Peel, crush and finely chop the garlic. Roughly crush the peppercorns. Mix together the crushed garlic, peppercorns, soy sauce, sherry and sugar and pour this marinade over the meat. Leave for 30 minutes.

● Remove the seeds from the chillies, rinsing them under the tap to ensure that none cling. Cut each chilli in half lengthways. Rinse your hands thoroughly once you have finished – chilli juice in the eye is painful.

● When you are ready to cook, heat the oil in a wok or frying-pan. When it is nearly spitting, add the chillies and stir-fry for 2 minutes, until the bright green colour begins to lighten. Stand well back, add the meat and the marinade and stir-fry for a further 3 minutes. Serve immediately.

BEEF MINCE

Minced beef is now available in a range of qualities, and is no longer the dumping ground for the remnants left over after butchering the cow. As a general rule, the less you are going to cook the mince, the better cut it should be produced from, and consequently the leaner it should be. It is, however, still difficult to find minced beef of sufficient quality for that ultimate fast food, steak tartare, unless you get your butcher to mince a piece of steak especially for you.

Lean meat is of course better for you, but remember that much of the flavour in beef comes from the fat, so extra-lean mince may not be the right choice for the more fully-flavoured dishes, especially those where the mince is subject to long slow stewing, such as spaghetti bolognese. Incidentally, this traditional student standby is no quick recipe when made properly, needing to simmer for 3–4 hours. For quicker dishes, make kebabs, hamburgers (have you tried them Korean style?) and meatballs.

Korean Hamburgers

The people of Korea like hamburgers too; they just season them slightly differently, using the South-east Asian trinity of garlic, ginger and chilli, with a dash of soy sauce, a swirl of sesame oil and plenty of their favourite spring onions. Each hamburger is much smaller than its American big brother, to ensure even cooking. Koreans would serve the burgers with the traditional *kimchi* – pickled, highly flavoured cabbage preserved in earthenware jars. You can try Chinese leaf flavoured with vinegar, sugar, salt and capers.

Preparation time: 20 minutes
Cooking time: 15 minutes
Grade: easy

Suggested accompaniments: Chinese leaf (see next page) and rice or bread

½ in (1cm) piece of fresh ginger	1 large or 2 small eggs
2 cloves of garlic	a few grinds of black pepper
1 or 2 small fresh green chillies, according to taste	1 dessertspoon dark soy sauce
	2 teaspoons sesame oil
8 small or 4 large spring onions	1½ lb (675g) beef mince
1 heaped tablespoon plain flour	1 tablespoon vegetable oil

● Peel the ginger and garlic; split the chillies and remove the seeds. Remove the green ends of the spring onions and peel the papery skin from the white bulb. Finely chop the ginger, garlic, chillies and onions.

- In a large bowl, thoroughly mix all of the ingredients except the vegetable oil. Using your hands, form the mixture into patties approximately 2in (5cm) across – you should have 12 in all.
- In a heavy-based frying-pan large enough to take all the patties, heat the vegetable oil over a medium flame. After 2 minutes, put in the patties. Fry for 6 minutes on each side. Remove from the pan, shaking off any oil, and serve.

Flavoured Chinese Leaf

Preparation time: 5 minutes, 30 minutes in advance of eating
Cooking time: none
Grade: easy

1 head of Chinese leaf	1 dessertspoon white sugar
2 tablespoons raspberry vinegar (*you can also use white wine vinegar*)	1 dessertspoon capers, rinsed
	1/4 teaspoon salt

- Shred the Chinese leaf and stir in the flavourings. Leave for 30 minutes before serving with the patties.

Meatballs in Spicy Lemon Sauce

Meatballs in the Middle East are most often made with minced lamb (or, more probably, goat), but beef is not unknown. In this recipe the meatballs themselves are lightly flavoured with paprika before being poached in a spicy sauce cut with lemon. The interesting thing about the sauce is the way grated onion is used to thicken it and butter to enrich it. Typically in Western cooking the onion would be fried in the butter before adding the liquid and spices, but in some Moroccan recipes all the ingredients for the sauce are put in the pot and boiled together before the meatballs are added for poaching.

Preparation time: 10 minutes, provided you have a food processor
Cooking time: 25 minutes
Grade: easy

Suggested accompaniments: rice flavoured with turmeric, and a tomato and onion salad

---

2 large Spanish onions
1lb (450g) minced beef
3 teaspoons sweet paprika ·
1 teaspoon freshly ground black pepper
1 teaspoon coarse salt
1 teaspoon ground ginger
1 teaspoon ground cumin
¼ teaspoon cayenne pepper
2oz (55g) unsalted butter
¾ pint (450ml) water
1 lemon
1 tablespoon chopped fresh parsley, if available

● Coarsely grate the onions (this is easiest with a food processor) and drain well. Combine the mince, 2 tablespoons of grated onion, 2 teaspoons of paprika and half the pepper and salt and process all together with a quick whizz so that you have a smooth mixture. Shape into meatballs about the size of a walnut.

● To make the sauce, choose a large heavy-based frying-pan or casserole with a lid, into which all the meatballs will fit in a single layer. Put in the rest of the grated onion, paprika, pepper and salt, the ginger, cumin, cayenne, butter and water. Bring to the boil, stir well, and leave uncovered to bubble gently for 5 minutes. Now turn down to a simmer, add the meatballs, cover, and simmer for 20 minutes. Add lemon juice to taste, sprinkle with parsley if available, and serve immediately.

Beef and Parmesan Sausages

Although we characteristically think of sausages as a mixture of minced meat (and all too often bread or rusk) contained within a skin, when making home-made sausages you can in fact dispense with that skin provided you have a sufficiently cohesive mixture. The Italians use fennel seeds to flavour their sausages and mix Parmesan into beef meatballs – all three ingredients come together here to make a sharp beef sausage.

Preparation time: 10 minutes
Cooking time: 15 minutes
Grade: basic

Suggested accompaniments: crusty bread, and a green or tomato and onion salad

1¼ lb (550g) lean minced beef
4oz (115g) finely grated
  Parmesan (*you could also use*
  Pecorino)
2 teaspoons whole fennel seeds
	1 large egg
	salt and freshly ground black
	  pepper
	1 lemon

- Pre-heat the grill to medium hot.
- Mix all the ingredients together except the lemon (it is better to do this in a bowl with a wooden spoon rather than in a food processor, which would break up the fennel seeds). Dampen your hands and fashion the mixture into 8 equal-sized sausage shapes.
- Grill the sausages close to the heat. After 7–8 minutes, by which time the top side should be nicely browned, drain off the fat and turn them over. Cook for a further 6–7 minutes, until browned all over, and serve very hot with quarters of lemon.

'Terrified' Beef with Spaghetti

In this rough and ready dish from Sicily, the beef is terrified by the aggressive garlic, chilli and anchovy mix which flavours the bacon-studded meatballs. Cooked in a simple tomato sauce, the strongly flavoured meatballs are served on a pile of soothing spaghetti.

Preparation time: 10 minutes
Cooking time: 25 minutes
Grade: basic

Suggested accompaniment: a green salad

---

2 cloves of garlic
4 small dried red chillies
2oz (55g) tin anchovies in olive oil
4oz (115g) pancetta or smoked streaky bacon, preferably thick-cut
1¼ lb (550g) beef mince
½ teaspoon freshly ground black pepper
2 tablespoons olive oil
14oz (400g) tin plum tomatoes
1 glass red wine
spaghetti (allow 3–4oz (85–115g) per person)

- Finely chop the peeled garlic, the chillies and the anchovies, reserving the oil. Cut the bacon into small dice, removing the rind. Mix these four ingredients with the mince and black pepper.
- Using your hands, form the meat into walnut-sized balls. Heat the oil in a heavy-based frying-pan, and when it is very hot fry the meatballs for 5 minutes, turning regularly, so that they are browned all over.
- Chop the tomatoes in the tin with a knife, then pour over the meatballs together with the wine. Bring to the boil, turn down to a simmer, cover and leave to cook for 20 minutes. Meanwhile cook the spaghetti.
- Take off the lid and reduce the sauce to taste. Pour over the spaghetti and serve.

VEAL ESCALOPES

Veal escalopes are expensive, but they also cook in the frying-pan in a matter of minutes, making them a good choice for a smart dinner party which you haven't enough time to prepare for. One problem is the butchering – it is often difficult to find veal escalopes cut sufficiently thinly, and they usually need plenty of beating. In particular, look for escalopes cut across the grain, which prevents the meat shrinking and curling during cooking.

I only buy veal meat from calves reared under British standards – that is, which have not been subjected to the cruel practice of crating. The more veal reared in this way that we, the consumers, buy, the fewer animals will be shipped overseas.

Veal Escalopes in a Lemon Sauce

This classic Italian recipe couldn't be easier, yet it is rarely prepared properly in restaurants, where the veal is too thick, the sauce too heavy, or the dish has been cooked too far in advance. For perfect results at home, there are two vital considerations – you must have good-quality veal sliced as thinly as possible, and you must cook the dish at the very last moment. This is a perfect dish for a summer's evening, requiring minimum time in the kitchen.

Preparation time: 5 minutes
Cooking time: 5 minutes
Grade: easy

Suggested accompaniments: in Italy the escalopes would probably be eaten all on their own, after a bowl of pasta; if you want to serve them with vegetables, try steamed new potatoes, fresh peas or fried slivers of courgette

---

8 small, thinly sliced veal escalopes, preferably cut on the bias
salt and freshly ground black pepper
2 tablespoons plain white flour

2oz (55g) unsalted butter
1 tablespoon olive oil
juice of 1 small lemon
1 tablespoon finely chopped fresh parsley

● Pre-heat the oven to 140°C/275°F/Gas Mark 1, and put in a large oblong serving plate to warm up.
● Beat the escalopes with a flat object until very thin. Season the flour, place on a plate, and lay each escalope in it, turning to make sure both sides are covered in a very thin coating of flour. Shake off any excess.

- In a heavy-based frying-pan large enough to take all the escalopes flat, heat half the butter with the olive oil over a medium high flame until it is nearly sizzling (a minute or two). Now add the escalopes and fry for no more than a minute on each side – by the time you have put the last escalope in the pan, it will be time to turn over the first one you put in. Remove the escalopes to the pre-heated serving dish to keep warm.
- Take the pan off the heat and add the lemon juice and remaining butter to the pan juices. Stir well, sprinkle in the parsley, pour the sauce over the escalopes and serve absolutely immediately.

Veal Escalopes in a Curry Cream Sauce

French cooks cleverly use a pinch of curry powder to give a lift and a touch of colour to cream sauces. The effect is quite unlike anything you will ever taste in India. This sauce is rapid and uncomplicated and goes especially well with veal escalopes. If the budget won't stretch to veal, try it with pork escalopes, which will need to be cooked a little longer.

Preparation time: 2 minutes
Cooking time: 8 minutes
Grade: easy

Suggested accompaniments: boiled long-grain rice; petits pois

8 small or 4 large veal escalopes, beaten very thin 1½ oz (45g) unsalted butter	4 tablespoons *crème fraîche* ½ teaspoon Madras curry powder

- Cut the veal into small medallions, about 3in (7.5cm) long.
- In a heavy-based frying-pan large enough to take all the veal, melt the butter. When the butter is fizzing, put in the veal and fry for a couple of minutes on each side. Take out the veal and put to keep warm.
- Pour the *crème fraîche* into the pan and stir in the curry powder. Season to taste and allow to bubble for a couple of minutes, stirring all the time. Put the veal escalopes back into the pan, turn to coat with the sauce and serve.

Veal Escalopes with a Wild Mushroom and Cream Sauce

Only a small quantity of dried wild mushrooms are needed to impart their earthy flavour to a sauce and provided they are fresh (yes, they can be fresh and dried at the same time) they rehydrate surprisingly quickly. This simple sauce goes with pork as well as veal escalopes, although then the dish will be a little less luxurious.

Preparation time: 15 minutes soaking for the mushrooms
Cooking time: 10 minutes
Grade: moderate

Suggested accompaniments: boiled long-grain rice and green beans

---

1oz (30g) dried porcini mushrooms (*ceps*)
2 shallots
1oz (30g) butter
½ tablespoon olive oil

8 small or 4 large veal escalopes
4fl oz (125ml) double cream
salt and freshly ground black pepper

- Soak the mushrooms for 15 minutes in a little warm water. Remove from the water and chop the mushrooms finely (reserve the soaking water). Peel the shallots and chop finely.
- In a heavy-based pan large enough to take all the escalopes, melt the butter with the oil over a medium high heat. When it is very hot, add the escalopes and fry for 2 minutes on either side. Remove from the oil with a slotted spoon and put to keep warm.
- Add the shallots to the oil and fry for 2 minutes, until soft. Now add the finely chopped mushrooms and fry for another minute. Pour in the double cream and the strained mushroom liquor and bubble hard for 2 minutes to reduce. Season, then return the escalopes to the pan, turn them in the sauce and serve immediately.

PORK

It may have received less publicity, but the taste of the meat from the pig has suffered just as much as that from the chicken as a result of the intensive rearing systems now widespread in our European 'economic' farming community. Good pork is a solid flavour-packed meat, providing not only delicious roasts and steaks but also sausages, bacon and ham which do not weep salty tears in the pan. It is worth paying more for 'traditionally' reared pork, that is, meat from an animal fed and allowed to mature naturally, without the assistance of growth hormones. This pork will not have been injected with water to increase its weight and will have plenty of fat to provide the flavour. Fortunately, supermarkets are increasingly stocking meat from properly brought-up pigs and bacon, sausages and hams prepared according to old-fashioned methods – they are worth the extra cost.

CHOPS

The best pork chops come from the loin of the animal, and are generally sold individually. Unfortunately, as a result of one of the more ludicrous EU regulations, there can no longer be a slice of the kidney attached. A little joint of loin of pork chops, with the chine bone (backbone) removed to simplify carving, makes an excellent roast for 2 or 3 people, whilst boned rolled loin of pork, stuffed with dried fruits or garlic and a few sprigs of fennel, is good for a larger party. For preference, choose larger joints than you need for the immediate meal at hand, so that you will be able to enjoy some of the meat cold, when to my palate it tastes even better than straight out of the oven. As with beef, much of the flavour of pork is contained in the fat; so even if you do not intend to eat it, leave the fat on the chop or joint during cooking.

Pork Chops with Juniper

An unexpected guest arrives for supper when you were planning to eat plainly grilled pork chops. Nothing wrong with that, and pork chops it will be, but you can make them more exciting by adding a coating of crushed juniper berries, giving the chops a slightly gamey flavour.

Preparation time: 5 minutes
Cooking time: 20 minutes
Grade: basic, if you can grill a pork chop, you can cook this dish

Suggested accompaniments: mashed potatoes and carrots

---

1 dessertspoon juniper berries
1 teaspoon coarse sea salt
½ teaspoon black peppercorns

4 thick pork chops
2 tablespoons olive oil

● Pre-heat the grill to maximum.
● In a pestle and mortar or with the flat side of a broad knife, crush the juniper berries, sea salt and peppercorns together, so that they are bruised and broken up but not powdered. Lay the pork chops on a metal tray and sprinkle over half the juniper mixture. Dribble over half the olive oil.
● Cook the chops close to the grill for 8–10 minutes, depending on thickness. Turn over, sprinkle the remaining juniper mixture on the other side and pour over the remaining olive oil. Cook for another 8 or so minutes – the chops are done when the fat is well browned and no blood runs when you pierce them with a fork. Allow to rest for 5 minutes before serving.

Pork Chops with a Cider and Apple Sauce

There is nothing new about the combination of pork and apples – it is simply one of those old-fashioned mixtures that really works. Roast whole, unpeeled eating apples alongside a joint of pork; make a tart sauce from cooking apples spiked with a couple of cloves and a pinch of nutmeg; fry apples in butter to go with a real pork sausage or a black pudding. To liven up pork chops, make a sauce with cider, preferably almost flat scrumpy from the West country or cidre bouchée from Normandy, in which you briefly stew slices of Cox's. The variety of apple is important – do not be tempted to use a cooking apple, which would be too tart, or to substitute a more watery, less flavourful apple such as Golden (less than) Delicious.

Preparation time: 5 minutes
Cooking time: 20 minutes
Grade: moderate, easy if you are familiar with roux-based sauces

Suggested accompaniments: baked potatoes and a green vegetable or salad

2 Cox's apples	½ oz (15g) plain white flour
salt and freshly ground black pepper	9fl oz (250ml) dry cider
4 pork chops	pinch of sugar
1oz (30g) butter	1 dessertspoon balsamic vinegar

- Peel and core the apples and slice the flesh thinly.
- The sauce can be made while the chops are grilling – simply season the chops well and pop under a hot grill for 10 minutes either side. Melt the butter over a gentle heat and then slowly stir in the flour. Cook over a low heat for 2 minutes until the roux takes on a little colour, stirring constantly to eliminate lumps. Now add the cider a little at a time, stirring constantly. When you have added all the cider, turn up the heat and bring to the boil. Bubble for 1 minute, then turn down the heat and add the slices of apple, the pinch of sugar and seasoning to taste. Allow to simmer uncovered for 10 minutes, until the slices of apple are tender but not falling apart.
- Just before serving, swirl in the balsamic vinegar, which gives colour, sweetness and depth to the sauce.

Pork Chops in Tomato Sauce with Gherkins

The affiliation of gherkins with pork products is best appreciated in France, to be enjoyed at its simplest form in a sandwich *saucisson sec aux cornichons*, served at the bar of a Paris café, or perhaps an *assiette de charcuterie* accompanied by a bowl of those pickled vegetables, interspersed with tiny onions, in a simple roadside restaurant. These small, crisp, tart gherkins are quite different from the fat, soft cucumbers of Jewish and Scandinavian tradition, and are now, happily, available in many British supermarkets. Gherkins need not be confined to cold meats, for they can do much to cheer up a miserably thin pork chop. I use them to add crunch and bite to the tomato sauce in which the chops are cooked.

Preparation time: 5 minutes
Cooking time: 30 minutes
Grade: moderate

Suggested accompaniment: a purée of lentils or mashed potato made with olive oil

---

1 large onion
4 cloves of garlic
4oz (115g) pickled gherkins
4 small sprigs of fresh thyme or
 ½ teaspoon dried thyme
2 tablespoons olive oil or, better

still, goose or duck fat
4 thin-cut pork chops
14oz (400g) tin tomatoes
salt and freshly ground black
 pepper

- Coarsely chop the onion but leave the garlic cloves unpeeled. Chop the gherkins across into thin slices and strip the leaves from the thyme if using the fresh herb.
- Heat the oil or fat over a medium high heat in a frying-pan large enough to take all the pork chops flat. When the oil is hot add the chops and fry for 1 minute on each side. Remove the chops and set aside.
- Add the chopped onion and the unpeeled whole garlic cloves to the fat in the pan and fry, stirring, for 5 minutes, still over a medium high heat, until the onion is lightly coloured. Now add the thyme and the contents of the tin of tomatoes. Break up the tomatoes in the pan with a wooden spoon, season well, and allow to bubble for a minute or two. Put the chops back in the pan, turn down the heat to low, cover and leave to cook for 10 minutes. Turn the chops over, add the chopped gherkins to the pan, replace the cover and cook for a further 5–8 minutes – the exact cooking time will depend on the thickness of the chops. If you are unsure, cut one of the chops across to make sure it is cooked through. The dish can stand for 10 minutes or so before you serve it.

Pork Chops with Lemon, Garlic and Spring Onion Butter Sauce

Spring onions briefly stewed in butter with garlic, are spiked with lemon juice, flavoured with rosemary and enriched with more butter. This sharp little sauce makes a grilled pork chop rather more exciting; it would also go well with a pork steak.

Preparation time: 10 minutes
Cooking time: 20 minutes
Grade: moderate

Suggested accompaniments: boiled new potatoes and peas

1 lemon	3oz (85g) unsalted butter, chilled
1 large bunch of spring onions, approx. 16 small or 8 large	4 pork chops
2 cloves of garlic	$\frac{1}{2}$ teaspoon sugar
1 small sprig of fresh rosemary	salt and freshly ground black pepper

● Squeeze the juice from the lemon. Finely chop the spring onions, including the green ends. Finely chop the peeled garlic cloves and the needles of rosemary. Cut 2oz (55g) of the butter into small cubes and keep in the fridge.

● Pre-heat the grill to medium hot and grill the chops for about 10 minutes on either side, until nicely browned. Meanwhile make the sauce.

● Melt 1oz (30g) of the butter in a small frying-pan and over a gentle heat cook the garlic for 5 minutes, stirring regularly. Take care that the garlic doesn't brown, or the sauce will be bitter.

● Add the spring onions and sweat gently for a further 5 minutes, until they are soft. Now add the sugar, rosemary and lemon juice, together with a pinch of salt and plenty of freshly milled pepper. Cook gently for a further couple of minutes then take the pan off the heat and stir in the chilled cubes of butter one at a time. Serve the sauce with the chops immediately – under no circumstance put the pan back over the heat or the sauce will curdle.

Chinese-style Roast Pork

The Chinese make the best roast pork, with crisp sweet dark skin and juicy meat. Often cuts of belly and streaky pork are used, involving many hours in the oven, but the method transfers well to a small joint of pork chops, basted with sugar and soy sauce and fiercely roasted.

Preparation time: 5 minutes
Cooking time: 45 minutes
Grade: easy

Suggested accompaniments: boiled rice, stir-fried vegetables

---

1 joint of loin of pork, chined, approx. 1½–1¾ lb (675–800g)
salt

2 teaspoons brown sugar
1 tablespoon dark soy sauce

- Pre-heat the grill to maximum and the oven to 200°C/400°F/Gas Mark 6.
- Bring a kettle of water to the boil and pour this over the skin side of the pork – it will shrink slightly. Score the fat with a sharp knife in a diamond pattern and rub well with salt. With a skewer, make holes through the meat.
- Grill the joint fat side up until the fat is lightly browned – this will take 6 or 7 minutes. Watch carefully to make sure it doesn't burn.
- Mix together the sugar and soy sauce and rub this all over the meat, including the fat. Roast in the oven for 40 minutes, turning once.

TENDERLOIN

Tenderloin is the fillet steak of pork, the long round strip of exquisite meat which lies underneath the loin bone. The meat is best cut across at regular intervals into thick slices, or *noisettes* as they are known in France. Although, unlike beef steak, it needs to be cooked through, this should be done as rapidly as possible to preserve the texture and flavour.

Herby Tenderloin with Mushrooms

Tenderloin benefits from even the quickest of dips in a powerful marinade followed by brief fierce cooking – preferably, as with fillet of beef, on a cast-iron skillet.

Preparation time: 10 minutes, at least 30 minutes before cooking
Cooking time: 15 minutes
Grade: moderate

Suggested accompaniments: buttered tagliatelle and a green salad

1½lb (675g) tenderloin	3 tablespoons extra virgin olive oil
2 sprigs of fresh rosemary	8oz (225g) brown cap mushrooms
4 sprigs of fresh thyme	2 cloves of garlic
freshly ground black pepper	salt

- Slice the pork into rounds ¾in (2cm) thick. Strip the leaves from the herbs and chop finely. Sprinkle the herbs, pepper and oil over the pork and leave to marinate for 30 minutes. Wash the mushrooms thoroughly and slice each across into 2 or 3 pieces. Peel the garlic and chop finely. Pre-heat the oven to 110°C/225°F/Gas Mark ¼.
- When you are ready to cook, heat a heavy-based frying-pan or skillet over a medium low heat. Strain the marinade from the pork into the pan and sweat the mushrooms and garlic, salted to taste, for 5 minutes. With a slotted spoon, remove mushrooms and garlic, leaving behind as much of the oil as possible, and put to keep warm in the oven. Now turn the heat up under the frying-pan and add the pork pieces. Fry for 4 minutes on each side over a high heat. Slice one piece through to check that it is fully cooked (the exact time will depend on the thickness of the meat, but it is important not to overcook) and serve as soon as it is ready.

Pork with Fennel

The marriage of pork and fennel can be appreciated at its best in the splendid Roman dish of *porchetta*, roast stuffed baby suckling pig. Once my brother and I, wandering around a town in the hills north of the city, sniffed out a small shop with a pig fresh from the oven, its skin a burnt orange, the green and white stuffing spilling out from the grainy meat, the air heady with pork fat and liquorice scents. We ate thick slices with our fingers and were in heaven. Ever since then I have lusted after pork cooked with fennel. You can stuff a roast with the feathery fronds, fry quartered bulbs in olive until caramelized to go with pork chops, or, at the very simplest, fry together slices of fennel and pork fillet.

Preparation time: 10 minutes
Cooking time: 20 minutes
Grade: moderate

Suggested accompaniment: mashed potatoes made with olive oil

1¼ lb (550g) pork tenderloin	1 glass dry white wine
2 fennel bulbs	salt and freshly ground black
2 cloves of garlic	pepper
2 tablespoons olive oil	

- Slice the meat across at 1in (2.5 cm) intervals, so that you have thick rounds. Slice the fennel into thin strips, discarding the core and reserving any feathery fronds. Peel the garlic and chop finely.
- Heat the oil over a high heat in a heavy-based frying-pan with a lid. When it is nearly spitting, add the meat and fry for 1 minute on either side, to brown. Now turn down the heat to medium and add the strips of fennel and the chopped garlic. Fry for 5 minutes, stirring regularly. Pour in the white wine, season well, and sprinkle in any reserved fennel fronds. Allow to bubble for 1 minute, then cover and turn the heat down to low. Leave to cook for 10 minutes then serve.

STEAKS

The tenderest pork steaks will be cut from the boned loin or leg and can be grilled, fried whole, or cut into strips for stir-frying.

Pork Pepper Steaks in a Mustard and Cream Sauce

Mustard goes as well with pork as it does with ham (cured pork). I roll pork steaks in coarsely crushed black peppercorns and serve them with a creamy mustard sauce sharpened with lemon juice and spiked with vermouth.

Preparation time: 5 minutes
Cooking time: 20 minutes
Grade: moderate

Suggested accompaniments: boiled new potatoes and green beans

1 tablespoon coarsely ground black peppercorns	*white wine*)
4 pork leg steaks, thinly cut, approx. 4oz (115g) each	1 tablespoon Dijon mustard juice of ½ a lemon
1oz (30g) butter	5fl oz (140ml) double cream or *crème fraîche*
2fl oz (50ml) white vermouth (*or*	

- Sprinkle the pepper over a plate and dip in the pork steaks so that they are evenly covered. Gently melt the butter in a frying-pan large enough to take all the steaks. Now turn up the heat to medium high and add the pork. Fry for 3 minutes on either side and then remove the pork. Discard the butter, which by now will be browned, and wipe the pan clean.
- Return the pan to a medium heat and add the vermouth or wine. As soon as it bubbles stir in the mustard. Now add the lemon juice and cream. Allow the sauce to simmer for a couple of minutes, stirring all the time, then return the pork to the pan, together with any juices which have run. Cook over a gentle heat for 5 minutes on each side and serve immediately.

Grilled Pork Steaks with Thyme, Orange and Garlic Butter

Flavoured butters transform grilled steaks of pork, beef, and lamb. I like thyme, orange and garlic butter with pork, but you can try many different combinations of spices and herbs – experiment to find your favourite.

Preparation time: 5 minutes
Cooking time: 15 minutes
Grade: basic

Suggested accompaniments: new potatoes; spinach with lemon juice and olive oil

2oz (55g) unsalted butter	4 large sprigs of fresh thyme
2 tablespoons fresh orange juice	salt and freshly ground black
1 teaspoon grated orange rind	pepper
½ clove of garlic	4 pork steaks

- Process the butter with the orange juice, orange rind, peeled garlic clove, leaves from the thyme and seasoning to taste. Leave to chill.
- Pre-heat the grill to maximum and grill the seasoned steaks close to the heat for 5–7 minutes on either side, until cooked through. Alternatively, cook them on an oiled cast-iron skillet.
- Put a knob of the flavoured butter on each steak and serve.

Peppered Pork and White Radish

The crunchy texture and relatively mild flavour of white radishes or moolis make them excellent ingredients for both salads and quickly cooked dishes. They combine especially well with pork, a fact recognized in both the West Indies and South-east Asia. This recipe is characteristically Thai, its origin recognizable from the plentiful use of garlic and black pepper. The pepper must be freshly ground for you to appreciate the full sweetness and bite of this vital spice.

Preparation time: 15 minutes
Cooking time: 10 minutes
Grade: easy, but you must give the stir-frying your full attention

Suggested accompaniment: stir-fried noodles (shrimp-flavoured noodles go very well) or rice

1¼ lb (550g) pork steaks	1½ teaspoons freshly ground
1 large white radish or mooli,	black pepper
approx. 10oz (280g)	1 teaspoon white sugar
6 cloves of garlic	light soy sauce (*Thai soy sauce if*
4 small dried red chillies	*you have it*)
2 tablespoons vegetable or	sesame oil
groundnut oil	

- Trim any fat from the pork steaks and slice very thinly into long strips. Peel the radish and slice across into rounds ¼in (5mm) thick. Now slice each round into slices ¼in (5mm) across so that you have oblongs. Peel the garlic and crush thoroughly. Leave the chillies whole.
- In a wok, or a large shallow thin-bottomed frying-pan, heat the oil over a high heat. When it is almost spitting, add the whole chillies and garlic and swirl around for a moment, until the garlic is just starting to take on colour. Now add the strips of pork and fry, stirring all the time, for 3 minutes. Add the strips of radish and continue to fry for another couple of minutes – the radish should heat through but retain its crunch. Finally stir in the black pepper and the sugar, together with a good splash of soy sauce and a few drops of sesame oil. Swirl all around and serve very hot.

Haitian-style Pork with Sweet Potato

In Haiti pork is braised in citrus fruit juices for the famous dish of *griots*, succulent pork with a syrupy orange glaze. The traditional accompaniment is fried sweet potatoes; I prefer to cook them with the pork itself, when they acquire an almost appley flavour whilst retaining a firm texture.

Preparation time: 15 minutes
Cooking time: 30 minutes
Grade: moderate

Suggested accompaniments: green beans steamed or boiled and then tossed with garlic and lemon juice, or a green salad

1¼ lb (550g) boned loin of pork, in one or two large pieces	2 tablespoons vegetable oil
12oz (350g) sweet potato	½ teaspoon dried thyme
1 fresh green chilli (*optional*)	4 allspice berries (*if available*)
4 oranges	½ teaspoon salt
1 lime	½ teaspoon freshly ground black pepper
1 bunch of spring onions	6fl oz (175ml) water

- Trim the pork of any fat and cut into 1½in (4cm) cubes. Peel the sweet potato and cut into ½in (1 cm) cubes. Finely chop the chilli if you are using it and squeeze the juice from the fruits. Coarsely chop the spring onions, including the green ends.

- In a heavy-based pan large enough to take the pork and potato, heat the oil. When it is nearly smoking, add the meat and cook over a high heat for 4 minutes, until it is well browned on all sides. Drain off the fat and add the remainder of the ingredients. Bring rapidly to the boil and then turn the heat down to medium low, cover, and leave to simmer for 20 minutes, by which time the sweet potato should be tender but not falling apart. Now remove the lid, turn up the heat and boil off any remaining liquid, stirring regularly, until you have a syrupy consistency (this should take about 5 minutes). Check the seasoning and serve.

MINCED PORK

I am a little dubious about the quality of much of the minced pork on offer, for I suspect it may still be regarded as something of a dumping ground for poor quality offcuts, as minced beef once was. Excessively fatty minced pork is best kept for pâtés and stuffings, but high-quality minced pork can make good meatballs, provided they are highly spiced to counteract the bland nature of the meat.

Green Pork Balls

Minced pork is used in Thailand with the 'green' ingredients of coriander, lime juice and chilli to make little balls which are traditionally deep-fried in batter. I prefer to roll them in flour and shallow-fry them, which still gives a nice crispy coating. You can serve these pork balls with a vinegar dipping sauce; and it may lack authenticity but I also like them with tomato ketchup.

Preparation time: 15 minutes, with 10 minutes standing time
Cooking time: 10 minutes
Grade: easy

Suggested accompaniment: coconut rice

3 small fresh green chillies	1 teaspoon sugar
2 cloves of garlic	½ teaspoon salt
1¼ lb (550g) minced pork	2 tablespoons plain white flour
3 tablespoons chopped fresh coriander, including roots if available	1 teaspoon freshly ground black pepper
juice of 1 lime	vegetable or groundnut oil
	1 tablespoon white wine vinegar

● Deseed the chillies and chop finely; peel the garlic and mince it. Mix the garlic and chillies with the pork, coriander, lime juice, sugar and salt (do not use a food processor or the texture will be too fine). With damp hands, shape the mixture into balls the size of walnuts. If you have time, leave to stand for 10 minutes for the meat to absorb the flavours.

● Stir together the flour and pepper and roll each of the balls in the mixture. Choose a pan large enough for all of them to fit, and pour in sufficient oil just to cover the bottom. Put over a high heat, and when the oil is nearly spitting, add the pork balls. Fry over a high heat for 4–5 minutes on either side, until nicely browned. Sprinkle with the vinegar and serve.

Steamed Pork Cakes

The Chinese use minced pork to make highly flavourful little balls which they steam and call cakes. Although they would typically be served in China as dim sum, slightly larger versions make a good if unconventional main course. The result is a compact, meaty mouthful with plenty of bite.

Preparation time: 10 minutes
Cooking time: 20 minutes
Grade: basic

Suggested accompaniments: boiled rice and stir-fried greens in oyster sauce

---

6 small spring onions
2 cloves of garlic
½in (1cm) piece of fresh ginger
3 or 4 small dried red chillies
1½ tablespoons dark soy sauce

2 teaspoons sugar
salt and freshly ground black pepper
1¼lb (550g) minced pork

- Wash the spring onions and chop them finely, including the green ends. Peel the garlic and ginger and chop finely.
- Mix all the ingredients into the minced pork and stir together very well. With your hands shape into 8 cakes, each approximately 2in (5cm) in diameter.
- Steam the cakes for 20 minutes (they may give off a little scum and liquid – drain this away). Sprinkle with soy sauce and serve.

SPARERIBS

It shouldn't be a surprise that all of the recipes given here for spareribs are derived from the enormous repertoire of the rib's biggest fans, the Chinese. Unfortunately ribs are rarely sold ready chopped into small pieces 1–2in (2.5–5cm) long, which is how they should be served in Chinese dishes (come on, supermarket buyers). The meat from sparerib chops is also sold boneless, and can be used in many of the recipes given previously for pork steaks.

Grilled Spareribs

The key to cooking spareribs is to boil them briefly first, so that the grill is used to crisp them up rather than cook them through. In this simple recipe the ribs are painted with a salt-sweet-sharp mixture which caramelizes under the grill. The Chinese serve spareribs with yet more salt to dip them in, an aromatic mixture of coarse sea salt spiced with a little ground black pepper and toasted in a dry pan for 3–4 minutes. If you find the salt too much, you could serve toasted sesame seeds alongside the ribs.

Preparation time: nil
Cooking time: 20 minutes
Grade: basic

Suggested accompaniment: the ribs make a good snack all on their own

---

3lb (1.3kg) spareribs
2 tablespoons dark soy sauce
2 tablespoons dry sherry

2 dessertspoons white sugar
2 teaspoons coarse sea salt

● Bring a large pan of water to the boil and boil the spareribs hard for 5 minutes. Drain and pat dry.
● Pre-heat the grill to maximum. Cover a large baking tray with foil and place the spareribs on it, making sure none of them are on top of each other. Mix together the remaining ingredients and paint half the mixture over the upper surface of the ribs. Cook close to the grill for 5–7 minutes, until the surface is lightly browned. Turn the ribs over and paint with the remainder of the sauce. Cook for a further 5–7 minutes, until nicely browned. Eat the ribs as soon as they are cool enough for you to pick them up.

Spareribs Roasted with a Honey Glaze

After a quick boil, the spareribs are rolled in lightly spiced honey and roasted in a hot oven. The result is almost black ribs, the sweet glaze concealing juicy meat.

Preparation time: 5 minutes
Cooking time: 25 minutes
Grade: basic

Suggested accompaniments: boiled rice, stir-fried greens in oyster sauce

3lb (1.3kg) spare ribs	4 tablespoons clear honey
2 teaspoons cornflour	2 teaspoons Chinese five-spice
juice of ½ a lemon	powder

- Pre-heat the oven to 200°C/400°F/Gas Mark 6.
- Bring a large pan of water to the boil and boil the ribs for 5 minutes. Drain and pat dry.
- Stir the cornflour into the lemon juice, making sure all lumps have dissolved. Mix the cornflour and lemon into the honey together with the spice powder. Roll the boiled spareribs in this glaze, making sure they are coated all over.
- Lay the spareribs on foil in an ovenproof tray, making sure none of them are touching. Pour over any remaining glaze. Roast in the oven for 20 minutes, basting half-way through. Eat as soon as they are cool enough to handle.

Noodle Soup with Spareribs and Cucumber

This is a substantial Chinese soup which peasants would eat as a meal on its own. Ideally the ribs would be cut into small sections, so that they could be put whole into the mouth, the meat chewed off and the remaining bone spat out. This is a tricky art for the uninitiated and you may well have to pick up the ribs with your fingers and chew them – especially if they have not been chopped up. The addition of chilli sauce at the end is optional; every restaurant in China has a dish of lurid red sauce, its fierceness depending on the region, sitting on the table for you to add as much or as little as you like.

Preparation time: 5 minutes
Cooking time: 30 minutes
Grade: basic

Suggested accompaniment: none needed

2lb (900g) spareribs (*if you are buying the ribs from a butcher, ask him to cut them in 1½in (4cm) lengths*)	2fl oz (50ml) dry sherry
	1 piece star anise
	2in (5cm) piece of lemon rind
1 Spanish onion	½ teaspoon freshly ground black pepper
1 large cucumber	
3 pints (1.7 litres) chicken stock	6oz (175g) egg noodles
3 tablespoons light soy sauce	Chinese sweet chilli sauce (*optional*)

- If you have full-size spareribs, use a sharp knife to detach the meaty end where the bones join. Do not attempt to cut up the ribs yourself unless you want fingers in the soup.
- Bring a large pan of water to the boil and blanch the ribs for 1 minute. Drain and discard the water.
- Finely chop the onion. Peel the cucumber and cut into 2 x ¼in (5 x 5mm) sticks.
- Put the blanched ribs, onion, stock, soy sauce, sherry, star anise, lemon rind and pepper into a large casserole dish. Bring to the boil, skim off any froth, turn down to a simmer and cover. Leave to cook over a gentle heat for 25 minutes.
- Bring back to the boil, add the noodles and stir with chopsticks or a fork until broken up. Now add the sticks of cucumber. Boil uncovered for 3–4 minutes, until the noodles are ready (taste to check). Stir in a teaspoon or two of chilli sauce to taste, and serve.

Braised Spareribs

Spareribs braised in sherry and soy sauce with garlic, ginger and chilli are particularly succulent.

Preparation time: 5 minutes
Cooking time: 30 minutes
Grade: easy

Suggested accompaniments: boiled rice and steamed greens

3lb (1.3kg) spareribs	1 teaspoon sugar
2 cloves of garlic	4fl oz (100ml) dry sherry
1in (2.5cm) piece of fresh ginger	2fl oz (50ml) dark soy sauce
2 small green chillies, deseeded	1 tablespoon rice or white wine
2 tablespoons groundnut oil	vinegar

- Bring a large pan of water to the boil and blanch the ribs for 1 minute, then drain and pat dry.
- Finely chop the peeled garlic and ginger and the deseeded chillies. Heat the oil in a wok or large frying-pan and when it is hot add the garlic, ginger and chillies. Stir-fry for 1 minute then add the ribs. Stir-fry for another minute then sprinkle with sugar. Stir-fry for a further 30 seconds, until the sugar caramelizes, then add the remaining ingredients. Bring to the boil, allow to bubble for 1 minute then turn down to a simmer, cover and leave to cook for 30 minutes, stirring once half-way through. Remove the lid, turn up the heat, bubble the sauce down to a syrupy consistency, and serve.

BELLY PORK

Our current aversion to fat leads many of us to ignore the meat from the belly of the pig. This is, in my opinion, a mistake, for not only is belly pork a very cheap cut, it also yields some of the best-flavoured meat. It is vital for pâtés but is worth cooking all on its own, either braised or roasted. Once again, many of the best recipes for belly pork come from China.

Glazed Pork Pieces

Briefly marinated pieces of pork are quickly roasted, producing dark brown chunks of succulent meat.

The flavourings are essentially Chinese, with the addition of some tomato paste.

Preparation time: 10 minutes, at least 40 minutes before you want to serve the pork, so that the meat can be marinated
Cooking time: 12 minutes
Grade: easy

Suggested accompaniments: green beans boiled and then tossed with garlic and ginger, or leeks steamed with garlic; boiled rice

1½ lb (675g) boneless streaky pork	juice of 1 lemon
2 tablespoons dark soy sauce	1 teaspoon sweet chilli sauce
1 tablespoon sesame oil	2 teaspoons brown sugar
2 tablespoons dry sherry	2 teaspoons tomato paste

- Bring a large pan of water to the boil and boil the whole pork slices hard for 5 minutes. Drain thoroughly and chop into bite-sized pieces, leaving the fat on.
- Mix together all the remaining ingredients and leave the pork in this mixture for at least 30 minutes, turning once.
- Pre-heat the oven to 220°C/425°F/Gas Mark 7. Cover a baking tray with foil and lay the pork pieces on it. Pour over any remaining marinade. Cook (at the top of the oven if it is not fan-assisted) for 5 minutes then turn the pork over. Cook for another 7 minutes, until the marinade has become a syrupy glaze. The pork is best hot but can also be served cold.

Braised Belly Pork with Star Anise

Chunks of belly pork braised until the liquid has almost evaporated, are tender, spicy and highly comforting.

Star anise is a key ingredient of Chinese five-spice powder, but here it is used all on its own.

Preparation time: 5 minutes
Cooking time: 40 minutes
Grade: easy

Suggested accompaniments: boiled rice and greens in oyster sauce

1½ lb (675g) pork belly
4 cloves of garlic
1 tablespoon vegetable oil
4 small red chillies
2 pieces of star anise

2 tablespoons dark soy sauce
2 tablespoons dry sherry
1 tablespoon white wine vinegar
pinch of sugar

● Chop the pork belly into bite-sized pieces. Peel the garlic and chop into fine flakes.

● Heat the oil in a casserole over a high heat and when it is sizzling add the flakes of garlic and the whole chillies and star anise. Cook, stirring, for 2 minutes, then add the pieces of pork. Stir-fry for a further 3 minutes, drain off the fat, then add the remaining ingredients. Turn the heat down to medium low, cover and cook for 30 minutes, with the sauce nicely bubbling. By the end of cooking the sauce should reduce to a nice glaze – take off the lid for the last 5 minutes of cooking if necessary. Leave to stand for 5 minutes, drain off any remaining fat and serve.

HAM AND GAMMON

Ham is not the weeping pink substance so many of us put up with. Never buy plastic-wrapped slices of processed ham – you are paying for water as much as meat. Look instead for thick slices cut straight from traditional British hams, the most beautiful of which are baked in honey and studded with cloves, and thin slivers from the air-dried hams of the continent.

Cold Ham with Mustard and Tarragon Sauce

A hot sauce poured over slices of cold meat makes a meal more enticing on a cold winter's day. Rare roasted cold beef is good with a warm béarnaise; thick slices of ham are enlivened by an old-fashioned white sauce flavoured with mustard and tarragon. The use of the grainy *moutarde de Meaux* in addition to the tarragon-flavoured Dijon mustard gives texture to the sauce.

Preparation time: none
Cooking time: 20 minutes
Grade: moderate, easy if you are used to making white sauces

Suggested accompaniment: boiled new potatoes

1oz (30g) butter
1 tablespoon plain white flour
2 teaspoons Dijon mustard
½ pint (300ml) milk
1 glass dry white wine
1 tablespoon *moutarde de Meaux*
1 teaspoon dried tarragon or 1

tablespoon chopped fresh tarragon
salt and freshly ground black pepper
4 thick slices of home–cooked ham

● Melt the butter over a gentle heat. Stir in the flour and cook, stirring, until the roux acquires a lightly golden colour. Now stir in the Dijon mustard and cook for a further minute. Pour in a little milk and stir well to amalgamate. Continue adding a little milk at a time until the mixture is smooth and lump-free. Now you can pour in the milk in a steady stream, still stirring continuously, until it is all added. Pour in the wine, turn the heat up to moderate, and keep at it with a wooden spoon until the mixture comes to the boil. Turn down the heat and allow to bubble for 3 or 4 minutes.

● If you have not stirred the sauce sufficiently assiduously and there is the odd lump, strain it at this stage. Off the heat stir in the grainy *moutarde de Meaux* and the tarragon. Season to taste and serve with the cold ham. You can prepare the sauce in advance and reheat it gently just before serving.

Ham and Eggs

Not exactly an unusual recipe, but turned into a luxury dish by the use of best-quality Italian, Spanish or French air-dried ham topped with eggs fried in olive oil. A slice of good bread rubbed with garlic and browned in yet more luscious olive oil completes the meal. For even greater sophistication you could use 2 or 3 quail eggs per diner instead of one laid by a hen. A favourite tapa in Southern Spain is a piece of bread topped with a sliver of *jamon serrano* and a cooked quail's egg.

Preparation time: minimal
Cooking time: 10 minutes
Grade: basic, provided you can fry an egg

Suggested accompaniment: none needed

1 clove of garlic	*jamon serrano, jambon de Bayonne*
4 slices of good-quality white	or other similar quality air-dried
bread	ham
5 tablespoons olive oil	salt and freshly ground black
4 eggs	pepper
4 good-sized slices of Parma ham,	

● Peel the garlic and cut in half; rub the bread on both sides with the cut side of the garlic. Heat 3 tablespoons of the olive oil in a non-stick frying-pan and fry the bread until lightly golden. Put on plates to keep warm. Heat the remaining olive oil and fry the eggs to your satisfaction. Put a slice of ham on each slice of fried bread, top with an egg, season well and serve.

Gammon in Sour Green Sauce

Gammon, a mild cut of bacon taken from the side of the hind leg, is usually served with sweet sauces and accompaniments. This needn't restrict you to a ring of tinned pineapple: try gammon basted with mustard and honey, blasted under the grill until the coating blackens. Personally, however, I prefer to mix sour flavours rather than sweet ones with the saltiness of the meat. This green paste is derived from a sauce served with pork in Goa.

Preparation time: 10 minutes
Cooking time: 10 minutes
Grade: easy

Suggested accompaniments: caramelized sweet potatoes; green salad

4 slices of gammon	juice of 1 lime
2 fresh green chillies	2 tablespoons groundnut oil
2 tablespoons fresh coriander	freshly ground black pepper
2in (5cm) piece of fresh ginger	

- Trim any fat from the gammon and cut the meat into 1in (2.5cm) squares. Deseed the chillies and chop coarsely. Pick over the coriander, removing any stalks, and peel the ginger.
- Process the chillies, coriander, ginger, lime juice and oil to a paste. Put a frying-pan over a high heat and fry the paste for 1 minute. Now turn the heat down to medium and add the squares of gammon. Fry, stirring regularly, for 6–7 minutes. Season with black pepper (but no salt) and serve.

PORK SAUSAGES

The sausage has for some years been nothing but a dumping ground for left-overs and cereals, rather than a product cherished in its own right. Fortunately, the sausage's day seems to be dawning again, marked by the opening of new shops specializing only in sausages and the availability of increasingly exotic varieties, from chicken and pistachio through seafood to venison sausages. Good though these are, they cannot replace an old-fashioned, meaty pork sausage.

Sausages with Fried Apples and Bacon

Fried or grilled apples are a well-known accompaniment to *boudin noir* in France, and go just as well with our own black pudding or plain pork sausage. As the apples, bacon and sausages cook together, the fruit picks up the meaty flavours.

Preparation time: 10 minutes
Cooking time: 25 minutes
Grade: basic

Suggested accompaniment: mashed potato, preferably with a parsnip or two in the mixture

4 eating apples, e.g. Cox's	sausages
4 rashers smoked streaky bacon	lard, dripping or goose fat
8 high meat content pork	

- Peel the apples and cut them vertically into quarters, or eighths if they are large. Dice the bacon, removing the rind. Prick each sausage several times with a fork.
- In a pan large enough to take all the apples and the sausages, melt a generous nugget of fat with the bacon. Cook over a moderate heat for 5 minutes, until the fat runs from the bacon. Now turn the heat up to medium and add the sausages and apples. Fry for 20 minutes, turning regularly, until both sausages and apples are nicely browned. Remove with a slotted spoon and serve.

Sausagemeat and Cream Sauce for Pasta

This immensely rich sauce from Bologna is a good way to make 4 pork sausages stretch to a meal for 4 people. They must, however, be quality sausages with a high meat content – spicy Italian sausages are the best of all. Never use the processed British variety that contain more rusk and bread than meat.

Preparation time: 10 minutes
Cooking time: 20 minutes
Grade: easy

Suggested accompaniment: this sauce should be served with a shaped pasta which will wrap the sauce round it

4 high meat content pork sausages	½ teaspoon freshly grated black
2 mild red onions	pepper
½oz (15g) butter	good pinch of freshly grated nutmeg
1 tablespoon olive oil	5fl oz (140ml) double cream

● Remove the skin from the sausages and chop the meat very finely. Slice the onions in half and then thinly across.

● Melt the butter and oil together in a frying-pan and add the onions. Cook over a gentle heat for 10 minutes, stirring occasionally, until the onion is soft but not browned. Now add the sausagemeat, pepper and nutmeg and cook for a further 10 minutes, again stirring occasionally. Stir in the cream, allow to heat through, check the seasoning and serve with the pasta of your choice.

Frankfurter and Potato Salad with Dill

High-quality vacuum-packed frankfurters are now available, as are small waxy salad potatoes – combine the two for a northern European salad.

Preparation time: 5 minutes
Cooking time: 20 minutes
Grade: basic

Suggested accompaniment: rye bread or pumpernickel

1lb (450g) salad potatoes, e.g. La Ratte or Belle de Fontenay	1 teaspoon German, Scandinavian mustard, or Dijon mustard
4 frankfurters	sweetened with a little sugar
½ a mild sweet onion	1 teaspoon paprika
4 tablespoons thick plain yoghurt	salt and freshly ground black
1 tablespoon chopped fresh dill	pepper

● Scrub the potatoes and boil them in salted water until tender. Meanwhile grill the frankfurters for 10 minutes, or according to the instructions on the packet. Peel the onion and dice the flesh.

● When the potatoes and sausages are cool enough to handle, chop both into bite-sized pieces and mix them with the onion. Whip together the yoghurt, dill, mustard, paprika and plenty of seasoning and pour this over the potatoes and sausages while they are still warm. Serve the salad either straight away or cold.

OFFAL

Offal, with the notable exception of calves' liver, is cheap in Britain, reflecting our inexcusable national disdain for some of the tastiest of meats.

KIDNEYS

Kidneys from the ox and the pig are delicious, but require long, slow cooking. Lamb and veal kidneys, on the other hand, are best cooked briefly so that they are still pink in the middle.

LAMB

Kidney Kebabs

Skewered pieces of lamb's kidney sprinkled with oregano and grilled or cooked over charcoal are popular in many parts of Greece. The important thing is to cook the kidneys quickly under or over a high heat, so that the meat stays juicy and doesn't toughen. I like to alternate the kidney pieces with chunks of spring onion, whose sweet flavour when grilled contrasts well with the slightly bitter kidney.

Preparation time: 15 minutes
Cooking time: 6–10 minutes
Grade: easy

Suggested accompaniments: pitta bread and halved tomatoes stuffed with slivers of garlic and grilled alongside the kebabs

8 large lamb's kidneys, 1–1¼ lb (450–550g)	coarse salt and freshly ground black pepper
8 spring onions	olive oil
dried oregano	8 kebab sticks

- Peel the fine membrane from the kidney if it has not already been removed, and with sharp scissors remove the fatty core. Cut each kidney across into 3 pieces. Wash the spring onions and cut the white of each into 4 pieces. Thread 4 pieces of spring onion and 3 pieces of kidney alternately on to a kebab stick.
- Pre-heat the grill to maximum. Place the kebabs on a metal tray and sprinkle all over with oregano, salt and pepper. Dribble over a little olive oil.
- Cook the kebabs close to the grill – if you are using wooden kebab sticks (which don't impart an unpleasant metallic tang), sprinkle the exposed ends with water before putting them under the grill and take

care they don't catch fire. Cook the kebabs for 3–5 minutes on each side, depending on how large the pieces of kidney are and whether you like the meat slightly pink. You will be able to see when the kidney is cooked through.

Roast Kidneys in Bacon

Halved kidneys can be wrapped in bacon and roasted in the oven until they are just cooked through. The bacon protects the delicate flesh of the kidney and provides the roasting fat. This is a pleasantly comforting dish for a cold winter's evening, especially if served with lentils.

Note: the same approach can be taken to the larger veal kidneys, which should be split in half lengthways and then in half vertically.

Preparation time: 15 minutes
Cooking time: 20 minutes (no attention needed)
Grade: basic

Suggested accompaniment: the kidneys are good served on a bed of green lentils cooked with diced carrots and onion and finished with a little butter and parsley

8 large lamb's kidneys, 1–1¼ lb, (450–550g) 8 rashers smoked streaky bacon	½ teaspoon freshly ground black pepper 2 teaspoons of paprika 16 cocktail sticks

- Pre-heat the oven to 200°C/400°F/Gas Mark 6. Peel the fine membrane from the kidney if it has not already been removed and with sharp scissors remove the fatty core. Cut each kidney in half across. Remove the rind from the bacon and cut each rasher in half across. Mix together the pepper and paprika and roll half a kidney in the spices so that it is well coated. Wrap a piece of bacon around the kidney half and secure with a cocktail stick. Repeat until you have 16 kidney rolls.
- Place the wrapped kidneys on a baking tray and cook in the pre-heated oven for 20 minutes. Serve very hot.

Kidneys with Mustard and Cream Sauce

This classic from France was an essential element of my cooking repertoire in student days, its attractions deriving from the cheap basic ingredient, the added luxury of cream and the ease of cooking. It remains a favourite in my household today. For added luxury, use thinly sliced veal kidneys instead of those from the lamb.

Preparation time: 10 minutes if the kidneys are not ready-prepared
Cooking time: 7–8 minutes
Grade: easy

Suggested accompaniments: boiled rice and a green vegetable

---

12 lamb's kidneys
1oz (30g) unsalted butter
6fl oz (175ml) double cream or *crème fraîche*
1 tablespoon *moutarde de Meaux* or

grain mustard (*1 dessertspoon if you are using fiercer Dijon mustard*)
salt and freshly ground black pepper

● Remove the core and the fine outer skin from the kidneys and slice each across into 4 or 5 pieces. Melt the butter in a large, heavy-based frying-pan and as soon as it is bubbling add the kidneys. Fry over a fierce heat for 1 minute on either side, then pour in the *crème fraîche*. Allow to bubble for 3 or 4 minutes, until the kidneys are just cooked through (i.e. they are still slightly pink at the centre). Stir in the mustard, season to taste and serve.

Kidney Curry

Indians are rather fond of lamb's kidneys, although you rarely see them served in British curry houses. In fact kidneys take particularly well to curry spices, having a sufficiently strong flavour to hold their own.

This recipe is for a 'dry' curry, with a relatively small amount of sauce to meat. Plenty of spice is used but don't let that put you off – the end result is flavourful rather than fierce.

Preparation time: 15 minutes
Cooking time: 25 minutes
Grade: moderate

Suggested accompaniments: boiled Basmati rice; small whole carrots, steamed and finished with butter, sugar and whole cumin seeds

1¼lb (550g) lamb's kidneys	2 teaspoons tomato paste
1 teaspoon salt	3 teaspoons ground cumin
juice of 1 lemon	1½ teaspoons ground coriander
2 large onions	¼ teaspoon cayenne pepper
3 cloves of garlic	1 teaspoon garam masala
1in (2.5cm) piece of fresh ginger	1 teaspoon white sugar
4 large tomatoes	2 tablespoons water
2 tablespoons vegetable oil	

- Wash the kidneys thoroughly and with a sharp knife cut them in half horizontally. With a pair of scissors remove the fatty white core; with a knife make a shallow cross in the rounded side of each kidney half. Sprinkle the kidneys with the salt and lemon juice and leave to stand while you prepare the sauce.

- Finely chop the onions, garlic and ginger. Cut the tomatoes into thin slices. Over a medium high heat in a large heavy-based frying-pan, warm the oil and fry the onions for 5 minutes, stirring regularly, until they are lightly browned all over. Add the chopped garlic and ginger and fry for another couple of minutes. Now add the sliced tomatoes, the tomato paste, the spices apart from the garam masala, and the sugar. Fry, stirring constantly, for another 2 minutes before adding the water. Turn the heat down to low and simmer uncovered for 5 minutes.

- Meanwhile take the kidneys out of their juice and pat dry. When the water has evaporated and the sauce taken on a reddish brown colour after its 5 minutes' cooking, turn the heat up to high and add the kidneys. Cook, stirring a few times, for 5 minutes, until the kidneys are cooked through. Stir in the garam masala in the last minute of cooking and check the seasoning. Allow the kidneys to sit for a few minutes before serving, to ensure that they are pink through.

LIVER

It seems to me that the Italians are the nation with the best grasp of liver. Calves' liver is their speciality, of course, but they do wonderful things with lamb and chicken liver as well. Perhaps this is because Italian cooks above all others understand the value of good ingredients quickly prepared. Half the secret of cooking liver is in the butchering: it should be sliced on the bias, as thinly as possible. Then the other half of the equation is easy to effect: rapid cooking, retaining the liver's succulence. The one liver that does require long slow cooking is the pig's.

CALVES' LIVER

The most unctuous, and expensive, liver comes from the veal calf, and the rapidity of its cooking makes calves' liver an especially good choice for the busy cook. Its price, however, restricts it to special occasions and it is not a good choice for large-scale dinner parties as it requires last-minute attention.

Venetian Calves' Liver with Lemon

Classic recipes gain their notoriety precisely because they have been perfected over the years. It is a brave, or perhaps foolhardy, cook who tampers with them. I hope purists will forgive this slight alteration (or adulteration, depending on your point of view) to the famous Venetian recipe for calves' liver with stewed onions and sultanas. In my defence I would say that cumin is hardly unknown to the cooking of a city which produced Marco Polo, and that I have seen the dish served *in situ* with a quarter of lemon on the side. The end result is a slightly sharp contrast to the sweetness which I find pleasing.

Preparation time: 5 minutes
Cooking time: 30 minutes
Grade: easy
Suggested accompaniment: for a small dinner party serve the liver with nothing more than a bitter green salad such as frisée after a first course of pasta or risotto; for an everyday dinner try accompanying it with mashed potatoes made with olive oil and stock rather than butter and milk, and spinach

3 large white onions	grated rind
3 tablespoons olive oil	salt and freshly ground black pepper
1 heaped teaspoon ground cumin	1lb (450g) calves' liver, sliced very thinly
1oz (30g) sultanas	
juice of 1 lemon plus 1 teaspoon	

- Slice the onions into very thin rings. Put the oven on low (you will use it to keep the sauce warm while you fry the liver) and warm up a serving dish. In a large heavy-based frying-pan, heat 2 tablespoons of the oil over a medium low heat. Add the onions and stew gently in the oil for 20 minutes, stirring occasionally, until they are very soft and just lightly browned. Now add the cumin, sultanas, grated lemon rind, lemon juice and salt and pepper to taste. Continue to fry for 2 more minutes then transfer the mixture to the serving dish to keep warm.
- Add the remaining oil to the pan and turn up the heat to high. After 1 minute add the liver to the pan. Provided it is finely sliced it should cook for no more than a minute on each side – there is nothing worse than overcooked liver. Pile the slices of liver on the onion and sultana mixture and allow to rest in the oven for a couple of minutes (but no more) before serving.

Calves' Liver in a Balsamic Vinegar Sauce

As the previous recipe indicates, the slight bitterness of calves' liver is complemented by sweet flavours. Balsamic vinegar lacks the harshness of the more ordinary wine vinegars, because of its long maturation in casks of differing woods. Although the balsamic vinegar we buy in our shops may have skipped a few years of wood age in favour of a spoon or two of sugar, this is in its favour when it comes to making sauces (and not just because it is so much cheaper than the older varieties, which you should keep for dribbling in tiny quantities over salads). Added to a hot pan, this vinegar caramelizes rapidly to form a thick, dark sauce which coats the liver. I like to add pinenuts and raisins for texture and sweetness, but if they are not available the sauce will do perfectly well on its own.

Preparation time: none
Cooking time: 5 minutes
Grade: easy

Suggested accompaniments: again, the dish is best served on its own after pasta; for a one-course meal, add some fried potatoes and green vegetables

8 thin slices of calves' liver	2oz (55g) pinenuts
salt and freshly ground black pepper	2oz (55g) raisins
2 tablespoons olive oil	4 tablespoons balsamic vinegar

- Season the liver. Heat the oil in a frying-pan large enough to take all the meat, and when it is very hot add the slices of liver. Fry for 1 minute on each side, then remove and keep warm.
- Put the pinenuts and raisins in the pan and fry, stirring for 2 minutes. Now add the vinegar (stand back as it will spit) and cook, stirring, for a further minute. Pour over the meat and serve.

CHICKEN LIVERS

Chicken livers are an underrated source of cheap, tasty dishes. The classic base for smooth pâtés, they are also good lightly fried and tossed over salads. Try them with different spices and oils – sprinkle green leaves for a chicken liver salad with toasted walnuts and dress with walnut oil, or roll the livers in flour mixed with paprika and cumin before quickly frying them in olive oil.

Chicken livers should be pink in colour, with no greenish tinges, each one plump with little gristle. Unfortunately they are generally sold frozen, which makes it difficult to asses their condition.

Chicken Liver Pilav

Many pilavs are vegetarian, with plenty of fruit and nuts for added interest, and are traditionally served as a side dish for roast meat. However, a pilav also makes an excellent one-pan supper, and unlike, say, a risotto, this is a rice dish which requires little attention during the cooking. When serving a pilav alone, I add some meat – chicken livers are especially successful, turning this into a rich dish. It is very important for perfect rice that you should soak and rinse it well beforehand.

Preparation time: 10 minutes
Cooking time: 25 minutes, 15 minutes before serving
Grade: moderate

Suggested accompaniment: green salad

8oz (225g) long-grain rice	2 tablespoons flaked almonds
1 onion	2 tablespoons currants
8oz (225g) chicken livers	1 teaspoon paprika
1 pint (600ml) water	salt and freshly ground black
2oz (55g) unsalted butter	pepper
1 tablespoon pinenuts	chopped parsley

- Put the rice to soak in water for 10 minutes. Meanwhile finely chop the onion. Chop the chicken livers into 1in (2.5cm) pieces.
- Melt half the butter in a large heavy-based lidded frying-pan. Fry the onion for 3–4 minutes over a gentle heat, until translucent. Now add the pinenuts, almonds and chicken livers. Fry for another 3 minutes and then remove the contents of the pan to a plate.
- Drain the rice and rinse twice under cold running water. Now melt the remaining butter in the pan and add the rice, currants and paprika.

Cook gently for 2 minutes, stirring all the time. Boil the water, pour into the rice, season well, stir just once, and cover. Leave to cook for 12 minutes over a low flame, until all the water is absorbed. During this time resist the temptation to lift the lid.

● Take the rice off the heat and stir the chicken liver and nut mixture in with the utmost care. Cover with a clean teatowel and replace the lid. Leave off the heat for 15 minutes. Now fluff the rice up with a fork, sprinkle with the parsley and serve.

Chicken Liver Sauce for Pasta

The Italians use chicken livers to make a rich sauce for pasta. Some recipes add minced beef or veal to the livers, giving a contrast of textures between the slightly grainy but creamy liver and the firmer mince, but personally I find the combination of flavours confusing and prefer to stick to just liver, tomato and red wine. The dish should be topped with plenty of freshly grated Parmesan before serving.

Preparation time: 10 minutes
Cooking time: 30 minutes
Grade: easy

Suggested accompaniments:
papardelle, tagliatelle or fettucine are the best pastas; a green salad is the only other dish I would serve

1 small onion	salt and freshly ground black
1 carrot	pepper
2 sticks of celery, including leaves	1 glass of red wine
2 tablespoons olive oil	14oz (400g) tin Italian plum
2 cloves of garlic	tomatoes
8oz (225g) chicken livers	3 or 4 sprigs of fresh thyme
½ teaspoon cinnamon	and/or rosemary
pinch of mace or nutmeg	Parmesan

● Chop the onion, carrot and celery, including the leaves, very finely. Heat the oil in a heavy-based saucepan over a medium heat and cook the chopped vegetables for 10 minutes, stirring occasionally, until lightly browned. Meanwhile, peel the garlic and chop finely; trim the livers of any gristle or greenish tinged pieces and chop coarsely.

● When the 10 minutes are up, add the garlic to the pan and cook for another couple of minutes. Now turn up the heat and throw in the chicken livers, the spices, salt and plenty of freshly ground black pepper. Stir for 2 minutes, until the livers are browned all over. Pour in the red wine and as soon as it starts to bubble add the tinned tomatoes and herbs. Chop up the tomatoes in the pan with your spoon, bring to the boil and then turn down to a simmer. Cover and cook for 15 minutes.

● Before serving, check the seasoning and put plenty of freshly grated Parmesan on the table.

Chicken Livers and Mushrooms on Toast

This is the sort of dish that was once served as a savoury after the meal but it makes an excellent supper all on its own.

Preparation time: 15 minutes
Cooking time: 15 minutes
Grade: easy

Suggested accompaniment: green salad

8oz (225g) brown cap mushrooms	1oz (30g) butter
1 clove of garlic	2 tablespoons olive oil
4 shallots	3 or 4 chopped leaves of fresh
4 slices of country bread,	sage, if available
preferably ciabatta	salt and freshly ground black
12oz (350g) chicken livers	pepper

● Wash the mushrooms and slice them across into 2 or 3 slices. Peel the garlic and shallots and chop both finely. Toast the bread and keep warm. Trim the livers of any gristle or greenish bits, then wash them well and pat them dry on kitchen towel.

● Heat the butter and oil in a large heavy-based frying-pan over a gentle heat. Stew the chopped shallots and garlic for 5 minutes, then add the sliced mushrooms and stew for a further 5 minutes. Turn up the heat and add the chicken livers and the sage (if you have it); cook fiercely, stirring all the time, for 3 or 4 minutes, until the livers are nicely browned. Season the contents of the pan well and pile on top of the slices of toast.

Lamb's Liver

Good quality lamb's liver is not a poor relation of calves' liver, but a delicacy in its own right. It too rewards quick cooking.

Lamb's Liver with Capers in Tomato Sauce

The astringency of capers offsets the richness of the liver in this North Italian dish, with a fresh tomato sauce to provide sweetness. In Italy this would usually be made with calves' liver, but the stronger flavour of the cheaper lamb's liver seems to me to stand up better to the powerful effect of the capers. You need paper-thin slices of liver for this dish, rather than the thicker chunks suitable for the salad right. If buying your liver in a packet from the supermarket, you should be prepared to use a sharp knife to slice the liver in half horizontally.

Preparation time: 10 minutes
Cooking time: 15 minutes
Grade: moderate

Suggested accompaniment: a slab of polenta, brushed with olive oil and grilled

6 large tomatoes	approx. 1–1¼lb (450–550g)
2 cloves of garlic	1 glass white wine
2 tablespoons capers	½ teaspoon of sugar
2 tablespoons olive oil	salt and freshly ground black
8 thin slices of liver, total weight	pepper

- Skin the tomatoes by pouring boiling water over them. Chop the flesh coarsely. Finely chop the garlic and rinse the capers thoroughly.
- In a pan large enough to take all the slices of liver flat, heat the oil over a high heat. Fry the liver for 30 seconds on each side, just enough for the flesh to turn opaque, and remove from the pan.
- Keep the pan over a high heat and add the chopped garlic to the oil. Fry for 1 minute, stirring, then add the chopped tomatoes. Break up the tomato flesh with a wooden spoon and cook for 3–4 minutes, until the tomatoes have started to break down. Now pour in the wine, allow to bubble for a minute, then turn down to a simmer. Add the sugar and the capers and cook for 5 minutes. Put the liver back in the pan, turning it to make sure it is well coated with the sauce, and cook for a further 2–3 minutes, until cooked through. Add plenty of salt and black pepper to taste and serve.

Spiced Lamb's Liver Salad

The Albanians spice lamb's liver with paprika, fry it briefly and serve it with sliced onion as a starter. I like to add extra vegetables in the form of cucumber and carrots to make a more substantial dish. The key to cooking lamb's liver is to do so very quickly – the meat should be browned on the outside but tender and still pink on the inside, its soft and juicy consistency contrasting with the crunchy vegetables.

Preparation time: 20 minutes
Cooking time: 5 minutes
Grade: easy

Suggested accompaniment: crusty bread

1 cucumber	1 tablespoon chopped fresh parsley
1 teaspoon coarse salt	1 tablespoon paprika
8oz (225g) carrots	$\frac{1}{2}$ teaspoon freshly ground black
2 small red onions or 1 large	pepper
Spanish onion	3 tablespoons olive oil
1¼ lb (550g) lamb's liver	1 tablespoon white wine vinegar

- Chop the cucumber into small cubes, sprinkle with the salt and leave to drain for 10 minutes. Peel the carrots and chop into small cubes. Slice the peeled onions into very thin half-rings. Wash and dry the liver and slice it into strips ½in (1cm) wide and 2in (5cm) long.
- When the cucumber has drained, rinse it thoroughly and mix it with the carrots, onions and parsley in a serving dish. Mix together the paprika and pepper. Roll the strips of liver in the spice mixture.
- Heat the oil in a frying-pan over a high heat. When it is almost smoking, add the liver pieces and fry very quickly, stirring all the time, for 3–4 minutes. Remove the liver from the pan and place on the vegetables. Turn the heat down, stand well back and add the vinegar to the pan – be careful, it will spit. Pour the pan juices over the salad and serve.

FISH
AND
SHELLFISH

FISH

Fish cooks quickly. It is good for you. Living on an island, we have (in theory) plenty of it near at hand. And the enormous number of species means that it is difficult to become bored with it. So, obviously, fish offers the ideal basis for a rapid supper.

Things aren't quite that simple. Yes, fish cooks quickly, but it is also tricky to prepare to perfection. There is little worse than overcooked fish, its flesh dry and rubbery. We may live on an island, but that does not appear to be a guarantee that our fish will reach us in prime condition – it is easier to buy excellent fish in Paris, far from the sea, than it is in, say, Dover or Edinburgh. The huge range of species is not generally represented in our supermarkets and fishmongers; although, to be fair, this situation is improving, so that we can now buy red mullet and squid as well as cod and plaice. But it remains true that when most of us eat fish, it has reached us via the food-processing industry, which swallows up much of the catch.

These are all reasons why we do not eat as much as fresh fish as we should. Reasons, but not excuses. It is up to us to demand better-quality fish of our retailers, and to learn how to treat it, so that we can enjoy to the full one of the best of ingredients.

COD

The ugly cod, Britain's most popular fish, has in recent years become beloved of restaurateurs as well as fish and chip shop owners. These days you can hardly enter a trendy eatery without spotting roast cod in olive oil on the menu. This enthusiasm is well founded, for a fresh piece of cod is surprisingly good – provided it hasn't been overcooked, as is so often its fate.

Cod is not a delicate fish, and responds well to tough treatment and strong flavours. Sear it in fruity olive oil, poach it in red wine, fiercely roast it with whole heads of garlic, coat it with spices and grill it – but personally I'd rather not deep-fry it.

Roast Cod with Salsa Verde

This uncooked sauce from Italy, a pungent mix of parsley, capers, anchovies and pickled gherkins, needs a bold partner. Cod roasted in olive oil is just the thing, and the white flesh set against the pool of green sauce looks as good as it tastes. The salsa verde is also excellent with cold, rare roast beef.

Preparation time: none
Cooking time: 10–15 minutes
Grade: basic

Suggested accompaniment: mashed potatoes

---

4 cod steaks
salt and freshly ground black
  pepper
2 tablespoons olive oil

For the salsa verde:
4 tablespoons chopped flat-leaved

parsley
2oz (55g) tin anchovies
1 tablespoon capers, drained
8 small gherkins
1 teaspoon grated lemon zest
4 tablespoons extra virgin olive
  oil

● Pre-heat the oven to 200°C/400°F/Gas Mark 6. Put the cod steaks in an earthenware baking dish, season them and brush the surface with the olive oil. Roast in the oven for 10–15 minutes, the exact time will depend on the thickness of the steaks. They are ready when the flesh flakes easily and a milky liquid starts to flow. Be very careful not to overcook.
● While they are cooking, make the salsa verde by simply putting all the ingredients in a food processor and giving them a quick whizz. The consistency of the sauce should be slightly bitty rather than smooth.
● Serve the hot roast cod with the cold salsa verde on the side.

Cod Steaks with Potato in Red Wine

This robust dish is perfect winter food: thick steaks of cod are simmered in a red wine sauce with diced potato to give substance and smoked bacon to enhance the flavour. In the Basque country, from which this recipe originates, small chunks of raw ham might be used in place of the bacon. A few juniper berries added to the dish give a herby scent of the mountains, and the final sprinkling of parsley adds a fresh taste as well as colour.

Preparation time: 10 minutes
Cooking time: 30 minutes
Grade: easy

Suggested accompaniment: a green salad

4 medium-sized waxy potatoes	9fl oz (250ml) red wine
1 Spanish onion	9fl oz (250ml) water
2 cloves of garlic	4 juniper berries
4 rashers smoked streaky bacon	salt and freshly ground black pepper
2 tablespoons olive oil	chopped fresh parsley
4 cod steaks	

- Peel the potatoes and cut them into ½in (1cm) dice. Rinse the potato under cold running water to remove some of the starch. Finely chop the onion and the garlic. Roughly chop the bacon and remove rind.
- In a deep-sided frying-pan large enough to take all the potatoes and the fish, heat the oil over a moderate heat. Fry the onion, bacon and the garlic, stirring occasionally, for 5 minutes until the onion is soft and beginning to take colour. Add the cod steaks to the pan and fry for 30 seconds on each side, to seal. Carefully remove the cod and put to one side. Throw in the potato dice and stir well to make sure that they are coated with oil.
- Pour the wine and water into the pan, add the juniper berries and plenty of seasoning, and bring the liquid to the boil. Turn down to a simmer, cover, and leave to cook for 10 minutes.
- Now put the cod steaks back in the pan, pushing them well down into the potato and onion mixture. Cover and cook for another 10 minutes. Take off the lid, boil off any excess liquid (but the mixture should still be quite soupy), sprinkle with parsley and serve.

Cod Steaks Grilled with a Mustard, Thyme and Breadcrumb Topping

This is essentially cod in breadcrumbs – except that the cod is in a thick steak, so that it remains juicy whilst the breadcrumbs crisp, the topping is stuck on with mustard instead of egg, and there is thyme instead of parsley. If you are nervous of bones, use filleted cod instead of steaks, but reduce the cooking time – fillets need only a few minutes on either side under a very hot grill.

Preparation time: 10 minutes
Cooking time: 20 minutes
Grade: easy

Suggested accompaniment: peas

2 teaspoons coarse salt	thyme or 1 teaspoon dried
4 cod steaks, each about 1in	thyme
(2.5cm) thick	½ teaspoon freshly ground black
½ a baguette, which should be	pepper
slightly stale	4 teaspoons Dijon mustard
a good handful of sprigs of fresh	2oz (55g) butter

● Rub the salt into the cod and leave to stand for 10 minutes. Pre-heat the grill to maximum. In a food processor (or using a grater) make fine breadcrumbs from the baguette. Strip the leaves from the stalks of thyme and mix into the breadcrumbs, along with the black pepper.
● Drain any liquid from the salted cod and rub off excess salt. Pat the surface of the fish dry with kitchen towel. Cook as close as possible to the grill for 5 minutes on each side. The fish should be lightly browned.
● Turn the grill down to medium. Rub a teaspoon of mustard into the uppermost surface of each steak. Now with your fingers carefully pack the breadcrumb mixture across the surface. Dot the butter over the breadcrumbs and return to the grill. Cook for another 6–7 minutes, until the surface is evenly browned – towards the end of this period watch carefully to make sure the coating does not burn. Serve immediately.

HADDOCK

The haddock may be widely used, but it deserves better treatment than it customarily receives. Poached in milk it is meant to be food for invalids, but frankly it would make me feel even more unwell. It needs strong, salty flavours to enhance its somewhat insipid nature. The taste of the fish is not overwhelmed, but rather brought out – haddock has an ability to absorb other flavours whilst retaining its essential fishiness.

Much of the catch of haddock in this country goes to the smoker. Undyed, best-quality smoked haddock is a British treasure, but the aggressively coloured, factory-produced version is best avoided.

Haddock Rolls

Briefly roasted with a herby, salty, fleshy stuffing of dill, tomatoes and black olives, fillets of haddock come into their own. This easy recipe looks impressive and is at home as a first or main course.

Preparation time: 15 minutes
Cooking time: 10 minutes
Grade: easy

Suggested accompaniments: new boiled potatoes and peas or another fresh green vegetable; or you can serve 1 roll apiece as a starter for a dinner party

4 small skinless boneless haddock fillets, approx. 1–1¼ lb (450–550g)	*to use stoned ones*)
freshly ground black pepper	1 tablespoon fresh dill
2 firm, flavourful tomatoes	2 tablespoons extra virgin olive oil
2oz (55g) black olives (*it is easiest*	8 wooden cocktail sticks

● Pre-heat the oven to 180°C/350°F/Gas Mark 4. Check the haddock fillets for stray bones and skin, then split each fillet in half lengthways with a sharp knife. Season with plenty of pepper. Dice the tomatoes and the olives finely and mix together. Add ¾ of the dill, finely chopped.

● Spread a little of the filling along each haddock fillet, roll up and secure with a toothpick (this is slightly fiddly – make sure you don't try to overfill the fillets). Place the rolled-up fillets in an ovenproof dish and dribble over the olive oil. Bake uncovered for 10 minutes – the fish is cooked when it starts to flake and give off a milky liquid. Sprinkle with the remaining dill and serve.

Haddock with Bacon and Mushrooms

This is fork food, a pile of sliced mushrooms interspersed with bacon and flecked with fish. It makes a rich and filling snack. Cod responds well to the same treatment.

Preparation time: 10 minutes
Cooking time: 10 minutes
Grade: easy

Suggested accompaniments: I pile the fish mixture into the well of lettuce leaves (raddichio looks good) and serve a potato salad on the side; it also goes well on toast

12oz (350g) skinless haddock fillets	**2 cloves of garlic**
8oz (225g) mushrooms (*shiitake mushrooms are especially good here*)	**2oz (55g) unsalted butter**
	2 teaspoons paprika
8 rashers smoked streaky bacon	**salt and freshly ground black pepper**

● Cut the haddock into bite-sized pieces. Slice the mushrooms across into 2 or 3 pieces each. Dice the bacon, removing the rind. Peel the garlic and chop finely.

● Melt the butter with the bacon and the garlic in a frying-pan over a gentle heat. Cook for 5 minutes, then turn up the heat to medium and add the sliced mushrooms. Fry, stirring, for 3 minutes, then add the pieces of haddock, the paprika and salt and pepper to taste (be careful with the salt, making allowances for the bacon). Continue to fry for 3–4 minutes, stirring regularly – the pieces of haddock will break up, but don't worry about this. Take off the heat, leave to stand for 5 minutes for the flavours to mingle, and serve.

HERRING

The herring is a fish popular with nutritionists, due to its high oil content. This oiliness means that it is better grilled or baked rather than fried. Other advantages of the herring are that it is both cheap and quick to cook, making it ideal for everyday suppers. The herring is briefly out of season in the spring.

Marinated herrings are useful store-cupboard items for quick snacks; my favourite are those pickled with dill, or the Scandinavian salted herrings which require soaking before serving.

Grilled Herring with Mustard Sauce

A fresh grilled herring is a dish many of us have forgotten about. Renew your acquaintance, for it is quite a treat, and a cheap one at that. Really the fish needs nothing more than a squeeze of lemon, but it was traditionally served with mustard to cut the richness. I like my mustard whipped into *smetana* to give a creamy sauce. If you have sweet German or Scandinavian mustard the effect will be particularly good.

Preparation time: none
Cooking time: 15 minutes
Grade: basic

Suggested accompaniment: a salad of radish and cucumber, dressed with white wine vinegar

---

4 herrings, approx. 10–11oz (280–325g) each, cleaned and gutted
1 dessertspoon German sweet mustard (*or failing that use Dijon mustard mixed with a teaspoon of* sugar)
9fl oz (250ml) creamed *smetana*, *crème fraîche* or sour cream
juice of ½ a lemon (*reduce to a squeeze if you are using sour cream*)

- Pre-heat the grill to maximum and cook the fish close to the heat for 7–8 minutes on either side.
- Meanwhile make the sauce by simply mixing together the remaining ingredients. You could add a little fresh dill or a teaspoon of dried dill.
- Remove the fish from the grill and peel off the skin. Season well, spoon the sauce over and serve.

Salted Herring

This very simple way of preparing herring is popular in Japan. The fish is rubbed with salt, which draws the liquid from the fish, firming up the flesh. Despite the large quantity of salt used, the flavour of the fish is unmasked. The herring should be very fresh; you could also use mackerel.

Preparation time: 5 minutes, 30 minutes before cooking
Cooking time: 15 minutes
Grade: easy

Suggested accompaniment: grated radish

| 4 herrings, gutted | 2 tablespoons coarse sea salt |

- Wash the fish and wipe it dry. With a sharp knife, make several slashes across the body down to the bone. Rub the salt all over the fish and leave to stand for 30 minutes.
- Pre-heat the grill to medium. Drain off any liquid from the fish, wipe off excess salt, and grill for 7–8 minutes on either side, until the skin is nicely blackened and the flesh flakes easily.

Herring, Beetroot and Potato Salad

Combining chopped marinated herring with beetroot and warm potatoes makes for a substantial Scandinavian salad, dressed with *crème fraîche* and fresh dill. If you have time to cook the beetroot yourself, roasting or boiling it in its skin, then it will taste all the nicer; if you are using ready-prepared beetroot, buy the variety cooked in salted water and vacuum-packed, rather than the kind preserved in vinegar.

Preparation time: 10 minutes, whilst the potatoes are cooking
Cooking time: 15 minutes
Grade: basic

Suggested accompaniments: rye bread or pumpernickel; a glass of iced vodka

---

1lb (450g) small salad potatoes
(*the waxy La ratte variety are particularly good*)
12oz (350g) cooked beetroot
2 x 9oz (250g) jars herrings
marinated in onion
1 tablespoon fresh dill
9oz (250g) *crème fraîche*
salt and freshly ground black pepper

● Boil the scrubbed potatoes in their skins for 15 minutes or until tender to the fork but not falling apart. Meanwhile, chop the beetroot into ½ in (1cm) cubes. Remove the herring fillets from the jar; discard the liquid but reserve the chopped onion with which they have been marinated. Cut each fillet in half lengthways and then cut across at ½ in (1cm) intervals. Finely chop the dill.

● Mix together the herring, reserved onion and beetroot. When the potatoes are cooked, drain them and as soon as they are cool enough to handle cut them into ½ in (1cm) cubes. Stir the hot potatoes, the fresh dill and the *crème fraîche* into the herring and beetroot mix, check the seasoning and serve.

JOHN DORY

The John Dory, or St Peter's fish as it is otherwise known, after the black thumbprint on its body, is a strange-looking beast, its massive head and jaw taking up nearly half of its length. Don't be put off by appearances, however, for it tastes very good. It can be baked or grilled, but is best of all fried in olive oil. Although the ratio of meat to bone is poor, the cooking is worth the effort. Some supermarkets have recognized this fact and now stock both whole John Dory and fillets from the larger fish. I think it is best cooked on the bone.

Fried John Dory with Potatoes and Garlic

Superior fish and chips – John Dory fried on the bone is one of life's treats and a few cubes of potato cooked in the same oil to absorb the fishy taste completes the dish.

Preparation time: 10 minutes
Cooking time: 25 minutes
Grade: moderate

Suggested accompaniment: a green salad
Serves: 2

1 large John Dory, approx. 2lb (900g)
2 large waxy potatoes
4 tablespoons olive oil
4 cloves of garlic, unpeeled
chopped flat-leaved parsley
1 lemon

- I normally like to cook my fish whole, but in this case you should have the head of the fish removed as it will probably be too large to fit in your frying-pan. (In any case, the massive jaw falls apart rather unattractively when put in hot oil.) The fish should also be skinned.
- Peel the potatoes and cut into ½in (1cm) cubes.
- In a large non-stick frying-pan, heat the oil over a high heat with the whole unpeeled garlic cloves. Add the potatoes and turn in the oil for 5–6 minutes. Now turn the heat down to medium, push the potatoes to the side of the pan and put in the fish. Fry for 10 minutes then turn over carefully, turning the potatoes at the same time. Cook for another 8–10 minutes, until the fish lifts easily off the bone. Season well, pour over the hot oil from the pan, surround with the potatoes and sprinkle with parsley before serving with wedges of lemon.

MACKEREL

Mackerel is one of the most attractive of fish, the black and green stripes leaping out at you from the gleaming silvery skin. You can almost see the fish slipping like a blade through the water. Well, when it is fresh, that it is. A tired, floppy, mackerel on a bed of ice is a dull thing, unlikely to lead you to flights (or plunges) of fantasy, especially when it has been cooked. So only buy mackerel which shine up at you from the counter, their flesh firm to the thumb.

A fresh mackerel tastes as good as it looks. It is a fatty fish, which means it is better grilled rather than fried. Best of all, barbecue whole fish and eat them with your fingers. Mackerel are also very good baked in cider or white wine with spices and served cold.

Grilled or Barbecued Mackerel with Mint and Citrus Juices

The Turks' favourite herbs are dill and mint – and they don't restrict themselves to dill when cooking fish. They also love mackerel, especially when it is barbecued or grilled, so that the skin bubbles up and blackens, leaving the flesh beneath still juicy and with a firm texture. To ensure firmness you should salt the fish in advance; for added flavour, and to cut the fattiness, I like to pour over lime and orange juice. The mint is sprinkled over the fish just before cooking.

Preparation time: 5 minutes, 15 minutes before you want to cook
Cooking time: 12 minutes
Grade: easy

Suggested accompaniment: good served all on its own after a vegetable starter such as artichoke or asparagus

4 small whole mackerel, gutted, head and tail left on	juice of 1 orange
1½ teaspoons coarse salt	2 teaspoons dried mint
juice of 1 lime	4 sprigs fresh mint, if available

● Wash the fish well. With a sharp knife, make 3 or 4 incisions across the flesh right down to the bone on either side. Lay the fish on a baking tray covered with foil. Rub the salt all over the fish then pour over the citrus juices, making sure as much as possible runs into the slashes in the flesh. Leave to stand for 15 minutes; meanwhile pre-heat the grill to maximum or get the barbecue coals glowing.

● When you are ready to cook the fish, sprinkle half the dried mint into the uppermost slashes and place a sprig of fresh mint, if you have it, in the cavity of each fish. Put the fish close to the hot grill or on the barbecue and cook for 6–7 minutes on one side, until the skin is blackened and the flesh falling away from the bone. Turn the whole fish over, sprinkle the remaining dried mint into the slashes, spoon over any juices from the tinfoil and cook for a further 5 minutes. Serve immediately.

Japanese Grilled Mackerel

The Japanese buy the very freshest fish and treat them with elegant simplicity. Mackerel can be grilled with salt or cooked teriyaki style, that is, brushed with soy sauce and lemon juice. The traditional skewering of the fish ensures it keeps its shape during cooking.

Preparation time: 10 minutes
Cooking time: 12–14 minutes
Grade: basic

Suggested accompaniments:
watercress and rice

4 small whole mackerel, cleaned and gutted, head and tail left on	preferably a Japanese variety
2 tablespoons fresh lemon juice	thinly pared lemon zest
2 tablespoons soy sauce,	8 wooden skewers

● Pierce each fish with a wooden skewer above the eye and carefully push the skewer the length of the fish, bringing the skewer out again on the same side above the tail. Do not pierce the flesh on the other side of the fish. Repeat the process on the same side with the second skewer, piercing at the end of the mouth and reappearing just below the tail.
● Mix the lemon juice and soy sauce together and brush this mixture all over the skewered fish. Pre-heat the grill to maximum and cook the fish for 12–14 minutes, turning several times during cooking and brushing with the lemon and soy mix. The fish is ready when the flesh flakes. Garnish with the lemon zest and serve.

Mackerel in Spiced Cider

Whole mackerel cooked in spiced cider is an old English favourite, competing with (and in my view beating) the French classic of *maqueraux au vin blanc*. The fish can be eaten straight from the oven, but are even better if allowed to cool down in the liquid and served either warm or completely cold.

Once cooked, the fish will keep for several days provided you leave them in the cider; if you remove them they will dry out. Half a mackerel per person makes a good starter, a whole fish an ideal summer supper.

Preparation time: 5 minutes
Cooking time: 20 minutes, preferably a while before serving or even the day before
Grade: basic

Suggested accompaniments: bread and a salad

4 small whole mackerel, head and tail left on	1 teaspoon allspice berries
1 teaspoon coarse salt	2 whole cloves
2 bay leaves	3 slices of orange
1 teaspoon black peppercorns	3 slices of lemon
	1 pint (600ml) dry cider

- Pre-heat the oven to 150°C/300°F/Gas Mark 2.
- Wash the mackerel and rub inside and out with salt. Arrange the fish head to tail in an ovenproof china or earthenware dish in which they will just fit. Tuck in the bay leaves, sprinkle over the peppercorns, allspice berries and cloves, lay the slices of fruit over the fish and pour in the cider. Cover with foil and bake in the pre-heated oven for 20 minutes. Allow to cool in the liquid and serve warm or cold.

MONKFISH

This is a gutsy fish. The way it looks, it probably needs to be. It certainly responds to forceful treatment. This is a fish not for gentle poaching, but for spicing and grilling in kebabs over the barbecue; instead of slowly baking it in foil, spike the whole tail with garlic and roast it naked in a fierce oven. In fact, treat it like meat.

You need less monkfish than you think for many recipes, because of its solidity. Given its recent rise to the category of expensive fish, this is a relief. If you are planning to cook kebabs, look for large pieces of fish, cut from the top or middle of the tail, so that there is little wastage when you cut your cubes.

Monkfish Wrapped in Bacon

Bacon wrapped scallops get my thumbs down. So does the oyster version, angels on horseback, although I don't mind the odd rasher wrapped around an apparently devilish prune. Prunes, instead of being overwhelmed like the delicate shellfish, can stand up to the salty, smoky flavour, indeed, make a powerful claim to be tasted above it. So does monkfish, which remains juicy and distinct inside its bacon casing, acquiring nothing more than a slight smokiness which only adds to its flavour. These kebabs make an excellent main course but can also be served as cocktail nibbles, one to a stick.

Preparation time: 15 minutes
Cooking time: 15 minutes
Grade: basic

Suggested accompaniment: flageolet beans heated with tomato and garlic

1½lb (550g) monkfish tail	kebab sticks
freshly ground black pepper	
6oz (175g) smoked streaky bacon	

● Remove any skin and bone from the monkfish and cut the flesh into 1in (2.5cm) cubes. Season with plenty of pepper. Remove the rind from the bacon. Wrap each cube of monkfish in sufficient bacon to just encircle it and secure on the kebab stick. Put 3 pieces of monkfish wrapped in bacon on each stick.
● Heat the grill to maximum. Grill the kebabs close to the heat for 15 minutes, turning regularly.

Monkfish with Chickpeas and Potatoes

The Catalans are keen eaters of monkfish. Here it is combined with a couple of their other regular ingredients, chickpeas and potatoes. The use of the *picada* at the end to thicken the sauce is characteristic of this region's cooking. It adds plenty of punch as well as texture – this is not a dish for those who are shy of garlic.

Preparation time: 10 minutes
Cooking time: 25 minutes
Grade: moderate

Suggested accompaniment: a green salad to follow

12oz (350g) monkfish, off the bone
1 large onion
2 cloves of garlic
1lb (450g) small new potatoes
2 tablespoons olive oil
14oz (400g) tin chickpeas
2 glasses dry white wine
salt and freshly ground black pepper

1 tablespoon chopped flat-leaved parsley, if available

For the picada:
2 cloves of garlic
1 tablespoon flaked almonds
1 slice dry white bread, crusts removed
1 tablespoon extra virgin olive oil

● Remove any skin from the monkfish and cut the flesh into 2in (5cm) pieces. Coarsely chop the onion and finely chop the garlic. Scrub the potatoes.

● Bring a pan of salted water to the boil and cook the potatoes until they are nearly but not quite ready, 10–15 minutes depending on size. Meanwhile heat the oil in a large, heavy frying-pan with a lid. Fry the onion for 5 minutes over a medium heat, until it is just colouring. Now add the monkfish and garlic and fry for a further couple of minutes. Tip in the contents of the tin of chickpeas, including the liquid, add the wine, turn the heat up and bring to the boil. Then turn down to a slow simmer, season, and cover.

● After 10 minutes add the almost-cooked potatoes. Cover again and leave to simmer for a further 5 minutes. Meanwhile make the *picada* by whizzing together the garlic, almonds, stale bread and oil (traditionally the bread is first fried in olive oil, but I prefer to cheat and simply add the oil to the mixture). Traditionally again, the *picada* is made in a pestle and mortar – if you are using a food processor, give a brief whizz. It should have a slightly lumpy consistency.

● Stir the *picada* into the pan and allow to cook for a further 3–4 minutes, still just simmering. Sprinkle with the parsley if you have it and serve.

Fried Monkfish Tail with Saffron

This straightforward dish shows monkfish off at its best, emphasizing the qualities which prompted the dubbing of the fish as poor man's lobster. As with many simple recipes, it relies on expensive ingredients, in this case best-quality olive oil and saffron.

Preparation time: none
Cooking time: 15 minutes
Grade: easy

Suggested accompaniments: boiled new potatoes and a green vegetable

2 small skinless monkfish tails, on the bone, approx. 10–12oz (280–350g) each salt and freshly ground black pepper	4 tablespoons extra virgin olive oil 8–10 saffron pistils or 1/3 teaspoon powdered saffron juice of 1/2 a lemon

● Season the monkfish well. Pour the oil into a heavy-based lidded pan large enough to take both pieces of fish and put over a high heat. When the oil is almost spitting, stand well back and add the monkfish. It will initially curl – don't worry about this. Fry the tail hard for 5 minutes on each side. Now turn the heat down to low and stir the saffron pistils and the lemon juice into the oil, turning the monkfish over once or twice so that it is coated with the yellow oil. Cover, leave to cook for 5 minutes over a low heat, then serve.

GREY MULLET

Grey mullet is a bargain in Britain compared to Turkey and Greece, where it is highly prized and priced accordingly. The salted roe of the mullet is used for the classic taramasalata, although these days smoked cod's roe is more common. It is a fish which takes especially well to baking, either simply with a few herbs and a slice or two of lime popped in its belly, or coated with a thick spicy paste in Turkish-style. It is also an excellent fish for the barbecue.

Whole Baked Mullet Turkish-style

In the fish restaurants which line the Bosphorus on the river trip from Istanbul, a whole baked fish is a distinguished (and expensive) choice, set aside on the menu from the selection of charcoal-grilled fish steaks and shellfish kebabs. Recipes vary from restaurant to restaurant, but the theory is the same: the fish, which might be grey mullet, bream or even sea bass, is coated in a thick sauce of olive oil, lemon juice, garlic, nuts and herbs before being baked in the oven or double-wrapped in foil and cooked over hot coals. Often the fish is prepared in advance and served cold, but it is even better straight from the oven. Be prepared to tinker with the version given below: try walnuts or almonds instead of pinenuts, or use mint instead of coriander or parsley.

Preparation time: 10 minutes (you do need a food processor or liquidizer)
Cooking time: 30 minutes, requiring no attention from the cook
Grade: easy

Suggested accompaniments: pitta bread and a tomato and cucumber salad

6 cloves of garlic	1 teaspoon ground cinnamon
1 small bunch of fresh coriander or flat-leaved parsley	1 tablespoon pinenuts
4fl oz (125ml) olive oil	1 large grey mullet, approx. 2½ lb (1.1kg), scaled and gutted
juice of 2 lemons	salt
½ teaspoon cayenne pepper	

- Pre-heat the oven to 180°C/350°F/Gas Mark 4.
- Peel the garlic cloves; remove the stalks from the bunch of herbs and discard. Put all the ingredients apart from the fish and salt in the food processor and whizz to a paste.
- Wash the fish well inside and out. Make 3 or 4 deep diagonal slashes

on each side and rub the fish well with salt. Find a baking tray into which the fish will just fit, or make a double-layered foil base, with the edges slightly turned up. Put some of the paste on the base of the baking tray or on the foil base and place the fish on top. Smear the remaining paste inside and over the top of the fish.

● Bake uncovered in the pre-heated oven for 40 minutes. The fish can be served hot or cold.

Barbecued or Grilled Grey Mullet with Tahina Sauce

Lightly charred on the outside, the white flesh peeping through the crinkly brown skin, a well-barbecued mullet is an appetizing sight. Achieving it, however, is something of an art form, perfected by Mediterranean café owners. The classic mistake is to put the fish on the barbecue too early – the charcoal should be no more than glowing. And you need a light touch to know when to turn the fish over. If all this is too much, use the grill.

Tahina sauce, a paste based on sesame seeds which is widely available in supermarkets, is a favourite accompaniment to barbecued fish all over the Mediterranean and the Arab world. It is also good with cold fried fish.

Preparation time: 5 minutes, provided you have a food processor or liquidizer
Cooking time: 15 minutes
Grade: easy

Suggested accompaniments: crisp Cos lettuce and crusty bread

2 small grey mullet, approx. 1–1¼ lb (450–550g) each, scaled and gutted	*of the fish)* 4 slices of lemon
salt	*For the sauce:*
2 tablespoons olive oil	3 tablespoons tahina paste
2 large sprigs of rosemary (*you could also use thyme, oregano, coriander, parsley or a mixture – you need enough to stuff the cavity*	juice of 1 lemon 3 tablespoons extra virgin olive oil 1 clove of garlic (*optional*)

● Get the barbecue coals glowing or pre-heat the grill. If using a barbecue, make sure that the grid is clean and well-oiled, to prevent the fish from sticking.

● Wash the fish, and with a sharp knife make 3 or 4 deep slashes diagonally across on either side. Sprinkle over plenty of salt and rub the surface with olive oil. Poke the rosemary and lemon slices into the cavity of the fish. Leave to stand (not in the fridge) for 10 minutes.

● To make the sauce, give the tahina, lemon juice, oil and garlic (if you are using it) a quick whizz in the processor, until you have a smooth paste. Slowly add just enough cold water to achieve a creamy texture – a few tablespoons should do.

● Cook the fish on the barbecue or close to the grill for 7–8 minutes on either side. Serve with the tahina sauce.

RED MULLET

Like mackerel, red mullet is one of those fish where 'the fresher the better' rule applies. This is not true for all species – skate, for example, is at its best 3 or 4 days after landing. But a red mullet deteriorates rapidly, and, what is more, takes unkindly to freezing. Look out for small red-orange mullet with a round glossy eye – if the eye is sunken or the colour dull, the fish is past its best. When you can find it, a fresh red mullet is a particular luxury.

Grilled Red Mullet with Anchovy Butter

Red mullet stands up well to pungent flavours – in the Mediterranean it is served grilled on a bed of burning fennel branches set on fire with pastis, or baked with salty black olives and sprigs of rosemary, or sprinkled with pickled capers and leaves of lemon thyme. The Niçois like to top the grilled fish with pats of anchovy butter. Anchovies are traditionally preserved in Nice in coarse salt scented with cloves; if you add a clove to the butter the effect is similar.

Preparation time: 5 minutes for the anchovy butter, provided you have a food processor, 5 minutes for the fish once they have been gutted.
Cooking time: 10 minutes
Grade: easy

Suggested accompaniments: for a dinner party, the mullet go well after a pasta starter; served alone, a bitter green salad such as chicory, endive and fennel is a good accompaniment, and so are fresh peas

---

4 medium-sized red mullet, approx. 2½ lb (1.1kg)
2 tablespoons best-quality extra virgin olive oil
coarse sea salt and freshly ground black pepper
a few sprigs of fresh parsley, chopped

For the anchovy butter:
2oz (55g) unsalted butter (*given the saltiness of the anchovies, it is vital that the butter be unsalted*)
3 anchovy fillets
1 whole clove
good pinch of cayenne pepper
juice of ¼ a lemon

● To make the anchovy butter, either whizz together the butter, anchovies, clove, cayenne pepper and lemon juice in a food processor, or pound in a pestle and mortar. Chill the butter until you are ready to use it – it will keep in the fridge for 3–4 days.

● If the mullet are ungutted, you may choose to leave the liver in when you remove the rest of the intestines. This gives a slightly gamey flavour to the fish which I personally enjoy. If you are unsure of your diners' preference, however, it is probably wise to remove the liver along with everything else. If the fish is already gutted, the choice will have been made for you – the liver will be gone. Scrape off the scales under running water with a broad-bladed knife.

● Wash the fish thoroughly and make 2 or 3 slashes across the flesh down to the bone, to promote even cooking. Mix together the olive oil and salt and pepper to taste – the fish should be quite highly seasoned. Rub this mixture all over the flesh, particularly into the slashes.

● When you are ready to cook, pre-heat the grill to maximum. Grill the fish close to the heat for 5 minutes on each side, until the flesh comes easily off the bone. Sprinkle each fish with chopped parsley, put a knob of anchovy butter on top and serve immediately.

Baked Red Mullet in Olive, Orange and Basil sauce

This is a good way to treat slightly tired red mullet. First briefly fried to seal them, the fish are then baked in a powerfully flavoured paste. This treatment soon brings them back to life.

Preparation time: 5 minutes, provided you have a food processor
Cooking time: 25 minutes
Grade: moderate

Suggested accompaniment: white tagliatelle dressed with extra virgin olive oil

---

4 medium-sized red mullet, approx. 2½ lb (1.1kg), scaled and gutted
2 tablespoons plain white flour
salt and freshly ground black pepper
2 tablespoons olive oil

For the sauce:
2oz (55g) stoned black olives

juice of 1 orange
2 tomatoes
1 or 2 fat cloves of garlic, (*preferably new season's*)
2 tablespoons extra virgin olive oil
a good handful of fresh basil leaves
freshly ground black pepper

● Pre-heat the oven to 180°C/350°F/Gas Mark 4.
● To make the sauce, process together all the ingredients so that you end up with a thick paste. Season this with plenty of freshly ground black pepper.

● Wash the fish inside and out and pat dry. Season the flour very well and roll the fish in it. In a non-stick frying-pan into which all the fish will fit, heat the oil over a high heat. When it is almost spitting, add the fish and fry for 2 minutes on either side, to seal. Remove the fish and discard the oil from the pan. Arrange the fish in an ovenproof dish (preferably earthenware) into which they fit snugly. Pour over the sauce and bake uncovered for 20 minutes. Serve very hot.

Red Mullet in a Parcel with Fennel

The affinity of fennel and red mullet is well known and to enjoy it you don't have to have fennel branches to throw on the barbecue. Wrapped up in a paper parcel with the fish and baked in the oven, a small amount of fennel imparts a delicate scent.

Preparation time: 10 minutes
Cooking time: 25 minutes
Grade: basic

Suggested accompaniments:
potatoes fried in olive oil with garlic, and a fennel salad

1 fennel bulb	salt and freshly ground black
4 medium-sized red mullet, scaled and gutted	pepper
4 tablespoons extra virgin olive oil	greaseproof paper

● Pre-heat the oven to 180°C/350°F/Gas Mark 4. Finely chop the fennel, including the feathery fronds if they are still attached. Lay each mullet on a piece of greaseproof paper, fill the cavity with some of the fennel and sprinkle more on top of the fish, dribble over a tablespoon of oil and season well. Fold over the paper to cover the fish and twist the ends to make a parcel. Repeat the process with the remaining fish.
● Bake the parcels in the oven for 25 minutes and give them to your diners to unwrap at the table.

PLAICE

Plaice is Britain's most popular flat fish, yet it receives scant attention in many cookery books, often suffering the scathing remark that 'plaice is a poor substitute for sole'. Rubbish – it is no substitute, but an individual fish, well worth individual attention. For best results it should, of course, be very fresh, for which reason I prefer to buy a whole fish, so that I can look it in the eye before the fishmonger fillets it. The best season for plaice is from early summer through to the New Year. If you are using a frozen fish or fillets, cook as soon as possible after defrosting to avoid waterlogging.

Fillets of Plaice Stuffed with Sultanas and Almonds

A good way to cook fillets of plaice is to roll them round a savoury stuffing and bake them. This recipe sounds faintly Middle Eastern but in fact owes more to medieval British cooking – the two cuisines have a great deal in common, especially in their use of dried fruits, nuts and spices.

Preparation time: 10 minutes
Cooking time: 10 minutes
Grade: easy

Suggested accompaniments: mashed potato spiked with a good pinch of cinnamon; carrots glazed in butter, lemon juice and brown sugar

4 skinless fillets of plaice	1 heaped tablespoon sultanas or
salt and freshly ground black	raisins
pepper	2 teaspoons paprika
1 heaped tablespoon flaked	2 tablespoons olive oil
almonds	
	8 cocktail sticks

● Pre-heat the oven to 160°C/325°F/Gas Mark 3.
● With a sharp knife, split the plaice fillets in half lengthways. Season well. Mix together the almonds and raisins and lay a little of the mixture at one end of a plaice fillet. Now roll it up and secure with a stick. Place the roll in an ovenproof dish into which all 8 rolls will fit snugly.
● Mix together the paprika and the oil and pour over the plaice rolls. Bake uncovered in the oven for 10 minutes, until the fish starts to give off a milky white liquid and is on the verge of flaking.

Fillets of Plaice in Spicy Breadcrumbs

A fillet of plaice dipped in egg and fresh breadcrumbs and fried in plenty of good-quality butter is a quite different taste experience from the commercially prepared breaded fish fillets – and takes hardly any longer to cook. I add spices to the breadcrumbs for extra interest, but the dish is also good quite plain.

Preparation time: 10 minutes
Cooking time: 8–10 minutes
Grade: easy

Suggested accompaniments: boiled or steamed new potatoes, and green beans

½ a slightly stale baguette or 3 thick slices of white bread
½ teaspoon turmeric
¼ teaspoon mace
¼ teaspoon cayenne pepper
salt and freshly ground black pepper
2 egg yolks
8 small or 4 large skinless fillets of plaice
2oz (55g) unsalted butter
1 lemon

- Make the bread into crumbs, either in a food processor or with a grater. Mix the spices into the breadcrumbs, adding plenty of seasoning.
- Beat the egg yolks with a fork and pour them on to a plate. Put the breadcrumbs on an adjacent plate. Pat the fillets of fish dry with some kitchen paper and dip them first into the egg yolk, making sure they are coated on both sides, and then into the breadcrumbs, again on both sides.
- Heat the butter in a non-stick frying-pan over a gentle heat. When the butter is foaming, add the breaded fillets and fry gently for 4–5 minutes on each side, until the coating is crisp. Serve immediately with quarters of lemon.

Baked Whole Plaice with Parmesan

The sharpness of Parmesan adds bite to plaice baked on the bone with a little white wine: this approach also works well with lemon sole.

Preparation time: 5 minutes
Cooking time: 20 minutes
Grade: basic

Suggested accompaniment: boiled new potatoes

4 small skinless whole plaice, 4 tablespoons white wine 1oz (30g) butter	salt and freshly ground black pepper 2 heaped tablespoons grated Parmesan

- Pre-heat the oven to 180°C/350°F/Gas Mark 4. Lay the plaice in an earthenware dish in which they will just fit and pour in the wine. Dot all over with butter, season well and cover with foil. Bake in the oven for 15 minutes.
- Now remove the foil and sprinkle over the Parmesan. Return to the oven until the cheese has melted and lightly browned, about 5–7 minutes. Serve very hot.

SALMON

Salmon is more popular than it has ever been. Available all year round, farmed salmon offers the potential for a wide range of healthy everyday dishes; wild salmon's rarity and price keep it in the special occasion category, but you can certainly taste the difference.

The traditional creamy, buttery sauces has always seemed to me to be at odds with the fatty quality of the salmon itself. Maybe this is because the original marriages of sauce and fish were made with the leaner wild salmon. I prefer my farmed salmon sharp or spicy, mingled with citrus juices or powerful scents, cooked as little as possible, and sometimes even served raw.

Salmon Steaks with Orange Sauce

Salmon steaks are baked in orange juice flavoured with star anise, producing succulent fish; the cooking liquid is then used to make a simple sauce which offsets the richness of the salmon. Give the juice a gloss with butter, stir in some chopped chervil to back up the flavour of the star anise, and there you are. Simple, but impressive – this is a good recipe for a dinner party.

Preparation time: none
Cooking time: 25 minutes
Grade: easy

Suggested accompaniments: boiled, buttered rice and a green vegetable

---

4 salmon steaks, approx. 6oz (175g) each
salt and freshly ground black pepper
4 whole pieces of star anise
9fl oz (250ml) orange juice (*long-life orange juice is actually better than fresh orange juice for this dish*)
juice of 1 lemon
1oz (30g) chilled unsalted butter
1 tablespoon chopped chervil

- Pre-heat the oven to 190°C/375°F/Gas Mark 5. Season the salmon steaks and place them in a dish into which they will just fit. Tuck in the star anise, pour over the orange juice and cover the dish with foil.
- Bake for 20 minutes. Pour the juice from the baking dish, including the pieces of star anise, into a saucepan and keep the salmon warm. Add the lemon juice to the pan and boil the sauce hard for a couple of minutes to reduce it – it should have a slightly syrupy consistency. Now remove the star anise and chop the chilled butter into cubes. Take the sauce off the heat, whip in the cubes of butter and stir in the chervil. Check the seasoning, pour the sauce over the fish and serve.

Spicy Salmon Kebabs with Root Vegetables

Fat cubes of salmon fillet are half-cooked with a brief dip in warm spicy oil, before finishing under the grill. Meanwhile the root vegetables on which the kebabs will be served braise in stock. The spices cut the fattiness of the salmon and accentuate its underlying flavour; the earthiness and bite of the root vegetables give texture and depth. In summer, when you won't have turnips and celeriac to hand, the kebabs are excellent on their own, served with pitta bread and a yoghurt and cucumber salad.

Preparation time: 10 minutes for the salmon, 15 minutes before cooking; 10 minutes for the vegetables
Cooking time: 5 minutes for the kebabs; 10–12 minutes for the vegetables
Grade: the kebabs are basic and the vegetables easy

Suggested accompaniment: bread or boiled new potatoes

For the salmon kebabs:
2 teaspoons ground cumin
1½ teaspoons ground cinnamon
2 teaspoons ground coriander
1 teaspoon freshly ground black pepper
½ teaspoon mace
crushed seeds of 6 green cardamom pods
4 tablespoons extra virgin olive oil
1½ lb (675g) salmon fillet
lemons
wooden skewers

For the root vegetables:
4 small turnips, total weight approx. 1lb (450g)
1 small celeriac, total weight approx. 1 lb (550g)
1 tablespoon olive oil
7fl oz (200ml) chicken stock
salt and freshly ground black pepper
pinch of sugar
1 tablespoon chopped parsley, if available

● For the salmon kebabs, mix all the spices together. (To extract the seeds from the cardamom pods, split open with a knife and winkle out the black seeds. Use the remaining pods to give coffee a Middle Eastern flavour.) Heat the oil in a frying-pan over a medium heat; when it is nearly spitting add the spices and fry, stirring, for 2 minutes. Leave the spicy oil to cool for 5 minutes while you prepare the salmon.

- Remove any remaining bones from the fish and cut into chunks about 1in (2.5cm) square. Thread 3 pieces of salmon on to each skewer. Pour the warm spicy oil over the kebabs and leave to stand for 15 minutes.
- Meanwhile prepare the vegetables – peel them and cut into cubes ½in (1cm) square. Heat the oil in a heavy-based pan over a high heat and toss the vegetables for a couple of minutes. Now add the stock and salt and pepper to taste and turn the heat down to low. Cook, covered, for 8–10 minutes, until the vegetables are al dente – tender but not falling apart. Take the lid off, turn up the heat and boil off the stock. Add the sugar, and the parsley, if you have it, and keep the vegetables warm.
- Heat the grill to maximum. Baste the kebabs with any remaining oil and cook them close to the hot grill for a couple of minutes on each side, basting again when you turn them over. Place the kebabs on top of the root vegetables and serve with quarters of lemon.

Warm Salmon and Potato Salad

This is a simple way to make a relatively small amount of salmon stretch between 4 people. The potatoes provide a soothing, bulky contrast to the salmon, which is barely cooked in olive oil. If you have very fresh salmon, you could even leave out the cooking altogether and simply marinate it in the oil and lemon juice.

Preparation time: 10 minutes
Cooking time: 15–20 minutes
Grade: easy

Suggested accompaniment: a green salad

1 onion	salt and freshly ground black
1½ lb (675g) red-skinned potatoes	pepper
1lb (450g) salmon fillet	juice of 1 lemon
3 tablespoons extra virgin olive oil	

- Finely chop the onion and put to soak in a bowl of cold water.
- Peel the potatoes and slice them across thickly (about ½in/1cm). Put them into a heavy pan with a good pinch of salt and just cover them with water. Bring to the boil and cook uncovered until they are soft but not falling apart and almost all the water has evaporated. This should take between 10–15 minutes, depending on the age and variety of the potatoes. Drain off any excess liquid and pile the potatoes on the serving dish.

- Remove any skin and stray bones from the salmon and chop it into bite-sized pieces. Over a medium high heat, warm the oil in the same pan as the potatoes were cooked in and when it is almost spitting add the salmon pieces. Cook for 2 minutes then turn off the heat, add seasoning to taste, and squeeze in the lemon juice.
- Drain the onions and sprinkle over the potatoes. Put the salmon pieces on top and pour the contents of the pan over the potato and salmon mixture. The salad can be served immediately or left to cool a little, although it is better warm than completely cold.

Whole Grilled Small Salmon

Small whole salmon are now very reasonable – much better value than salmon steaks or fillets. Many people are put off buying a whole fish because they think it will take a long time to cook – but this is not the case if you grill it. Whole salmon in fact grills much better than individual pieces, as the delicate flesh is protected by the skin. It is important to make slashes on each side of the fish, so that it cooks evenly. I tuck sprigs of thyme in the slashes – if you have lemon thyme, it adds an especially good flavour. However, if you don't have any thyme, you can cook the fish perfectly well without it; instead tuck a few slices of lemon in the cavity of the fish.

Preparation time: 5 minutes
Cooking time: 20 minutes
Grade: easy

Suggested accompaniments: boiled or steamed new potatoes; a green vegetable (samphire, also known as sea asparagus, is especially delicious with salmon – it is in season in early summer)

1 small whole salmon, gutted, approx. 2lb (900g) salt and freshly ground black pepper	8–10 sprigs of fresh thyme, preferably lemon thyme 2 tablespoons extra virgin olive oil 1 lemon

- Pre-heat the grill to maximum.
- Wash the gutted fish well. With a sharp knife, make 4 or 5 slashes across on each side, right down to the bone. Rub the fish all over with salt, making sure plenty gets down into the cracks. Poke a sprig of thyme into each of the cracks. Put the fish on a piece of foil and pour over half the oil.

● Cook the fish near to the grill for 10 minutes. Take it out and check that side is cooked – the flesh should lift easily away from the bone. The easiest way to turn the fish over is to lay another piece of foil over it and then turn the whole package over. Now remove the piece of foil on top, so that the uncooked side of salmon is uppermost. Dribble over the remaining oil, return to the grill and cook for a further 8–10 minutes. Season with plenty of pepper and serve with chunks of lemon.

Salmon and Pear Salad

This salad originated when I had nothing but left-over cold salmon and slightly under-ripe pears in the house. With a dressing of soy sauce, vinegar and sesame oil and topped with sesame seeds, the mixture was surprisingly successful. The soft, pink salmon contrasts in colour and texture with the crisp white pear and the crunchy toasty-brown seeds, the dressing adds sweetness, sharpness, nuttiness and saltiness all at once, the raw ginger gives bite, yet all the flavours remain satisfyingly distinct. But this is no new invention, for many South-east Asian salads combine fish and meat with fruit. Still, there aren't many recipes for salmon and pears. You may, or may not, consider this a good thing.

Preparation time: 15 minutes
Cooking time: none
Grade: basic

Suggested accompaniment: you could serve the salad with a little cold vinegared rice but bread is fine

---

For the salad:
½ in (1cm) piece of fresh ginger
1lb (450g) cooked salmon, skin removed
6 spring onions
4 large, crisp pears
For the dressing:
1 tablespoon dark soy sauce

1 tablespoon rice or white wine vinegar
1 tablespoon sesame oil
1 teaspoon white sugar
½ teaspoon coarse salt
½ teaspoon black pepper
For the topping:
1 tablespoon toasted sesame seeds

● Crush and mince the ginger very finely. Flake the salmon, being careful to remove any stray bones. Remove the green ends of the spring onions and chop the white part finely. Peel and core the pears and slice the flesh finely. Mix all these ingredients together in a serving dish, being careful not to break the pear slices.
● To make the dressing, put all the ingredients in a screw top jar and shake well until the sugar and salt have dissolved.
● Pour the dressing over the salad, sprinkle with the toasted sesame seeds and serve at room temperature.

SARDINES

A fresh sardine is a cheap delicacy. Quality and supply are highest in the summer months, which is lucky because the sardine is ideal for the barbecue. A fatty fish, it grills well and is also good served as in Italy, filleted and stuffed with herbs and garlic before baking. If fried, however, it tends to be greasy.

Spicy Sardines with Coriander and Cumin

The Portuguese are fond of spices, and use them to give a crispy coating to their national fish. I have eaten sardines rolled in paprika, even cinnamon, but I like best this Arab combination of coriander and cumin, with a few leaves of fresh coriander tucked in the cavity of each fish.

Preparation time: 5 minutes
Cooking time: 8 minutes
Grade: easy

Suggested accompaniments: bread, and a tomato and onion salad

8 large fresh sardines	2 teaspoons ground cumin
2 tablespoons chopped fresh coriander	1 teaspoon coarse salt
2 teaspoons ground coriander	2 lemons

- Pre-heat the grill to maximum.
- Gut the sardines if they are not already prepared and wash well. Stuff a little coriander in the cavity of each. Mix together the spices and salt and roll the coriander-stuffed sardines in the mixture, so that they are thinly coated.
- Grill for 4 minutes on either side – or, better still, cook on the barbecue. Serve with quarters of lemon.

Garlic and Herb Stuffed Fillets of Sardine

Some supermarkets now sell filleted sardines, which makes this Italian dish very simple to prepare. I like to use a stuffing mix of parsley, basil and oregano, but you could include other herbs such as chives or rosemary (although the latter should be used only in moderation). The sardines are as good cold as hot, and you could serve them as a starter or as a main course.

Preparation time: 5 minutes, provided you don't have to fillet the fish yourself
Cooking time: 15 minutes
Grade: basic, provided you have filleted sardines

Suggested accompaniments: bread, and a tomato and onion salad

8 fresh sardines, filleted	zest of ½ a lemon, preferably unwaxed
2 cloves of garlic	salt and freshly ground black pepper
2 tablespoons chopped flat-leaved parsley	2 tablespoons extra virgin olive oil
1 tablespoon chopped fresh oregano	1oz (30g) fresh white breadcrumbs
1 tablespoon chopped fresh basil	

- If you have to fillet the sardines yourself, first cut off the head and tail. With a sharp knife slit the fish all the way along its belly. Turn it over and with your thumbs press down on the backbone, to flatten the fish out. Turn it back over and peel out the backbone, taking care to pick out any stray bones. Now cut the fish in half lengthways, so that you have 2 fillets. With luck, though, you will be able to buy your sardines ready filleted.

- Finely chop the peeled garlic cloves and mix with the chopped herbs. Finely grate the lemon zest and add this to the herb and garlic mixture, together with plenty of seasoning.

- Pre-heat the oven to 220°C/425°F/Gas Mark 7. Grease an earthenware dish with a little of the olive oil and lay half the fillets across the base, skin side down. Spread the herb and garlic mixture over the surface of the fish then lay the other fillets on top, flesh to flesh, so that the skin side is uppermost. Sprinkle all over with the breadcrumbs, dribble over the rest of the olive oil and bake in the oven for 15 minutes, until the top is nicely browned and the fillets cooked through. Serve very hot.

SEA BASS

A very superior fish, the sea bass – a superiority unfortunately reflected in its price. This is not a fish you will eat every day, but it is my favourite for an occasional treat. I prefer to buy smaller fish, which cook quickly and don't require a fish kettle for poaching, the best way of preserving the delicate flavour in cooking. For a more robust dish, try grilled sea bass; the fish is also good roasted or baked in foil.

Poached Sea Bass

Small whole sea bass, poached in white wine and sauced with their cooking juices enriched with butter and tarragon, are the ultimate dish for a small summer dinner party. Small because, given the cost of sea bass, there is no way you will want to share them with anyone other than your closest friends; or, better still, friend.

Preparation time: 5 minutes
Cooking time: 30 minutes
Grade: easy

Suggested accompaniments: boiled new potatoes and fresh peas

2 small sea bass gutted and cleaned, approx. 1lb–1¼lb (450–550g) each	8 black peppercorns
1 red onion	½ teaspoon dried tarragon
3oz (85g) unsalted butter, well chilled	pinch of salt
14fl oz (400ml) white wine	2 sprigs of fresh tarragon, if available
	1 teaspoon tarragon vinegar

- Wash the sea bass well and remove the scales if the fishmonger has not already done so. Choose a deep, wide pan into which both fish will fit side by side – you may need to remove the heads and tails. Chop the onion roughly. Cut the chilled butter into small pieces.
- Put the wine, chopped onion, peppercorns, dried tarragon and a pinch of salt into the pan and bring to the boil. Turn down to the slowest possible simmer and slip in the fish. Cover and cook for 10 minutes, then gently turn over the fish. Cook for a further 10 minutes, then remove the fish carefully from the pan and peel away the skin. Put the fish to keep warm.
- To make the sauce, strain the poaching liquid and reduce by fast boiling until you have 6–8 tablespoonfuls. Take off the heat and stir in the butter a piece at a time, until it is all used up. Add the chopped fresh tarragon if you have it, and the tarragon vinegar. Pour a little sauce over the fish.

Sea Bass Baked with Saffron Butter

The use of saffron with fish was traditional in medieval Britain, when the spice was even more fearfully expensive than it is now. It is a habit which has been retained in Middle Eastern cooking, which today bears the closest resemblance to the culinary habits of our forebears. The honeyed quality of the saffron, mixed with plenty of excellent butter, is at its very best with sea bass – after all, one expensive ingredient deserves another.

Preparation time: 5 minutes
Cooking time: 25 minutes
Grade: basic

Suggested accompaniments: boiled buttered samphire or green beans, new potatoes

2 small sea bass gutted and cleaned, approx. 1–1¼ lb (450–550g) each 4oz (115g) best-quality unsalted butter	½ teaspoon saffron pistils salt aluminium foil

- Pre-heat the oven to 180°C/350°F/Gas Mark 4. Wash the fish well, removing the scales if the fishmonger hasn't already done so and pat dry. Pound together the butter and saffron.
- Lay the fish on two separate pieces of foil, big enough to wrap them in. Salt the fish well inside and out. Divide the butter into two equal-sized nuggets; dot both over and in the fish. Wrap up the foil parcels.
- Bake in the oven for 25 minutes. Unwrap the parcels at the table so that everyone shares the wonderful honeyed aroma of saffron. Pour a little butter over each portion of fish.

SEA BREAM

There are many sea fish in the bream family, and they range in colour from a pinky-red to a bluey-grey with yellow stripes down the body. Varieties of the fish are found in many different waters, from the Mediterranean and the Atlantic to the Caribbean and the Pacific. The finest tasting, by general consensus in Europe at least, is the Mediterranean gilt-head bream, so called for the golden line between its eyes. Sea bream is best cooked whole, either grilled or baked.

Baked Sea Bream with Tomatoes and Oregano

This is a very simple and good way to treat many whole fish from the Mediterranean. The tomatoes form a little sauce around the baked fish, which is topped with crispy breadcrumbs.

Preparation time: 5 minutes
Cooking time: 25 minutes
Grade: basic

Suggested accompaniment: good bread
Serves: 2

---

salt and freshly ground black pepper	4 sprigs of fresh oregano, or ½ teaspoon dried
1 whole skinless sea bream, approx. 2lb (900g), scaled and gutted	4 tablespoons fresh white breadcrumbs
4 large tomatoes	2 tablespoons extra virgin olive oil

● Pre-heat the oven to 180°C/350°F/Gas Mark 4.
● Season the fish inside and out. Wash the tomatoes and slice across finely. Put a layer of sliced tomatoes across the base of an earthenware dish in which the whole fish will just fit, and either tuck in a couple of sprigs or oregano or sprinkle with half the dried herb. Lay the fish on top and cover with the remaining tomato and oregano. Sprinkle with the breadcrumbs, dribble over the oil and bake in the oven for 25 or so minutes, until the flesh lifts easily off the bone.

SKATE

Pink-tinged wings of skate are a lovely sight. This is one of the few fish which does not gain from being served absolutely fresh – it is at its best a few days after leaving the water, when it starts to give off a characteristic ammoniac smell. The fish is of the highest quality in the autumn and through to early spring. It is classically served with black butter and is best poached or fried. Cooked strips of skate are an excellent component of a wide range of salads.

Skate Wings in Orange, Garlic and Chilli Sauce

This is one of those dishes which starts in your own kitchen, and then sets you wondering whether you mightn't have tasted it before. I am not even sure whether this recipe is new-fashioned or old. The olive oil, the orange juice, even the chilli, point towards the 'Mediterranean style' which has recently become so popular. On the other hand the flaming in brandy is distinctly 1970s. I like to think of the dish as the sort which might be served in an upwardly mobile Spanish kitchen.

Preparation time: 5 minutes
Cooking time: 20 minutes
Grade: moderate

Suggested accompaniments: saffron rice, green salad
Serves: 2 (*you are unlikely to have a pan into which you can fit 4 wings of skate*)

1 large mild green chilli	2 small wings of skate
2 cloves of garlic	2 tablespoons brandy
juice of 2 oranges plus the zest of 1/8 of an orange	salt and freshly ground black pepper
3 tablespoons extra virgin olive oil	

- Deseed the chilli and chop the flesh finely. Finely chop the garlic and the orange zest.
- In a long-handled pan with a lid, gently heat the oil together with the chilli and garlic. After 5 minutes turn the heat up, and when it is almost spitting add the wings of skate. Cook for 1 minute on either side, turning over carefully with a spatula. Now warm the brandy, set light to it, stand well back, and pour it into the pan. Shake until all the flames have died down.

● Pour in the orange juice, sprinkle in the zest and seasoning to taste, give the pan a good shake to amalgamate the oil and juice, cover, and leave to cook over a moderate heat for 10–12 minutes, until the fish is cooked through (test to see that the strips of flesh lift easily away from the bone).

Skate and Potato Salad with Caper Dressing

We all know that astringent capers go well with the powerful skate, but the combination does not have to be restricted to that classic dish of skate with black butter. Skate is the ideal fish for salads, having no difficult bones to worry about – which is lucky, for this combination of strips of the fish laid over warm potatoes and dribbled with caper dressing encourages aggressive eating.

Preparation time: none
Cooking time: 20 minutes
Grade: easy

Suggested accompaniment: a green salad

1lb (450g) of waxy salad potatoes, e.g. *La Ratte* or *Belle de Fontenay*	pinch of sugar
2 small wings of skate	salt and freshly ground black pepper
2 tablespoons capers, drained	6 tablespoons extra virgin olive oil
1 teaspoon Dijon mustard	chopped fresh parsley
juice of 1 lemon	

● Boil the potatoes for 20 minutes or until tender. Pre-heat the grill to maximum and grill the skate for 5–7 minutes on each side, until the flesh lifts easily off the bone. To make the dressing, process the capers, mustard, lemon juice, sugar, seasoning and oil until you have a thick emulsion.
● Remove the fish from the bone in strips and lay over the warm potatoes. Pour over the dressing, sprinkle with parsley and serve.

SOLE
—

When is a sole not a sole? When it's a lemon sole, of course. Strictly speaking, the Dover sole is a true sole, the lemon sole a pretender. Certainly the latter cannot match the finesse of the greatest of British fish, which in my view should be treated with simplicity. A Dover sole swamped in a thick creamy sauce is anathema to those who have tasted the fish grilled to perfection and served with nothing more than a delicately flavoured butter. Greater liberties can be taken with the lemon sole, which is available filleted as well as whole.

Grilled Dover Sole with Lime and Chervil Butter
―――――

The traditional butter to serve with a grilled Dover sole is one flavoured with lemon and parsley, but I find lime and chervil a sharper, more interesting mix.

Preparation time: 5 minutes, preferably 30 minutes in advance
Cooking time: 10 minutes
Grade: easy

Suggested accompaniments: boiled new potatoes and peas

1 tablespoon fresh chervil 4oz (115g) best-quality unsalted butter 1 tablespoon lime juice	salt and freshly ground black pepper 4 small skinless Dover sole, approx. 10oz (280g) each 1 lime

- First prepare the butter. Chop the chervil as finely as possible, discarding any stalk. Combine 3oz (85g) of the butter with the chervil, lime juice and a little seasoning. Put to chill.
- When you are ready to cook the fish, pre-heat the grill to medium. Melt the remaining butter and brush half of it over each sole. Grill for 5 minutes, then carefully turn over and brush the other sides with the remaining butter. Grill for another 5 minutes and serve with pats of the butter on top and perhaps a wedge of lime.

Fillets of Sole Fried with Egg

In Italy, tiny sole no more than a few inches long are available, to be deep-fried in olive oil for *fritto misto* or dipped in egg yolk and fried in butter. Although we find it hard to obtain the same size of fish, we can treat fillets of sole in the same way. The egg forms the lightest of protective barriers, the butter its own sauce. You must use the very best butter for this dish.

Preparation time: 5 minutes,
Cooking time: 5 minutes
Grade: easy

Suggested accompaniments: boiled new potatoes (not scented with mint, which would overpower the subtle flavour of the sole), green beans with lemon

3 egg yolks salt and freshly ground black pepper	2oz (55g) unsalted butter 8 skinless fillets of sole

- Mix together the egg yolks and season well. Melt the butter over a gentle heat in a frying-pan large enough to take all the fillets of sole. Dip each fillet in the egg yolk, turning to make sure it is coated on each side, and transfer to the pan of melted butter. By the time you have put in the last fillet, the first will be ready to turn over. Each should be fried over the gentle heat for 2–3 minutes on either side.
- Serve the fillets with the melted butter from the pan, making sure you scrape out any eggy residue.

Lemon Sole with Ginger

Fresh ginger has a lemony, only mildly hot flavour which combines well with white fish, providing sharpness without becoming overpowering. Used here with lemon sole, it also goes well with plaice and cod. I prefer to use small whole lemon sole, cooked on the bone, but you could also try this recipe with fillets of fish, which should cook for only a couple of minutes on each side.

Preparation time: 5 minutes
Cooking time: 10 minutes
Grade: moderate

Suggested accompaniments: boiled new potatoes and a green salad
Serves: 2 (*you are unlikely to have a pan large enough to cook more than 2 fish at once*)

2 small skinless lemon sole, total weight approx. 1lb (450g) salt 1in (2.5cm) piece of fresh ginger	1 lemon (*preferably unwaxed*) 2 tablespoons extra virgin olive oil

- Wash the sole well and season with salt. Peel the ginger and grate it finely. Grate the zest from the lemon and then squeeze out the juice.
- Heat the oil in a non-stick frying-pan. When it is almost spitting put in the fish, side by side. Fry over a medium heat for 4–5 minutes on one side, shaking the pan frequently. Now carefully turn the fish over with a spatula and fry on the other side for another 3–4 minutes, until just cooked through. Put the fish to keep warm.
- If the fish are whole remove any pieces of bone from the pan with a spatula. Keep the oil over a medium heat and stir in the grated ginger and lemon zest. Cook for 1 minute, stirring, then pour in the lemon juice. Cook for another minute, pour the contents of the pan over the fish, making sure you scrape out any bits of ginger and zest, and serve piping hot.

Grilled Caramelized Sole with Chilli

This unusual South-east Asian treatment of fish is well worth trying. You could use plaice, instead of sole, but a flat fish which cooks quickly is needed, or the sugar will burn. Do make sure you cook the fish on foil to avoid having to scrape off caramelized sugar from your grill pan.

Preparation time: 5 minutes
Cooking time: 8 minutes
Grade: basic

Suggested accompaniment: finely sliced raw white cabbage, dressed with soy sauce and sesame oil

4 small lemon sole	1 large fresh red chilli
juice of 1 lemon	4 tablespoons brown sugar
1 teaspoon coarse salt	

● Pre-heat the grill to absolute maximum. Rub the fish all over with the lemon juice and salt. Deseed the chilli and cut into very fine strips.

● Lay the fish on a sheet of foil on a baking tray and sprinkle half the sugar over the surface, followed by half the chilli. Cook close to the grill for 4 minutes – the sugar will bubble up, the skin of the fish blacken in places. Turn the fish over, sprinkle with the remaining sugar and chilli and cook for another 4 minutes. Serve immediately.

SQUID

I hesitate to include squid, as many cooks find its preparation too offputting to contemplate. However, the supermarkets have come once more to the rescue of the timorous with their ready-prepared squid, the bodies relieved of their slimy interiors, the tentacles rendered inoffensive once they are separated from the beak. Inevitably the squid offered in this manner are frozen, which does not benefit the larger ones caught off our own waters but appears to be less detrimental to the very tiny squid from the Pacific, often no more than a couple of inches long. These are the perfect squid for grilling or frying, needing only a few minutes of cooking. Any more and they will go tough and rubbery, so be careful.

Grilled Squid with Chilli and Garlic

Squid briefly marinated in good olive oil made powerful with garlic and red chilli are then flashed under a very hot grill or on a skillet. They need only a minute on either side, just enough to warm the flesh through without causing it to toughen. You can also cook squid prepared in this way on the barbecue, keeping the olive oil to dribble over the charred squid as soon as it is cooked. Use only the bodies for this dish and keep the tentacles for a recipe for a warm squid salad, such as the one given next.

Preparation time: 10 minutes, at least 30 minutes before serving
Cooking time: 5 minutes
Grade: basic

Suggested accompaniments: good bread and a rocket salad

24 small bodies of squid, approx. 1–1¼ lb (450–550g)	coarse sea salt and freshly ground black pepper
3 small fresh red chillies	2 tablespoons chopped fresh coriander
3 small dried red chillies	2 lemons
4 fat cloves of garlic	
4 tablespoons of extra virgin olive oil	

- Wash the bodies of the squid well and with a sharp knife lightly score them through with 1 or 2 slashes on either side. Remove the seeds from both fresh and dried chillies and chop the flesh finely. Finely chop the peeled garlic.
- Place all the squid flat on a tray that can go under the grill. Sprinkle

over the chillies and garlic, and pour on the olive oil. Season well and leave to marinate for 30 minutes, turning half-way through.

- Heat the grill to absolute maximum or place a skillet over a high heat. When you are ready to eat, cook the squid for no more than a minute or two on either side. The squid should just turn opaque. Sprinkle with the coriander and serve immediately, with all the oily, spicy juices and quarters of lemon on the side.

Warm Squid and Tomato Salad

Squid briefly cooked in olive oil makes an excellent salad. You can do perfectly well with just these two ingredients but I like to flavour the oil with shallots and garlic, and to stir in some tomatoes and herbs for colour and flavour, with a final touch of balsamic vinegar. The salad should be served warm rather than hot, allowing time for the juices to spread and the flavours to mingle.

Preparation time: 10 minutes
Cooking time: 15 minutes, 5–10 minutes at least before serving
Grade: moderate

Suggested accompaniment: bread

4oz (115g) shallots or 1 small red onion	2 tablespoons extra virgin olive oil
2 cloves of garlic	salt and freshly ground black pepper
1lb (450g) small squid, including plenty of tentacles	1 tablespoon chopped flat-leaved parsley (*you could also add a few leaves of basil*)
12oz (350g) small flavourful tomatoes	1 dessertspoon balsamic vinegar

- Finely chop the shallots or onion and the garlic. Wash the squid well and cut the bodies into ½in (1cm) rings, leaving the tentacles whole provided they are small. Cut the washed tomatoes into quarters.
- In a large frying-pan or a casserole dish which will go on the heat, warm the oil. Gently fry the onion, if that is what you are using, for 5 minutes. Now add the garlic and fry for another 5 minutes – if you have shallots cook them and the garlic together, leaving out the first stage.
- Turn up the heat and throw in the squid. Stir-fry for 2 minutes, until the tentacles curl, then add the quartered tomatoes. Cook over a medium heat for 2 minutes, until the tomatoes are warmed through and their skins just starts to shrivel, and take off the heat. Season well, add the chopped parsley (and basil if you are using it) and the balsamic vinegar, and leave to stand for at least 5–10 minutes before serving.

TROUT

There is a risk that as the farming of the rainbow trout becomes ever more intensive, the product will go the way of the battery-reared chicken. That is, we shall simply forget what a trout should taste like. Already it is hard to find a truly flavoursome trout, one that will reward you if served *à la meunière* or lightly poached. The fish simply isn't what it used to be, and as a result needs unsubtle cooking.

On the bright side, to compensate for this increase in size and change in flavour there has been a substantial decline in the price of the fish, and as a commodity product it has become available from the supermarket neatly filleted.

Marinated Barbecued Trout

Farmed rainbow trout are fatty fish, and take well to the barbecue. I prefer to use trout fillets, which soak up the marinade more rapidly and cook quickly, reducing the risk of charring, but you could also use small whole fish for this recipe. The marinade, with its characteristic use of sesame, is based on a Korean recipe.

Preparation time: 10 minutes, 30 minutes before cooking
Cooking time: 6 minutes
Grade: easy

Suggested accompaniments: boiled white rice, slivered spring onions

4 large fillets of trout (*you could also use whole fish*)	1 tablespoon sesame oil
2 cloves of garlic	1 dessertspoon white sugar
˙in (1 cm) piece of fresh ginger	pinch of cayenne pepper
1 tablespoon sesame seeds	½ teaspoon freshly ground black pepper
2 tablespoons dark soy sauce	

- With a sharp knife, split the trout fillets in half lengthways. Remove any stray bones. If you are using whole fish, make several slashes on each side to allow the marinade to penetrate.
- Finely chop the peeled garlic. Peel the ginger and grate it on the finest hole of the grater, being careful to keep any juice. Heat a dry frying-pan over a moderate heat and carefully toast the sesame seeds for a minute, stirring all the time. They are ready as soon as they start to pop.

- Lay the trout fillets or whole fish in a dish into which they will just fit. Mix together all the remaining ingredients and pour over the trout. Leave to stand (not in the fridge) for 30 minutes.
- When you are ready to cook, the barbecue coals should be glowing or the grill or skillet pre-heated to medium hot. Cook the trout fillets skin side down on the barbecue or skillet, or skin side up to the grill for 4 minutes. Turn over, baste with the marinade and cook for a further 2 minutes. If you are using whole fish, double the total cooking time and cook evenly on each side. Serve with a little of the marinade spooned over.

Trout with Cucumber, Lime and Dill

Cooked cucumber is even nicer in my view than the raw vegetable. Provided it does not spend long in the pan, it loses little of its crunch. This pretty dish of green and white strips of cucumber and pink trout, flecked with the green of lime and dill, is good both as a hot dish or a salad, but do not serve it straight from the fridge.

Preparation time: 10 minutes, 10 minutes before cooking
Cooking time: 5 minutes
Grade: easy

Suggested accompaniment: bread

4 fillets of trout	juice and zest of 1 lime
1 large cucumber	2 tablespoons olive oil
salt and freshly ground black pepper	$\frac{1}{4}$ teaspoon sugar
	2 tablespoons chopped fresh dill

- With a sharp knife, cut the trout fillets into strips $\frac{1}{2}$in (1cm) wide by 2in (5cm) long. Wash the cucumber and cut it into sticks $\frac{1}{4}$in (5mm) by 2in (5cm). Salt both the trout and the cucumber well and leave each to stand for 10 minutes. This helps to firm them up for cooking.
- Wash the lime and grate its zest. Squeeze the juice.
- When you are ready to cook, heat the oil in a large frying-pan over a medium heat. Add the cucumber and stir-fry for 1 minute. Now add the strips of trout skin side down and cook for 3 minutes, until the skin starts to brown. Stir-fry for a further minute then add the lime juice, sugar and zest. Stir all together, take off the heat and add the chopped dill and some black pepper.

Tuna

Fresh tuna is expensive but worth it. The firm texture and slightly oily nature of this monster fish make it an ideal candidate for roasting, grilling and barbecuing. The thicker the steak, the better it will cook. Many supermarkets have an annoying habit of cutting their tuna thin and wide, which is fine for frying but not so good for the oven or the grill. If you are buying from the fishmonger, get him to cut one thick slice and then divide it across into smaller pieces, so that you have chunky steaks.

The recipes here are for the fresh fish, but tinned tuna is a vital store-cupboard item. Buy the best you can afford, preferably preserved in olive oil, and use it for pizzas, stuffed tomatoes (see page 286) or salade niçoise.

Roast Tuna with Red Peppers

You can roast your tuna plain, but it is particularly good on a bed of red peppers, whose sweetness will bring out that of the fish. Cod is also good cooked in this way.

Preparation time: 10–15 minutes
Cooking time: 20 minutes
Grade: basic

Suggested accompaniments: wilted spring greens; bread or rice

salt	1 tablespoon chopped fresh
4 thick-cut tuna steaks	coriander (*you could also use flat-*
2 large or 3 small red peppers	*leaved parsley*)
2 tablespoons extra virgin olive oil	1 lime

- Salt the tuna steaks well and leave to stand for 10 minutes. Chop the red peppers in half, remove the core and stringy pith and chop the flesh into ¼in (5 mm) cubes. Pre-heat the oven to 220°C/425°F/Gas Mark 7. Wash the salt from the tuna.
- Lay the peppers in a large earthenware dish, dribble over half the oil, and put in the pre-heated oven to roast for 5 minutes. Now lay the tuna steaks on top of the red peppers, dribble over the remaining oil, turn the oven down to 200°C/400°F/Gas Mark 6 and roast the red peppers and the tuna for 15 minutes. This is for steaks 1in (2.5cm) thick – thinner ones may be cooked in only 10 minutes. The fish is ready when it flakes readily.
- Serve straight from the dish, sprinkled with the coriander and the lime juice.

Tuna in Hot Tomato Sauce

Plenty of tuna is caught off the coast of Sicily, where it is often served in a tomato sauce spiked with the small dried red chillies of which Sicilians are especially fond.

Preparation time: 5 minutes
Cooking time: 30 minutes
Grade: easy

Suggested accompaniment: spaghetti

1 large onion	2 x 14oz (400g) tins Italian plum
2 tablespoons olive oil	tomatoes
2 cloves of garlic	salt and freshly ground black
3 or 4 small dried red chillies	pepper
1 glass red wine	4 thin tuna steaks

● Chop the onion finely and in a heavy frying-pan with a lid fry it in the olive oil for 5 minutes, stirring occasionally. Meanwhile, finely chop the garlic and the chillies (removing the seeds if you don't want the dish too hot). Add them to the onion after 5 minutes and fry for a further minute or two before pouring in the red wine. Allow to bubble for a couple of minutes then add the tinned tomatoes and their juice. Season to taste, turn down to a simmer, cover and cook for 15 minutes.

● Now add the tuna to the sauce, cover and cook for another 5–10 minutes, depending on the thickness of the steaks. The fish is ready when it starts to flake.

Tuna and Mushroom Kebabs

The woody flavour of mushrooms complements many different kinds of fish and shellfish (see prawn and mushroom casserole, page 184). Tuna is one of the few types of fish with the right texture for kebabs (another is monkfish) and is no exception to the mushroom rule. I paint the kebabs with a mixture of walnut oil, soy sauce and lemon juice before grilling them – if you have time, you can marinate them in the mixture in advance of cooking, but it isn't vital.

Preparation time: 10 minutes
Cooking time: 15 minutes
Grade: easy

Suggested accompaniment: a rice salad

1¼ lb (550g) fresh tuna, cut in 2 or 3 thick slices 8oz (225g) mushrooms, preferably in the form of 2 or 3 large field mushrooms	2 tablespoons walnut oil 1 tablespoon dark soy sauce juice of 1 lemon cocktail or kebab sticks

- Trim the tuna of any skin and cut it into bite-sized cubes, about 1in (2.5cm) square. Be careful to cut across rather than with the grain, so that the fish does not flake. For the same reason do not cut the pieces too small.
- Wash the mushrooms well. If you have large field mushrooms, trim the stalk and cut the mushroom into pieces 1½in (4cm) or so, i.e. slightly larger than the pieces of tuna. If you are using smaller mushrooms, leave them whole.
- Thread pieces of tuna and pieces of mushroom on to each kebab stick, adding extra mushroom if you have too many pieces.
- Pre-heat the grill to maximum. Mix together the remaining ingredients and paint the kebabs with the liquid. Grill the kebabs for 4–5 minutes on either side, basting regularly. The kebabs are ready when the fish is opaque and looks ready to flake.

WHITING

Whiting, unless extremely fresh, does not really taste of much apart from a general sense of fishiness and is therefore not worth getting excited about. It does, however, pick up other flavours well, so if you happen to have some to hand, combine it with powerful ingredients such as bacon or capers.

Whiting with Capers and Parsley

Preparation time: 5 minutes
Cooking time: 10 minutes
Grade: easy

Suggested accompaniments: plain boiled potatoes and a green vegetable

plain white flour	2 tablespoons capers
salt and freshly ground black pepper	2oz (55g) butter
8 skinless fillets of whiting	1 tablespoon chopped fresh parsley

- Season the flour well and roll the fillets of fish into it. Rinse the capers very well. Pre-heat the oven to low.
- In a frying-pan large enough to take all the fish, melt the butter over a gentle heat. When it is liquid, turn up the heat to moderate and add the fillets of fish. Fry for 3–4 minutes on either side.
- Transfer the cooked fish to the oven. Add the capers to the butter and cook for 1 minute to warm through. Turn up the heat to make the butter fizz and go golden brown, pour immediately over the fish, sprinkle with the parsley and serve.

SHELLFISH

I long for the day when our supermarkets sell oysters, as they do in France, where there is usually even someone available to open the oysters for you, stacking them on neat little trays to hold them upright until you get them home to suck out their juicy flesh. To me this seems the perfect TV dinner – for because of the volume in which oysters are sold, they are not expensive over there. But, lack of oysters apart, there is an excellent range of cheap shellfish available in our shops, almost all of it quick and easy to cook and good to eat – provided you avoid those unfortunate specimens marinated in vinegar and look instead for the creatures in their shells.

PRAWNS

Given that prawns cook so quickly (even the largest of Pacific prawns need no more than a few minutes under a hot grill or on the skillet, or a brief boil), it seems a little odd that so many of us persist in buying them ready-cooked. One reason is that they are simply the most available, for many Atlantic fisherman now boil their catch on board ship, before even arriving back at land. The result is the virulent pink frozen prawns which taste of nothing at all when cold; these prawns need to be combined with strong flavours if they are to be worth eating. Look out for the raw tiger prawns from further afield, now stocked in most supermarkets – they too will be frozen, but they certainly have an improved taste and texture as a result of cooking at home, when their blue-grey stripes will turn rapidly pink. Also not to be ignored are our tiny brown native shrimps, best nibbled with a slice of good bread and butter.

Prawn and Mushroom Casserole

Sweet prawns and earthy mushrooms go well together – try skewering them alternately on a kebab. In winter I cook mushrooms slowly in plenty of olive oil flavoured with garlic and chilli before stirring in ready-cooked prawns for a quick 'casserole'. The sharp taste of coriander completes the dish.

Preparation time: 10 minutes
Cooking time: 25 minutes
Grade: easy

Suggested accompaniment: boiled rice

12oz (350g) mushrooms	24 large raw shelled prawns
2 small fresh green chillies	salt and freshly ground black
3 cloves of garlic	pepper
3 tablespoons extra virgin olive	2 tablespoons chopped fresh
oil	coriander

- Wash the mushrooms and slice each across into 3 or 4 pieces. Deseed the chillies and chop finely. Peel the garlic, crush and chop finely.
- Heat the oil gently in a heavy-based casserole. Add the chillies and garlic and cook gently for 5 minutes. Now add the sliced mushrooms, cover and leave to stew over a low heat for 15 minutes. Turn up the heat, stir in the prawns and cook for a further 5 minutes. Season to taste, stir in the coriander and serve.

Prawn and Aubergine Slice with Tomato Salsa

Treat a slice of grilled aubergine like the base of a mini pizza, and you can create a wide range of interesting supper dishes. Prawns and aubergine are often used together in curries and the combination translates well to other culinary styles. The accompanying salsa gives this rich dish a touch of sharpness.

Preparation time: 5 minutes, plus 10 minutes for the salsa (*which can be prepared whilst the aubergines are cooking*)
Cooking time: 20 minutes
Grade: basic

Suggested accompaniment: hot bread

---

2 aubergines
extra virgin olive oil
10oz (280g) mozzarella
8oz (225g) cooked peeled prawns
salt and freshly ground black
  pepper

For the salsa:
4 large tomatoes
1 fresh green chilli
1 teaspoon white sugar
½ teaspoon salt
2 tablespoons chopped fresh
  coriander
juice of 2 lime

- Pre-heat the grill to maximum. Cut the aubergines across into slices about ³/₄in (2cm) thick, discarding the ends. Line an oven tray with foil and place the aubergine slices on it. Brush the upper surface lightly with olive oil and grill for 7 minutes. Turn over, brush the other side with oil and grill for a further 7 minutes.

- While the aubergine slices are grilling, make the salsa. Pour boiling water over the tomatoes to loosen their skins and slip them off. Dice the tomato flesh. Chop the chilli very finely. Mix together the diced tomato, chilli, sugar, salt, coriander and lime juice.

- Slice the mozzarella so that you have a piece for every slice of aubergine, which by this time will be lightly browned and soft to the touch. Lay a slice of the cheese on top of each aubergine slice and return to the grill for a couple of minutes until the cheese is just beginning to bubble. Now sprinkle a few prawns on top of each aubergine slice and return to the heat for a minute, to just warm the prawns through. Season with salt and plenty of black pepper, put a pile of the salsa on the side of each plate, and serve immediately, before the cheese becomes rubbery.

Sweet and Spicy Prawn and Okra

This is a very pretty dish, especially if you have the time to use unshelled prawns, which should be served with the heads left on. The turmeric gives the prawns a slightly yellow hue which contrasts with the brown of the onions and the sultanas, and the okra and parsley provide a splash of green. The mixture of sweet and spicy flavours, and the different textures of the shellfish and the vegetables, make sure it is more than just good to look at.

Preparation time: 15 minutes if you are using prawns in the shell, plus 15 minutes
Cooking time: 20 minutes

Grade: moderate
Suggested accompaniment: boiled long-grain rice or pitta bread; a cucumber salad

1½lb (675g) cooked prawns, preferably in the shell	1 teaspoon turmeric
2 large Spanish onions	1 teaspoon salt
1lb (450g) small fresh okra	4oz (115g) sultanas
3 cloves of garlic	4 tablespoons cold water
1 or 2 small fresh green chillies	1 tablespoon chopped fresh
2 tablespoons olive oil	parsley, preferably flat-leaved

- If you have prawns in the shell, remove the shell and legs from the body but leave the heads on (this makes the dish particularly attractive). Rinse well. Chop the onions coarsely. Top and tail the okra, cutting any particularly large ones in half across, and wash thoroughly. Chop the garlic and chillies very finely.
- In a large heavy-based frying-pan, heat the oil over a medium high heat. Add the chopped onions and fry, stirring regularly, for 10 minutes until they are browned all over. Now add the okra, garlic and chillies to the pan. Continue to fry over a medium high heat for 5 minutes, stirring all the time, until the okra have softened and taken on a dark green hue. Now turn the heat down to medium and add the turmeric, salt, sultanas, prawns and the water. Stir all together well and allow to simmer uncovered for 3–4 minutes until almost all the water has evaporated. Stir in the chopped parsley and serve.

Prawn and Melon Salad

Salting melon for 10 minutes before using it in a salad makes the flesh crisper, providing a good contrast to the slightly soggy consistency of defrosted prawns. As with the salmon and pear salad on page 163, this dish originates in South-east Asia, where shellfish and fruit are common mixtures, often spiked with chilli and coriander. The raspberry vinegar is a European introduction which is rather good.

Preparation time: 15 minutes
Cooking time: none
Grade: basic

Suggested accompaniment: makes a good light lunch on its own, or can be served as part of a selection of salads

---

1 large, ripe melon, well-chilled
  (*Galia are good for this dish*)
½ teaspoon coarse salt
2 fresh green chillies
1lb (450g) large shelled cooked
  prawns

2 tablespoons raspberry vinegar
1 teaspoon white sugar
2 tablespoons sunflower oil
2 tablespoons chopped fresh
  coriander

● Cut the melon in half and scrape out the seeds. Cut the flesh into bite-sized chunks, removing the skin. Sprinkle the melon with the salt and leave to drain for 10 minutes.
● Meanwhile deseed the chillies and chop very finely. Wash the prawns thoroughly. Mix together the raspberry vinegar and sugar and then stir in the sunflower oil drop by drop, until the dressing emulsifies.
● Mix all the ingredients together and the salad is ready. If you are preparing the salad in advance, do not add the coriander and the dressing until you are about to serve.

COCKLES AND MUSSELS

I am besotted with mussels, probably as a result of an upbringing in Belgium; but in spite of my enthusiasm I have to admit that although they may be quick to cook, mussels are a bore to prepare, especially in the quantities needed for a main course. Let us be practical and not suggest that you roll up your sleeves and set to with a mound of bivalves of an evening. To appreciate the flavour without the chore, either scrub just a few mussels to add to a shellfish risotto or to a tomato sauce for pasta or buy them cleaned and ready-prepared from a large supermarket. Cockles require rather less effort to prepare but they are unfortunately more difficult to get hold of – few supermarkets stock them, despite the fact that they are plentiful off British shores.

Always discard any shellfish with cracked shells and never eat any mussels, clams or cockles which do not open when cooked.

Spanish-style Cockles

Cockles, clams or mussels are all good served Spanish-style, cooked with chunks of red pepper and bacon and moistened with a slug of dry sherry.

Preparation time: 20 minutes
Cooking time: 20 minutes
Grade: easy

Suggested accompaniment: good bread is essential; follow the dish with a salad

6lb (2.7kg) cockles in the shell (*you can also use Venus clams or mussels*)	4 leeks
	1 large Spanish onion
	2 fat cloves of garlic
8 rashers smoked streaky bacon	1 large glass dry sherry
2 tablespoons olive oil	salt and freshly ground black pepper
2 red peppers	chopped fresh parsley

- Scrub the cockle shells under cold running water (if you are using mussels or clams you will preferably have given them a preliminary soak and will have to debeard them). Remove the rind from the bacon, but leave the fat on, and chop into 1/2in (1cm) pieces.
- Gently heat the oil in a pan large enough to take all the shellfish, and add the bacon. While it is cooking, remove the core from the red peppers and chop the flesh into 1/4in (5mm) squares; finely chop the leeks, including the green ends; finely chop the onion and garlic.
- When the fat from the bacon begins to run, which will take 5–8

minutes, add the onion, red pepper and garlic to the pan. Cook, stirring occasionally, over a medium heat for 5 minutes, until the onion turns translucent. Now add the shredded leeks and cook for a further 3 minutes. Turn up the heat to high and pour in the sherry. When it starts to bubble, put the cockles in the pan. Cover and cook for a further few minutes, until the cockles open. Season with salt and pepper, sprinkle with some finely chopped parsley, and serve.

Mussel and Tomato Sauce for Spaghetti

Since you need a good 6–8lb of mussels for a main course for 4 people, each one to be scrubbed and debearded, they aren't really the thing for a quick supper, unless you have a sous-chef. But a small quantity of mussels can eke out a basic tomato sauce for pasta, when their juice is as important as the mussel meat itself. As long as each diner has a few mussels to look at on top of their spaghetti, they will be happy. If you happen to have a few unshelled prawns handy, throw them in at the same time as the mussels. The same sauce is very good with tinned or bottled clams (*vongole*).

Preparation time: 15 minutes
Cooking time: 25 minutes
Grade: easy

Suggested accompaniment: spaghetti

2lb (900g) mussels	2 x 14oz (400g) tins Italian plum
1 large onion	tomatoes
2 tablespoons olive oil	salt and freshly ground black pepper
2 cloves of garlic	extra virgin olive oil
	balsamic vinegar

- Under cold running water, scrub the mussels well and debeard by pulling out the weedy attachments at one side of the shell.
- Chop the onion finely and fry it in the olive oil in a heavy-based frying-pan over a high heat for 5 minutes, stirring regularly.
- Meanwhile peel and chop the garlic. When the onion is ready, add the garlic to the pan and fry for a further couple of minutes before pouring in the contents of the tins. Break up the tomatoes with a wooden spoon, season well, turn down to a simmer, cover and leave to cook for 15 minutes. Meanwhile cook the spaghetti.
- When the sauce is nearly ready, add the mussels and cover. When the mussels have opened (which should take 3 or 4 minutes – pick out and discard any that don't), add a swirl of extra virgin olive oil and a few drops of balsamic vinegar and the sauce is ready.

CRAB

I adore eating crab from the shell, scraping out the brown flesh from the body, cracking the claw to get at the white meat, sucking the sweet juices from the long spindly legs and then fishing in the hole left at the juncture of the body to extract the last few strands of flesh. Give me a small crab, some crusty bread and a glass of white wine for lunch on a summer's day and I'm happy.

But not everyone shares my enthusiasm, for a squeamishness has crept into our national palate which means that we are wary of serving anything that looks like it was once alive, that requires tearing apart to get at the meat, that makes a mess when you eat it. Many people prefer to buy their crab ready-dressed. Which is a shame, for not only are they paying more, but they are missing much pleasure. Crab in the shell needs nothing to go with it beyond a little dedication, but dressed crab, particularly if it has been frozen, requires some attention.

Crab and Cucumber Salad

Crab and mayonnaise is too lush a combination for my taste. I prefer to add a touch of sharpness, in the form of vinegar or lemon juice rather than oil, to cut the slightly cloying nature of the meat. The Japanese have a wonderful vinegared crab salad, of which this is a loose adaptation. As always with Japanese dishes, there is a contrast of textures and colours, this time between the smooth brown and white crabmeat and the crunchy white and green cucumber.

Preparation time: 10 minutes, 30 minutes before serving
Cooking time: none
Grade: basic

Suggested accompaniments: bread or boiled sticky rice

---

1 cucumber	2 tablespoons dry sherry
1 teaspoon coarse sea salt	1 tablespoon cold water
3 tablespoons rice or white wine vinegar	2 teaspoons sugar
2 tablespoons dark soy sauce	4 small or 2 large dressed crabs

---

- Peel the cucumber in strips, leaving alternate strips of skin for colour, and slice very thinly. Sprinkle with the salt and leave in a colander to drain for 30 minutes.
- Mix together the vinegar, soy sauce, sherry, water and sugar to make a dressing. Remove the crab meat from the shells and mix the

dressing into it. Allow to stand for the same time as the cucumber.
● Rinse the cucumber well and arrange on a serving plate. Lay the crab mixture over the top and serve.

Crab and Cheese Grill

The combination of crab and cheese was popular on canapés and bakes in pre-war Britain, and retains a nursery-food feel to it. Toast topped with crabmeat and melted cheese makes a comforting snack.

Preparation time: none
Cooking time: 10 minutes
Grade: basic

Suggested accompaniment: a green salad

4 slices good bread (*I like to use a ciabatta loaf cut in half lengthways and then in half across*) 2 teaspoons Dijon mustard	8oz (225g) crab meat 6oz (175g) grated hard cheese, e.g. Emmenthal, Gruyère freshly ground black pepper

● Toast the bread on one side until lightly browned. Spread a little mustard on the untoasted side of each slice, followed by some crab. Top each slice with grated cheese and grill until the cheese is bubbling. Season with black pepper and serve.

Scallops

Scallops are ideal fast food, needing only the briefest cooking. They lend themselves to a wide variety of methods; scallops can be steamed, fried, grilled, baked, poached – you name it, as long as it is quick.

The very best scallops are collected by divers rather than dredged, and bought still live on the shell. It is a quick, if messy, matter to prepare them. With a sharp knife, sever the connection to the shell at the base. Now remove the frilly skirt and the black sack, leaving only the white flesh and the coral if there is one. Rinse well and you are ready to cook. It is more likely, however, that you will buy ready-prepared scallops. Try to find ones which have not been frozen; the frozen variety have a slightly soggy consistency and give off water during cooking. And look out for queenies, tiny scallops which are especially sweet.

Fried Scallops on Potato and Celeriac Rosti

The trouble with eating scallops is that, just like the cooking, it is brief. One or two delectable mouthfuls and that's it, they have all gone. To extend the scallop into a main course something more substantial is needed as an accessory. I serve scallops on a rosti of potato and celeriac, finished with a dollop of creamy sauce spiked with vermouth, the traditional poaching liquor for scallops. As a general rule, root vegetables go surprisingly well with fish and shellfish (see the salmon kebabs on page 160).

Preparation time: 25 minutes provided you have a food processor (of which 15 minutes do not require any effort from the cook)
Cooking time: 20 minutes
Grade: moderate

Suggested accompaniment: green beans

1½ lb (675g) potatoes	2 tablespoons olive oil
1½ lb (675g) celeriac	8 large scallops
1 teaspoon coarse salt	2fl oz (50ml) dry white vermouth
2 tablespoons chopped fresh coriander (*you could also use dill, in which case you need only 1 tablespoon*)	5fl oz (150ml) double cream
	freshly ground black pepper

- Peel the potatoes and celeriac and grate finely (a food processor makes this job a good deal easier). Mix together, put in a colander and sprinkle with the salt. Leave for 15 minutes for the starch to drain away.
- With your hands, squeeze the liquid from the grated potato and celeriac. A fair quantity of starchy white water should come out. Mix in ³/₄ of the chopped coriander, reserving the remainder for the sauce. Now fashion the grated mixture into 8 little pancakes, each about ¹/₂in (1cm) thick.
- In a non-stick pan large enough to take all the rosti, heat the oil over a medium heat. Add the patties and fry for 6–7 minutes on each side, until lightly crisped. Meanwhile heat the oven to very low.
- When the rosti are ready, pat them dry on kitchen paper and transfer them to the oven to keep warm. Turn the heat up under the pan and in the oil left over from cooking the rosti fry the scallops for no more than a minute on each side. Add the vermouth and allow to sizzle for 1 minute. Fish out the scallops and put on top of the rosti to keep warm.
- Add the cream to the vermouth in the pan and boil together until the sauce is reduced to the required consistency (a minute or two). Stir in the remaining chopped coriander, add plenty of black pepper, and spoon over the scallops and rosti.

Scallops and Pasta

This is a luxury pasta dish which is extremely quick to prepare. If it was served to you in an expensive restaurant, you would consider it a real treat, yet, like so much Italian food, it is easy to prepare at home, relying only on best-quality ingredients. In summer rocket grows very easily in pots but you can also buy it in small quantities from the supermarket. Its slight bitterness offsets the sweetness of the scallops very successfully, lifting the whole dish. One word of warning: many of the 'fresh' packaged and chilled pastas take longer to cook than the instructions suggest.

Preparation time: 5 minutes
Cooking time: as long as it takes to cook the pasta
Grade: easy

Suggested accompaniment: none needed

1lb (450g) scallops (*the small queenies are especially good in this dish*)
2 good handfuls of rocket
2 fat cloves of garlic
1 small green chilli (optional)
fresh egg tagliatelle (*allow 3–4oz (85–115g) per person*)

4 tablespoons extra virgin olive oil
1 dessertspoon balsamic vinegar (*less if you have a really good-quality, powerful vinegar*)
salt and freshly ground black pepper

- Wash the scallops well. If you are using large scallops, slice them vertically into 3 or 4 pieces, according to size. If you have queenies, you can cook them whole. Wash the rocket well.
- Chop the garlic finely, and the chilli if you are using it. Bring a large pan of salted water to the boil. Cook the pasta al dente – packaged 'fresh' pastas can take up to 10 minutes, truly fresh pasta will take only 2 or 3 minutes.
- While the pasta is cooking, prepare the scallops. Gently heat the oil in a heavy frying-pan. When it is hot, add the chopped garlic and chilli. Fry for 1 minute, stirring, then turn up the heat and put in the scallops. Fry, stirring, for 2 minutes, then take off the heat and add the balsamic vinegar and seasoning to taste.
- Drain the pasta and stir in the rocket. Pour the contents of the pan, including all the oily juices, over the top and serve.

Scallop, Broad Bean and Bacon Salad

This warm salad is a classic combination of textures and flavours: smooth, delicate scallops, sweet juicy beans, crisp salty bacon. It is, of course, nicest made with tiny new season's broad beans straight from the pod, but frozen broad beans are perfectly good.

Preparation time: 5 minutes, provided you are using ready-shelled broad beans
Cooking time: 15 minutes
Grade: easy

Suggested accompaniment: good bread

---

8 rashers smoked streaky bacon
2lb (900g) broad beans in the shell or 12oz (350g) frozen beans
8 large scallops
4 tablespoons extra virgin olive oil

juice of 1 lemon
salt and freshly ground black pepper
fresh basil, if available

- Remove the rind from the bacon, but leave the fat on. Chop the bacon into small oblongs. Shell the beans if they are in their pods. If you have large scallops, use a sharp knife to slice them across into 3 or 4 pieces.
- Put a heavy-based frying-pan over a gentle heat and fry the bacon with no added fat – sufficient fat should run from the bacon itself. Fry for 10 minutes until crispy.
- Meanwhile cook the beans in a little salted water until just tender. The exact cooking time will depend on whether you are using fresh or frozen beans, and on their size. An average would be 3–4 minutes, but taste to check.
- Remove the crispy bacon from the fat and drain the beans; combine the two together. Heat the olive oil over a high heat and briefly fry the scallops, no more than a minute on each side. Pour the scallops and the oil from the pan over the beans and bacon. Squeeze over the lemon juice to taste, add seasoning and shredded basil if you have it, and serve.

SMOKED FISH

Fish was once smoked in order to preserve it, but today smoked fish has become a delicacy in its own right. Not just smoked salmon, but Finnan haddock, Craster kippers and smoked trout are justifiably regarded as great British foods. The best need nothing more than a squeeze of lemon, but they can also be eked out with other ingredients.

SMOKED HADDOCK

The best smoked haddock is undyed, a pale cream colour rather than a virulent yellow. It is more expensive but increasingly available, and worth the extra cost for reasons of both health and taste. Cold-smoked Finnan haddock is very good thinly sliced and dribbled with olive oil. Smoked haddock makes a delicate soup when cooked with milk; it is the key ingredient of that Anglo-Indian dish, kedgeree; and it goes very well with eggs, as Arnold Bennett and the Savoy knew.

Smoked Haddock and Cucumber Salad

I like the texture of smoked haddock shredded and mixed with raw spring onions and chives, spiked with a little lime juice. This fish tartare mixture is good all on its own, but you can also pile it on top of a cucumber and yoghurt salad for added texture and flavour.

Preparation time: 15 minutes
Cooking time: none
Grade: basic

Suggested accompaniment: bread; this makes a good starter or light lunch

1lb (450g) undyed smoked haddock	salt and freshly ground black pepper
4 large spring onions	1 cucumber
juice of $3/4$ of a lime	4fl oz (125ml) thick, plain, creamy yoghurt
3 tablespoons extra virgin olive oil	
1 tablespoon snipped chives	

● Remove any skin and bone from the fish. Cut the spring onions, including the green ends, into the finest possible rings. Give the fish the quickest of whizzes in a food processor – it should be shredded, not reduced to a paste. Mix in the lime juice, olive oil, spring onions, chives and plenty of pepper.

- Finely slice the cucumber (this is easiest in a food processor) and mix in the yoghurt. Season well with salt. Arrange some of the cucumber salad on each plate and put a dollop of the haddock mixture on top.

Smoked Haddock with Potatoes and Scrambled Egg

This is comforting nursery food of the best kind.

Preparation time: 5 minutes
Cooking time: 25 minutes
Grade: moderate

Suggested accompaniment: none needed

1lb (450g) waxy potatoes	salt and freshly ground black
8oz (225g) undyed smoked	pepper
haddock	6 large eggs
½ pint (300ml) full cream milk	2oz (55g) butter
	chives, if available

- Peel and dice the potatoes. Bring a large pan of salted water to the boil and cook them for 5 minutes or until just tender but not falling apart, then drain.
- Remove any skin from the haddock and gently poach it in the seasoned milk for 15 minutes, until tender. Remove the fish from the liquid (reserve milk) and flake the flesh.
- Beat the eggs with the slightly cooled haddock milk. Melt the butter in a heavy-based pan and add the diced cooked potatoes. Toss them in the butter, then add the egg and milk mixture. Cook, stirring, until the egg just starts to scramble. Take off the heat, stir in the flaked fish and allow to finish cooking from the heat of the pan. Check the seasoning, stir in the chives if you have them, and serve.

SMOKED SALMON

Good-sized slices of best-quality smoked salmon, pale in colour and oily to the touch with a light hint of oak on the palate, need just a squeeze of lemon and a few slices of brown bread. For the recipes given below I suggest you use offcuts of smoked salmon, which retain the flavour but do not have the elegance of whole slices. They are also agreeably cheap.

Tabbouleh with Smoked Salmon

Tabbouleh is strictly speaking a mixture of burghul wheat and fresh herbs, with more of the latter than the former. But the basic dish can be reinforced with extra ingredients.

My favourite is to mix strips of smoked salmon into the swollen wheat, the slightly nutty nature of which offsets the rich, oily fish.

Preparation time: put the burghul to soak 20 minutes before you want to eat
Cooking time: it takes 5 minutes to assemble the salad
Grade: basic

Suggested accompaniment: pitta bread

6oz (175g) fine-grain burghul wheat	parsley
4oz (115g) smoked salmon	juice of 1 lemon
3 tablespoons chopped fresh dill	salt and freshly ground black pepper
2 tablespoons chopped fresh	extra virgin olive oil

- Just cover the burghul wheat with warm water and leave to soak for 15–20 minutes, until the wheat is puffed up.
- Drain any excess water from the burghul. Chop the salmon into little pieces. Mix the salmon, dill and parsley into the burghul, add the lemon juice, seasoning and plenty of olive oil and serve.

Smoked Salmon and Bean Salad

Beans and fish go well together – think of the classic Italian salad of tuna fish and white beans or try scallop and broad bean salad (page 195). In this recipe beans add slippery bulk to the cloying oiliness of smoked salmon, which is cut by the sharp taste of coriander. There is a risk of too many soft textures, so I add crunchy spring onions and sprinkle crisp olive oil croûtons over the top. The salad benefits from being put together a little in advance so that the beans absorb some of the flavour of the salmon, but do not add the croûtons until the last minute.

Preparation time: 10 minutes
Cooking time: 10 minutes for the croûtons
Grade: basic

Suggested accompaniment: rice salad

4oz (115g) smoked salmon	4 tablespoons extra virgin olive oil
14oz (400g) tin white haricot beans	salt and freshly ground black pepper
6 spring onions	juice of 1 lime
1 tablespoon fresh coriander	
4 slices of white bread	

- Pre-heat the oven to 180°C/350°F/Gas Mark 4.
- Chop the smoked salmon into bite-sized pieces. Drain the beans and rinse with water. Finely chop the spring onions. Coarsely chop the coriander leaves. Remove the crusts from the bread and chop into croûtons. Put them in a bowl with 2 tablespoons of the olive oil and plenty of salt and stir to make sure all the croûtons are coated.
- Sprinkle all the croûtons on a baking tray and put in the oven for 8–10 minutes, until nicely crisp. Be careful – they burn very easily. Mix together all the remaining ingredients, season well, and sprinkle the croûtons on top of the salad.

Smoked Salmon and Pasta

This sauce couldn't be easier and doesn't require any cooking – you just stir the smoked salmon and *crème fraîche* into the pasta when it is cooked. The result is luxurious, perfect for a summer supper. If you don't have star anise, don't worry about it too much. The light hint of aniseed in the pasta does, however, add an extra dimension to this simple dish.

Preparation time: 5 minutes
Cooking time: as long as it takes to cook the pasta
Grade: basic

Suggested accompaniment: a green salad to follow

6oz (175g) smoked salmon
1 teaspoon black peppercorns
salt
2 whole pieces star anise
egg tagliatelle (*allow 3-4oz*

(*85–115g*) *per person*)
6fl oz (175ml) *crème fraîche* (*you could also use double cream, but I prefer the slight sharpness of* crème fraîche)

- Cut the smoked salmon into bite-sized strips. Roughly crush the peppercorns.
- Bring a large pan of water to the boil, with plenty of salt and the pieces of star anise. Cook the pasta, drain and remove the star anise.
- Immediately stir the *crème fraîche* into the pasta, so that it is well coated. Add the strips of salmon and the crushed peppercorns, and serve.

EGGS
AND
CHEESE

EGGS

Eggs is eggs, it's said – well, up to a point. A fresh egg from a free-range hen fed on a diet of corn is a different proposition from a stale one laid by a factory bird whose diet has impregnated the egg with a mild taste of fish. Buy the best of what is one of the most versatile ingredients in the kitchen, keep them cool but not in the fridge, where they will absorb the flavours of the foods surrounding them, and use them quickly to make sure they are fresh. All over the world eggs are poached and fried, boiled and scrambled with different herbs and spices, creating endless choices for the cook.

Spanish Scrambled Eggs

It is by no means easy to achieve perfect scrambled eggs British-style. The key (apart from the use of rather more cream and butter than is strictly good for you) is to remove the pan from the heat before the eggs have fully set, in fact just as they are beginning to coagulate. They will continue to cook in the pan heat, rapidly reaching the perfect consistency. If you observe this rule, then you will have no need to go to the lengths of some perfectionists, who cook scrambled eggs in a double boiler.

Easier still, though, is to prepare scrambled eggs as they are served in the tapas bars of Spain. These are rather different scrambled eggs from the British version – the fat comes from olive oil rather than butter, the eggs are quickly scrambled in a frying-pan rather than being slowly heated through until they coagulate, this method being made possible because no milk is added, and the Spaniards flavour the eggs with their favourite trio of onions, garlic and tomato.

The most famous dish is the Basque *piperrada*, where peppers are cooked, often in goose fat, to form a thick sauce before the eggs are added. For a lighter (and quicker) dish, the tomatoes can be heated through with the fried onions and garlic rather than cooked until they dissolve, so that the scrambled egg is studded with pieces of juicy red tomato flesh. For extra colour and flavour I add fresh herbs to the eggs.

Preparation time: 10 minutes
Cooking time: 10 minutes
Grade: basic

Suggested accompaniments: serve with good bread for a snack; for a more substantial supper add to each plate a couple of slices of *jamon serrano*, Spain's equivalent of Parma ham, or, failing that, good-quality cooked ham.

2 red onions or 1 large Spanish onion	salt and freshly ground black pepper
2 cloves of garlic	1 tablespoon snipped fresh chives
4 large juicy tomatoes	(optional – you could also use
6 eggs	parsley)
	3 tablespoons olive oil

- Chop the peeled onions and the garlic very finely; wash the tomatoes and dice finely. Break the eggs into a bowl, season with salt and plenty of freshly ground black pepper, add the chives, if you have them, and stir well with a fork (but do not beat the eggs).
- Heat the oil in a large, heavy-based frying-pan over a medium heat. Add the onions and garlic and fry, stirring, for 5 minutes, until tender and lightly coloured. Now add the diced tomatoes and fry for 1 minute more, so that the tomatoes are well coated with the oil. Pour in the egg and chive mixture and stir all together until the eggs scramble – a minute or two. Serve immediately.

Parsee Scrambled Eggs

The Parsee population of Bombay, with its Persian origins and its wealth, has developed one of the most interesting of the regional cuisines of India. Parsee cooking boasts many egg dishes, and one of my favourites is this slightly curried version of scrambled eggs. Although the ingredients and the cooking method are similar to the Spanish egg dish above, the chilli, spices and sugar turn the eggs into something quite different. Parsees would eat this for breakfast, but you will probably prefer it as a lunch or supper dish.

Preparation time: 10 minutes
Cooking time: 15 minutes
Grade: easy

Suggested accompaniment: toast

1 Spanish onion	½ teaspoon ground cumin
1 large beef tomato	pinch of turmeric
2 cloves of garlic	salt
1 fresh green chilli	½ teaspoon of sugar
6 eggs	1 tablespoon fresh coriander
1 tablespoon vegetable oil (or ghee if you have it)	

● Chop the onion very finely. Cut the tomato into small dice. Peel the
garlic cloves and chop finely; cut the chilli into very fine rings,
removing the seeds if you don't want the dish to be too hot. Lightly
beat the eggs.

● In a heavy-based frying-pan, heat the oil or ghee over a medium
flame. Add the chopped onion and fry until it is lightly golden (10
minutes). Now add the chilli, garlic, cumin, turmeric and salt to taste;
stir into the onion and fry for 2 minutes before adding the diced
tomato and the sugar. Fry for another minute then turn the heat down
to low and add the beaten eggs. Stir the mixture continuously until
the eggs are lightly scrambled, which shouldn't take more than a
minute or two. Stir in the chopped coriander and serve on toast.

Scrambled Eggs with Tuna

This version of scrambled eggs comes from Sicily, where large quantities of tuna were traditionally landed in the spring. Unfortunately today the catch is declining, but wherever your canned tuna comes from, for a Sicilian flavour it should be preserved in fruity olive oil rather than brine.

Preparation time: 5 minutes
Cooking time: 7–8 minutes
Grade: easy

Suggested accompaniments: bread and a salad

6 large eggs	2 tablespoons olive oil
8oz (225g) canned tuna	pinch of ground cumin
2 onions, preferably red	salt and freshly ground black
2 cloves of garlic	pepper
2 small dried red chillies	lemon juice

● Lightly beat the eggs. Drain the tuna and flake the flesh with a fork.
Finely chop the onions, garlic and chillies.

● Heat the oil in a large frying-pan over a high heat and fry the onion
for 3 minutes, until soft. Add the garlic and chillies and fry for a
further minute. Now add the cumin, tuna and plenty of seasoning.
Stir, then pour in the eggs. Continue to stir until the eggs are cooked
through – this will take no more than a couple of minutes. Finish
with a squeeze of lemon and serve.

Parsee Hard-boiled Eggs

Another Parsee special, this time creating something quite exceptional out of hard-boiled eggs and store-cupboard ingredients. The key to the mixture is the flaked almonds and the sultanas, which add unexpected crunch and fruit. Hard-boiled eggs will never seem the same again.

Preparation time: 10 minutes, provided you already have hard-boiled eggs (otherwise you need to add another 10 minutes)
Cooking time: 15 minutes
Grade: easy

Suggested accompaniment: Indian bread such as chappati or nan

8 hard-boiled eggs	2 tablespoons of ghee (*if you don't have ghee, use vegetable oil*)
2 large onions	
2 cloves of garlic	1 teaspoon cumin seeds
1 small fresh green chilli	2 tablespoons flaked almonds
2 large tomatoes	2 tablespoons sultanas
1 tablespoon fresh coriander	salt

● Shell the eggs and quarter them. Slice the onions into fine half-rings. Finely chop the garlic and chilli. Roughly chop the tomatoes. Chop the coriander.
● In a large frying-pan heat the ghee over a moderate to high heat and fry the onions, stirring occasionally, for 10 minutes, until lightly browned. Add the garlic, chilli and cumin seeds and fry for another 2 minutes, stirring all the time. Now add the tomatoes, almonds and sultanas and fry for a further minute or two, until the tomatoes start to lose their shape and the almonds take on a touch of colour. Add the quartered eggs and the coriander, toss for 2 minutes to heat the eggs through, add salt to taste and serve.

Eggs Vindaloo

Vindaloo is now associated, in Britain at least, with the hottest of curries, but in fact this Goanese-style of cooking relies on the use of plenty of vinegar rather than massive quantities of chilli. The wine brought by the Portuguese rapidly soured in the heat of Goa and was then used in cooking, often as a preservative. The most famous vindaloo is cooked with pork, but eggs are also prepared in this way. The result is sweet and sour and only slightly hot.

Preparation time: 10 minutes
Cooking time: 20 minutes
Grade: moderate

Suggested accompaniments: rice, poppadums and mango chutney

6 large eggs	2 whole cloves
2 onions	1 teaspoon freshly ground black
2 cloves of garlic	pepper
2in (5cm) piece of fresh ginger	1 teaspoon coarse salt
1 large fresh green chilli	2 tablespoons brown sugar
2 teaspoons ground cumin	4fl oz (125ml) red wine vinegar
1 teaspoon cinnamon	2 tablespoons vegetable oil
½ teaspoon turmeric	1 teaspoon garam masala
⅛ teaspoon cayenne pepper	6fl oz (175ml) water

- Hard-boil the eggs by covering them with cold water, bringing slowly to the boil and then cooking for 7 minutes. Drain the eggs and place them immediately in cold water.
- Peel and roughly chop the onions. Finely grate the peeled garlic and the ginger. Deseed the chilli and chop the flesh very finely. Mix together the garlic, ginger, chilli, cumin, cinnamon, turmeric, cayenne, cloves, black pepper, salt and sugar. Add 2 tablespoons of vinegar to this spice mixture, which should be sufficient to create a paste.
- Shell the eggs and cut them in half lengthways. Heat the oil in a pan and fry the onions over a medium heat for 7–8 minutes, until they are just starting to brown. Now add the spice paste, standing well back as it may spit. Continue to cook, stirring all the time, for 3 minutes then sprinkle over the garam masala. Pour in the remaining vinegar and the water and bring the sauce back to the boil, still stirring. Turn down to a simmer and place the eggs in the sauce, yolk side up. Spoon some of the sauce over the eggs and leave the pan, uncovered, over a moderate heat for 10 minutes, to allow the eggs to warm through and absorb the flavours while the sauce reduces. When the sauce is fairly thick, the dish is ready to serve.

Poached Eggs in a Red Wine Sauce

In Burgundy a dish of poached eggs is turned into a meal with a butter-enriched sauce of red wine, onion and bacon. The use of lavish quantities of red wine with such a basic ingredient as an egg may seem extravagant as well as unusual, but be assured that it is worth it.

Preparation time: 5 minutes
Cooking time: 30 minutes for the sauce, 5 minutes for the eggs
Grade: moderate

Suggested accompaniments: a crisp green salad of bitter leaves such as frisée, and plenty of French bread

---

4 rashers smoked streaky bacon
4 shallots, or 1 medium-sized onion
3oz (85g) unsalted butter
14fl oz (400ml) red wine (*technically it should be Burgundy, but any good-quality fruity red wine will do well*)
9fl oz (250ml) chicken or beef stock

8 large free-range eggs, as fresh as possible
2 tablespoons white wine vinegar
1 clove of garlic (*optional*)
4 slices of good-quality white bread
salt and freshly ground black pepper

● Trim the bacon of fat and chop into small pieces. Finely chop the shallots or onion. Melt $\frac{1}{2}$oz (15g) of the butter in a heavy-based saucepan and stew the bacon and onion or shallots over a gentle flame for 7–8 minutes, until tender. Chop the remaining butter into small cubes and chill.

● Now add the wine and stock to the bacon and onion, bring to the boil and allow to boil swiftly, uncovered, until reduced by two-thirds (this will take 10–12 minutes).

● To poach the eggs, fill a large pan with water, add the vinegar (but no salt, which would stop the whites from coagulating), bring to the boil and then turn down to a rolling simmer. While the sauce is reducing, poach the eggs in two batches. Break each egg into a cup, slip into the water and leave to cook for 3–4 minutes before removing with a slotted spoon. Try to remember the order in which you put in the eggs, so that you can take them out in the same order. Put the first batch of eggs in a low oven to keep warm while you poach the second batch.

● Cut the garlic in half lengthways, if you are using it, and rub the sides of the bread with the cut sides. Toast the bread lightly on both sides.

● When the sauce is reduced, remove it from the heat, add seasoning to taste, and gradually beat in the cubes of butter. Put 2 poached eggs on each piece of toast, pour over the sauce, and serve immediately.

Thai Fried Egg Salad

This recipe was given to me by my local Thai restaurant, the Pearl of Siam in London's East End. A simple combination of raw vegetables, fresh coriander and lightly fried eggs, the key is in the slightly sweet and sour dressing of sugar, soy and lemon juice. Make sure you keep tasting until you get the proportions exactly as you like them.

Preparation time: 15 minutes chopping
Cooking time: 5 minutes
Grade: basic, provided you can fry an egg

Suggested accompaniment: can be served as part of a Thai meal, or alone as a quick snack with bread

---

1 cucumber
2 red onions (*white onions are too strong in flavour*)
2 red peppers
1 bunch of spring onions
2 tablespoons chopped fresh coriander
2 teaspoons sugar, or to taste

juice of 1 large or 2 small lemons, or to taste
2 tablespoons light soy sauce (*preferably Thai soy sauce*), or to taste
2 tablespoons vegetable oil
8 large fresh eggs

● Peel the cucumber and the onions. Deseed the red peppers. Chop all the vegetables into small chunks and combine. Add the coriander, sugar, lemon juice and soy sauce. Taste to check the seasoning – it is a question of balance, and you may need to add a little more of one or the other.
● Heat the oil in a non-stick frying-pan and quickly fry the eggs until the white is set but the yolk runny, turning them over to seal. Place the eggs on a plate, pour over the vegetables and sauce and serve immediately.

Anatolian Fried Eggs

This is the way fried eggs are sometimes served in central Turkey, turning an ordinary dish into something exotic. It is important that you use good-quality thick yoghurt – my favourite is the Greek-style strained yoghurt which is now widely available, preferably the variety made from sheep's milk. You can draw patterns over the white yoghurt and the yellow yolk with the melted butter stained red with paprika, making the dish particularly attractive as well as tasty.

Preparation time: none
Cooking time: 10 minutes
Grade: basic

Suggested accompaniment: makes a good snack all on its own

9oz (250g) thick plain yoghurt	4 slices of good bread
1 teaspoon ground cumin	2½ oz (75g) butter
½ teaspoon salt	4 large eggs
½ teaspoon freshly ground black pepper	2 teaspoons paprika

- Beat together the yoghurt, cumin, salt and pepper. Toast the bread. Heat 1oz (30g) of butter in a non-stick frying-pan. Quickly fry the eggs over a high heat, until the yolk is just set, and carefully transfer one egg onto each piece of toast. Put a dollop of yoghurt alongside each egg on the toast.
- Discard the butter in which the eggs have been fried and melt the remaining butter over a gentle heat. As it starts to foam, take off the heat and stir in the paprika. Pour the red butter over the eggs and serve straight away.

Herb Eggah

Omelette aux fines herbes Moroccan-style. The egg mixture, packed with herbs, is cooked very slowly in butter, so that it browns and solidifies, acquiring a cake-like texture. The eggah has three main advantages over the omelette for the busy cook – enough for 4 or 6 can be made at once in one pan; it can be made in advance and reheated, or served cold; and it has a high ratio of filling to egg, making it suitable for one-course meals. It does, however, lack the light fluffiness of an omelette and takes longer to cook, although requiring little attention. Once you have mastered the technique, all sorts of vegetable fillings can be used in an eggah; try leeks first softened in a little butter, spinach briefly cooked and chopped or green pepper fried until tender.

Preparation time: 5 minutes
Cooking time: 25 minutes
Grade: easy

Suggested accompaniments: plain thick yoghurt, spiced with paprika and/or cumin; pitta bread; a salad

1 red onion or ½ a large Spanish onion	*whatever you have and try to use a mixture of at least 2 or 3 herbs)*
3oz (85g) fresh green herbs (*my favourites for this dish include celery leaves, chives, coriander, dill, lovage, mint and flat-leaved parsley, but use*	6 large eggs
	salt and freshly ground black pepper
	2oz (55g) butter

- Finely chop the onion. Remove the stalks from the herbs and coarsely chop the leaves.
- Lightly beat the eggs in a bowl. Add the herbs and the onion and season well.
- Choose a large, heavy-based, lidded frying-pan and melt the butter over the lowest possible heat. Add the egg mixture, cover and cook for 15 minutes. Now put a large plate, concave side down, over the pan and carefully invert, making sure that hot fat does not drip down your arm. Slide the eggah back into the pan, unbrowned side down. (If all this sounds too complicated, you can also brown the top of the eggah under a low grill). Cook for another 10 minutes. The eggah can be served hot or cold.

EGGS AND CHEESE

An omelette filled with a smattering of Gruyère, a *frittata* with a slice or two of Pecorino or a *fonduta* of Fontina cheese, a cheese soufflé or a *tarte au fromage*, all rely on the combination of eggs and cheese. This combination has its advantages for texture as much as taste – often the whipped egg whites are used to lighten the heaviness of the cooked cheese, whilst the egg yolks increase the richness of the mixture (try adding a yolk or two to Welsh rarebit).

Italian Cheese Omelette

The Italian omelette or *frittata* is cooked more slowly than the French variety, and should have a solid rather than a light and fluffy consistency when ready to eat. It is served flat, like the Spanish tortilla, rather than folded over. The flavouring is often fried in the pan before the eggs are added – here I use cheese, but you can apply the same principle with slices of ham or slivers of vegetables, artichokes and courgettes being favourite choices in Italy. You should use a non-stick frying-pan.

Preparation time: 5 minutes
Cooking time: 15 minutes
Grade: moderate

Suggested accompaniments: bread and a green salad
Serves: 2

---

4 large eggs
salt and freshly ground black
    pepper
2 tablespoons olive oil
	4 thin slices of young Pecorino
	    cheese (you could also use
	    Fontina or *Emmenthal*)

- Beat the eggs with plenty of seasoning. Add the oil to the pan and warm gently. Put in the slices of cheese and fry until just beginning to turn up at the corners. Now pour in the eggs and cook gently for 10 minutes, until nearly set. Invert the *frittata* by placing a plate over the pan and turning it upside down, being careful not to let any hot oil drip down your arm. (As with the eggah, a less complicated alternative is to finish the *frittata* under the grill). Slide the *frittata* back into the pan uncooked side down and cook for another 3–4 minutes before serving.

Macedonian Omelette

I first ate this dish in Northern Greece, and was intrigued by what appeared to be a cross between a soufflé and an egg custard, with a surprising sharpness and a very light touch of spice. According to my aged informant, wearing the inevitable black, the dish, which she called an omelette, originates from Macedonia. The sharpness comes from the yoghurt and the feta mixed in with the eggs; I think the spices were cumin and paprika, but I could be wrong. Anyway, they work well in my version of this unusual egg dish.

Preparation time: 10 minutes
Cooking time: 25–30 minutes
Grade: easy

Suggested accompaniments: serve for supper with bread and a salad; this is a good dish to serve with a selection of salads, as part of a mezze table
Serves: quantities are sufficient for 4 as part of a mezze, generous for 2 for supper

olive oil
4oz (115g) feta cheese
5 large eggs
10fl oz (300ml) plain yoghurt (*it will be especially good if you use sheeps' milk yoghurt*)
½ teaspoon ground cumin
½ teaspoon paprika
freshly ground black pepper

● Pre-heat the oven to 200°C/400°F/Gas Mark 6. Grease a shallow baking dish (preferably earthenware) with a little olive oil. If the feta is firm enough, grate it finely; otherwise crumble it with your fingers.
● Mix together the eggs, the yoghurt, the crumbled or grated cheese, the spices and pepper to taste. You do not need to add salt, as the feta itself is very salty. Whip until slightly creamy, or give a quick whizz in a food processor. Pour the mixture into the oiled baking dish.
● Cook in the centre of the oven for 25–30 minutes, until the mixture has risen up and is lightly browned on top. It will sink back slightly when removed from the oven. Sprinkle with a little paprika and serve immediately.

Scrambled Eggs with Manchego Cheese

I like to stir a little of the sharp Spanish cheese, Manchego, into my scrambled eggs. If you can't find Manchego, Parmesan also serves well.

Preparation time: 5 minutes
Cooking time: 10 minutes
Grade: moderate

Suggested accompaniment: toast

8 eggs	3oz (85g) grated Manchego
4fl oz (125 ml) double cream	cheese
2oz (55g) butter	freshly ground black pepper

● Break the eggs (which should be at room temperature) into a large bowl and beat them lightly with a fork. Stir in the cream. Choose a saucepan with a relatively thin base to allow you to regulate the heat more easily, place it over a medium heat and add the butter. When it is foaming, add the egg and cream mixture and swirl around with a wooden spoon. Continue stirring until the eggs just start to set – the exact time this takes will depend on the thickness of your pan. As soon as there is the slightest sign of setting, take the pan off the heat and add the grated cheese. Continue stirring until the eggs have reached the consistency you like (I prefer a very soft set, others like their scrambled eggs rather more lumpy). Season with plenty of black pepper and serve on toast.

Fried Eggs with Feta

The saltiness of feta goes well with eggs, as the Macedonian omelette (page 212) shows. An egg fried in olive oil with a topping of melted feta cheese is a simple treat.

Preparation time: 5 minutes
Cooking time: 5 minutes
Grade: easy

Suggested accompaniment: toast

| 4oz (115g) feta cheese | 2 tablespoons olive oil |
| 4 large eggs | |

● Crumble the feta. Break the eggs into 4 cups. Heat the oil in a non-stick frying-pan and when it is very hot slide in the eggs one at a time, using a spatula to keep the whites from running together. Immediately sprinkle the feta over the white of the eggs, and follow up with a few grinds of pepper. Fry for 3 minutes, until the eggs are nearly set and the feta has become embedded in the white, then carefully turn the eggs over with a spatula. Fry for a further minute and serve.

Baked Eggs with Parmesan

One of the simplest ways of cooking eggs also has one of the most delicious results. Buttery baked eggs, removed from the oven just at the moment when the white has lightly set but the yolk still remains runny, are the perfect nursery tea. Forget boiled eggs – this is the way to cook them when you want to dip in toast soldiers. For a little more sophistication and a hint of sharpness, mix in some grated Parmesan.

Preparation time: 5 minutes
Cooking time: 12–15 minutes
Grade: basic

Suggested accompaniments: toast and a green salad

| 1½oz (45g) unsalted butter | 4 large eggs |
| 2oz (55g) Parmesan, grated | freshly ground black pepper |

● Pre-heat the oven to 180°C/350°F/Gas Mark 4. Grease 4 ramekins with a little of the butter. Sprinkle the base of each with a little Parmesan then carefully break in an egg. Put a knob of butter, a further sprinkling of Parmesan and a good grind of pepper on top of each.

- Place the ramekins in an ovenproof dish and add sufficient water to come half-way up the side of the ramekins. Bake in the oven for 10–12 minutes, until the surface develops a light film and the white is set. The yolk should still be runny – serve immediately or it will continue to cook in the heat from the ramekin.

Poached Eggs on Stilton Toast

Most people know that grilled Stilton on toast makes a good snack (try it with mango chutney) and everyone has had poached eggs. I like all three together.

Preparation time: 5 minutes
Cooking time: 5 minutes
Grade: easy

Suggested accompaniment: a green salad, perhaps sprinkled with crispy bacon

1 tablespoon of white wine vinegar ½ a baguette	4oz (115g) Stilton 4 eggs

- Pre-heat the grill to hot. Bring a large pan of water, with the vinegar, to the boil. Cut the baguette in half, first vertically and then horizontally, so that you have 4 pieces. Toast the rounded side of these, then sprinkle the untoasted side with the Stilton and return to the grill until the cheese is just melted – this will take 2–3 minutes.
- Meanwhile poach the eggs as in the recipe for poached eggs in a red wine sauce (see page 207). When the eggs are ready, lift them out with a slotted spoon and place each on top of a piece of Stilton toast.

Cheddar, Egg and Potato Bake

This is a rich, indulgent dish which is immensely satisfying on a cold winter's evening.

Preparation time: 10 minutes, provided you have a food processor with a grater attachment
Cooking time: 40 minutes
Grade: basic

Suggested accompaniment: a few green leaves on the side

6oz (175g) mature Cheddar	1½oz (45g) butter, softened
3 large eggs	salt and freshly ground black
2lb (900g) floury potatoes	pepper
4fl oz (125ml) double cream	2 teaspoons walnut oil

- Pre-heat the oven to 200°C/400°F/Gas Mark 6.
- Finely grate the cheese. Lightly beat the eggs. Peel the potatoes and grate them finely (this is easiest in a food processor), then squeeze out the liquid with your hands and discard.
- Mix together the grated potato, cheese, cream and beaten eggs, with plenty of seasoning.
- Put the mixture in a well-buttered shallow earthenware dish and dot with the remaining butter. Sprinkle with the walnut oil and bake in the pre-heated oven for 40 minutes, until the top is lightly browned. Serve very hot.

CHEESE

The selection of cheeses now available to the shopper is vast. There are cheeses for cooking with, either under the grill or in a pan; cheeses for grating; cheeses for straight eating; cheeses for all three uses (one of my favourite after-dinner cheeses is a slice of young Parmesan).

Whatever type of cheese you buy and whatever use you intend to put it to, make sure that it has been properly looked after before it reaches your kitchen. That means not wrapped in heavy duty plastic, which only encourages sweating, nor over-chilled, which will 'kill' a cheese which is still maturing. Keep good-quality cheese in a cool place, but preferably not the fridge, and eat it quickly. Cooking with cheese does not mean using cheeses that are of lower quality or past their best, nor can you substitute one cheese for another – just as you wouldn't prepare a Welsh rarebit with Gruyère, nor should you try to cook a fondue with Caerphilly or sprinkle Cheddar on pasta. Regionality applies to cheese above all other ingredients, and when cooking with cheese the best principle is to use a local cheese for a local recipe.

Feta and Dill Strudel

Feta cheese is not just a Greek favourite – it is just as popular, if not more so, in Turkey, where it is often used with dill to fill the tasty little pastries known as *boreks*. To make a batch of individual *boreks* is not, however, a job for the cook in a hurry. You can cheat by rolling the whole into a strudel shape – the flavour will be the same, although you will have to sacrifice a little of the crispy texture of the *boreks*.

Preparation time: 15 minutes
Cooking time: 35–40 minutes
Grade: easy

Suggested accompaniment: a crisp green salad

4oz (115g) feta cheese
2 tablespoons chopped fresh dill
freshly ground black pepper
3oz (85g) unsalted butter
8 large sheets of filo pastry

- Pre-heat the oven to 200°C/400°F/Gas Mark 6. Crumble the feta and combine with the chopped dill. Season with plenty of black pepper.
- Melt the butter and skim off any scum. Lay a sheet of filo on a greased oven tray, making sure you keep the remaining pastry covered with a damp cloth. Brush melted butter over the surface of

the pastry. Lay another sheet on top of the first and again brush with butter, making sure you don't apply any pressure – the aim is to keep as much air as possible between sheets. After 4 sheets are used up, lay the cheese and dill mixture all over the surface, leaving a gap 1in (2.5cm) around the edge. Lay the other 4 sheets on top, buttering each one.

● Carefully roll the pastry up into a long sausage shape from the long side. Place it on the baking sheet with the join underneath and brush the surface with any remaining butter.

● Bake in the pre-heated oven for 15 minutes, then turn the heat down to 180°C/350°F/Gas Mark 4 and bake for a further 20–25 minutes, until the top is crisp and brown.

Blue Cheese and Walnut Sauce for Pasta

Traditionally walnuts and the wickedly rich mascarpone cheese are served together, but I prefer the combination of nuts and blue cheese. Not any blue cheese, but the Italian Gorgonzola or the milder Dolcelatte.

Preparation time: 5 minutes
Cooking time: 10 minutes
Grade: easy

Suggested accompaniments: tagliatelle and a green salad

6oz (175g) Gorgonzola or
  Dolcelatte
1oz (30g) butter
5fl oz (150ml) double cream

freshly ground black pepper
2oz (55g) shelled chopped
  walnuts

● Chop the cheese roughly. Melt the butter over a gentle heat and add the chopped cheese. Cook, stirring until the cheese has melted. Add the cream and heat slowly, stirring all the time. When the sauce is smooth and nearly boiling, take off the heat and add plenty of pepper and the walnuts. Pour over the cooked, drained pasta.

Ricotta and Lemon Sauce for Pasta

Creamy white ricotta cheese is used in both savoury and sweet dishes in Italy. A slice of really fresh ricotta, with the characteristic grainy texture, makes an excellent pudding served with a dollop of cream and some squashy summer fruits. The ricotta available in Britain is generally creamed and processed so that it keeps far longer, but as a consequence it is best used in cooking rather than its natural state. Stirred into pasta it makes a rich sauce, lightened and sharpened with plenty of lemon zest.

Preparation time: 5 minutes, while the pasta is cooking
Cooking time: 15 minutes
Grade: easy

Suggested accompaniment: a chicory and walnut salad

12oz (350g) shaped pasta, such as the spiral fusilli or the bow-shaped farfalle
2 lemons, preferably unwaxed
6oz (175g) ricotta
nutmeg

salt and freshly ground black pepper
½oz (15g) butter
2oz (55g) Parmesan

● Bring a large pan of salted water to the boil and cook the pasta for just slightly less than you would usually – 8 minutes rather than the 10 given for many brands.
● Pre-heat the oven to 150°C/300°F/Gas Mark 2. Finely grate the zest from the lemons. Season the ricotta with a pinch (or better still a grating) of nutmeg and plenty of salt and pepper and beat it with a fork until it is creamy. Stir in the lemon zest.
● Drain the pasta and stir in the butter and the ricotta mixture. Top with grated Parmesan and put in the oven for 5 minutes, until the cheese is just melted.

Rice Salad with Manchego Cheese and Chickpeas

This substantial salad comes from Spain, where the rice is often cooked in the chickpea water. Chickpeas straight from the tin are fine, provided they are treated with a little warmth and a few additional ingredients, such as spices, oil and garlic, to help them lose their tinned taste. The basic salad can be enhanced with whatever you have to hand – bite-sized pieces of chorizo or *jamon serrano* are especially good additions.

Preparation time: 5 minutes
Cooking time: 10 minutes
Grade: basic

Suggested accompaniment: any of the additions suggested above, plus good bread

8oz (225g) Manchego cheese	good pinch of cayenne
14oz (400g) tin chickpeas	salt and freshly ground black pepper
1 clove of garlic	
2 tablespoons extra virgin olive oil	juice of ½ a lemon
1 teaspoon paprika	8oz (225g) cooked long-grain rice
1 teaspoon cumin	

- Remove the black rind from the Manchego and cut the cheese into small cubes. Drain the chickpeas and rinse well. Peel the clove of garlic and cut in half.
- Heat the oil gently with the garlic for 3–4 minutes, so that the garlic flavour infuses the oil. Now remove the halves of garlic and turn up the heat. When the oil is nearly spitting stir in the spices and salt and pepper to taste. Cook, stirring, for a minute, then add the chickpeas and lemon juice. Turn the heat down to low, cover, and leave to cook for 5 minutes. Now remove the lid and add the rice. Stir everything together for a minute or two, until the rice is just warmed through. Take off the heat, add the cubes of cheese and serve.

Cheshire Cheese Purée with Salad Potatoes

In the Vosges, a thick purée based on salted white cheese enriched with eggs and thickened with flour is a traditional peasant accompaniment to boiled potatoes. The interesting thing about this purée is that it is prepared in reverse order to the way cheese sauces are made in Britain – the cheese is melted before the flour is added, and the milk or cream comes last of all. The result is thicker, smoother and cheesier. Given the difficulty of finding salted white cheese in Britain, I have sacrificed my usual rule of regionality and as a consequence found that the mild Cheshire cheese works well when treated in the same way.

Preparation time: none
Cooking time: 20 minutes
Grade: easy

Suggested accompaniment: a green salad

1½lb (675g) waxy salad potatoes, e.g. La Ratte, Linzer Delicatess, Pink Fir Apple 9oz (250g) Cheshire cheese 2 large eggs	1 dessertspoon plain white flour *crème fraîche* salt and freshly ground black pepper dill and/or chives (*optional*)

- Boil the potatoes in their skins in salted water until just tender.
- Melt the cheese over a very low heat, stirring occasionally. Meanwhile beat the eggs well and then fold in the flour. When the cheese is melted add the flour and egg mixture very slowly, stirring constantly. Cook over a low heat, stirring all the time, for 8–10 minutes, until you have a very thick mixture. Now take off the heat and beat in just enough *crème fraîche* to bring the mixture to a pouring consistency. Season well and spoon over the potatoes. You can add a few chopped herbs – dill and/or chives go well.

Fondue

Most people associate the fondue with Switzerland but there are versions from all over the Alps, using the local cheeses and alcohols. In some places fondue is even made with cider rather than dry white wine. The principle, however, remains the same: a smooth mixture of melted cheese is brought bubbling to the table for diners to dip in pieces of bread or sometimes potatoes. Fondue is surprisingly easy to prepare, although it does require constant attention, and is a perfect winter supper.

Preparation time: 5 minutes
Cooking time: 30 minutes
Grade: basic

Suggested accompaniments: slightly stale bread cut into cubes; boiled salad potatoes; gherkins

8oz (225g) Gruyére	*Gewürztraminer good*)
8oz (225g) Emmenthal	1oz (30g) butter
1 teaspoon cornflour	12fl oz (350 ml) dry fruity white
2fl oz (50ml) of kirsch or another	wine (*Apremont from the Savoie*
white alcohol (*I find Marc de*	*is particularly good*)

- Remove any rind from the cheeses and chop them into very small pieces (resist the temptation to grate them or the texture will be wrong). Whisk the cornflour into the kirsch, taking care to eliminate lumps.
- Put the cheese, butter and wine in a heavy-based pan over the gentlest possible heat (if you have gas, it is a good idea to use a heat-diffuser). Once the cheese starts to melt, start stirring the mixture with a wooden spoon and continue doing so until you have a smooth mixture which is just on the verge of boiling. Now whisk in the alcohol and cornflour mixture. Continue to cook, stirring, until the mixture thickens slightly. Transfer to the table, preferably over a spirit lamp to keep the fondue bubbling while you eat.

Mozzarella Toasts

This is Italian cheese on toast, and just as easy to prepare as the British variant. What makes the difference, and allows restaurants to serve this to you at a price, is the use of good-quality bread and extra virgin olive oil. Best of all, use mozzarella made as it should be, from buffalo's rather than cow's milk.

Preparation time: 5 minutes
Cooking time: 10 minutes
Grade: basic

Suggested accompaniment: a green or tomato and onion salad

---

2 x 9oz (250g) packets mozzarella, drained
1 clove of garlic
1 ciabatta loaf cut in half across and then each half split lengthways, or 4 slices of good-

quality country bread
8 large leaves of basil
coarse salt and freshly ground black pepper
4 tablespoons extra virgin olive oil

- Slice the mozzarella across thinly. Cut the garlic clove in half and rub the cut sides over both sides of the bread.
- Pre-heat the grill to hot. Toast one side of the bread lightly (if you are using ciabatta, toast the crust side).
- Lay 2 basil leaves on the untoasted side of each slice of bread, then top with the mozzarella slices, making sure all the bread is covered. Season well with plenty of freshly ground black pepper and a little coarse salt, then dribble over the oil. Toast under the grill until the cheese is melted and slightly browned. Serve immediately.

Toasted Goat's Cheese with Little Gem Lettuce

The factory-processed logs of goat's cheese which are now widely available may not compare with artisanal goat's cheeses, but they do provide a relatively cheap cheese which is good to cook with. Toast the cheese on rounds of French bread and serve on a salad of crispy, slightly bitter Little Gem lettuce for an easy and complete snack. If you don't have Little Gem, other bitter leaves such as raddichio, rocket or frisée are also excellent, but the point of the salad is slightly lost if you use the limp, sweet, round lettuce.

Preparation time: 10 minutes
Cooking time: 5 minutes
Grade: basic

Suggested accompaniment: none needed – this makes an all-in-one snack; it is also a good starter

6oz (175g) goat's cheese	extra virgin olive oil
1 teaspoon Dijon mustard	2 Little Gem lettuces
salt	8 slices of baguette
tarragon or white wine vinegar	freshly ground black pepper

- Slice the goat's cheese into 8 thin slices. Remove the rind.
- Make a salad dressing with the mustard, plenty of salt and 1 part vinegar to 4 parts oil. Arrange some salad leaves on each plate and dress.
- Pre-heat the grill to hot. Toast 1 side of the rounds of bread. Turn over and lay a slice of goat's cheese on top of each piece of bread. Return them to the grill and cook until the cheese is bubbling and lightly browned. Put 2 pieces of cheese on toast on top of each pile of lettuce, season with plenty of freshly ground black pepper and serve.

Halloumi Salad

Halloumi is a solid, salty sheep's milk cheese popular in Greece, Turkey and the Middle East. It has unusual cooking properties, retaining its shape under the grill or in the frying-pan rather than melting. Cubes of halloumi can be grilled as part of a vegetarian kebab; slices of halloumi browned under the grill and dribbled with olive oil are often served as part of a selection of mezze. They also make a good snack when served on top of crisp lettuce hearts.

Preparation time: 5 minutes
Cooking time: 10 minutes
Grade: basic

Suggested accompaniment: plenty of good bread

8oz (225g) piece of halloumi	extra virgin olive oil
4 lettuce hearts or 2 Little Gem lettuces	1 lemon

- Pre-heat the grill to maximum.
- Slice the halloumi across into slices $\frac{1}{4}$in (5mm) thick – you should have 8 slices. Cook close to the grill for about 5 minutes on either side, until lightly browned. Meanwhile wash the lettuce well. Top each pile of lettuce with a couple of slices of cheese, dribble over some olive oil and serve with a quarter of lemon on the side of each plate.

VEGETABLES

You don't need to be a vegetarian to enjoy vegetables for a main course. In fact, it often helps if you are not. In Europe vegetables have long been the food of the poor, who without the effete sensitivities of our urban culture developed dishes in which vegetables were enhanced with the offcuts, or even the fat, from meat, typically that peasant staple, the pig. From this tradition are derived Italian bean stews flavoured with pancetta, chicory wrapped in ham, mushrooms cooked in bacon fat. And then there are the stuffed vegetables of Greece and Turkey, fat peppers and aubergines spillng over with spiced rice and minced lamb. The staple vegetable or grain absorbs the fat, and the flavour, from the smallest quantity of meat.

The fat, however, need not necessarily come from an animal. Other fats will do the trick – olive oil for grilled vegetables, ghee for dribbling over curried lentils, butter for mashed potato – and better still if they are flavoured with spices or herbs. For the most purist and in my opinion delicious vegetarian cuisine look to Southern India, where the combination of spicy vegetables, thick creamy yoghurt and freshly baked breads will keep even the most ardent carnivore happy. As with most vegetarian cultures two or three different dishes are usually served at once, rather than one large portion.

The recipes which follow, for main courses using vegetables as key ingredients, are not intended specifically for vegetarians (although there are plenty of dishes which use nothing but vegetable or dairy products). A vegetable should be viewed by the cook in much the same way as a cut of meat or a fillet of fish – well, I've got pork chops/slices of plaice/a cabbage or some carrots, and the shops are shut. What can I do to this to feed 4 people? The answer is, usually, quite a lot.

ASPARAGUS

Although asparagus is available from somewhere on the globe virtually all year round, British asparagus with its short season in May and June retains the edge on the interlopers. The fat white stalks from the Mediterranean and Alsace are also very good. At the beginning of the season you will want to serve your asparagus perfectly plainly, steamed or poached and sauced with butter or hollandaise, or perhaps roasted in extra virgin olive oil. When (or rather if) you tire of this simplicity, or you need to stretch the precious stalks into a more substantial dish, the following recipes may come in useful.

Asparagus and New Potatoes with Scrambled Eggs

In Southern Spain wild asparagus is cooked in stock with saffron and finished with scrambled or poached eggs. The method translates well to our own cultivated asparagus, or indeed to Spanish imports. In particular, the fact that the asparagus is chopped into lengths before cooking eliminates the problem of getting both the tips and the stalks right – you simply add the tips later. To make a more substantial dish I add tiny new potatoes.

Preparation time: 5 minutes to scrub the potatoes; the asparagus takes another 10 minutes, which can be done while the potatoes are cooking
Cooking time: 25 minutes
Grade: moderate

Suggested accompaniment: bread

12oz (350g) tiny new potatoes (*Jersey Royals are the best*)	good pinch of saffron
1½ pints (850ml) chicken stock	1 tablespoon hot water
1½lb (675g) asparagus (*the smaller sprues are good for this dish*)	4 eggs
	freshly ground black pepper

- Scrub the potatoes very well and put them into a large deep lidded frying-pan. Pour over the stock, bring to the boil, turn down to a steady simmer and cover. Cook for 10 minutes.
- Trim the asparagus of their woody ends; with a potato peeler remove the tough fibrous outer layer if the stalks are large. Cut the asparagus into 1½in (4cm) lengths.

- After 10 minutes, the potatoes should be verging on the tender. Add the asparagus stalks, but not the tips, to the pan and cook for a further 5 minutes, covered. Now add the tips – if there is little liquid, add just enough water to cover the base of the pan. Cover again and cook for a further 2–3 minutes, or until all the ingredients are tender. At the end of this time, if there is any liquid left, take off the lid and boil the liquid away.
- Stir the saffron into the hot water. Break the eggs and stir them with a fork. Pour the saffron water and the eggs into the pan and cook, uncovered, stirring carefully to make sure you don't break up the asparagus, until the eggs are lightly scrambled. Season with black pepper – you are unlikely to need salt because of the stock – and serve.

Asparagus in Filo Pastry

Thick stalks of asparagus are rolled in buttery filo pastry and baked in the oven. The crisp casing becomes imbued with the scent of the asparagus, the buttery juices of which drip out as you bite. This makes a hugely indulgent first course or light lunch.

Preparation time: 15 minutes
Cooking time: 15–20 minutes
Grade: easy

Suggested accompaniment: none

16 fat spears of asparagus	salt and freshly ground black
4oz (115g) unsalted butter	pepper
16 sheets of filo pastry	

- Pre-heat the oven to 180°C/350°F/Gas Mark 4. Wash the asparagus well and trim the bases. With a potato peeler, remove the tough outer coating of the last few inches of the stalk. Melt the butter and skim off any scum.
- Lay out a sheet of filo pastry and brush the surface with the melted butter. Place an asparagus spear at one edge of the narrower end and season well. Now roll up the pastry, starting from the asparagus end, into a cigar shape. Trim excess pastry and brush the surface with butter.
- Repeat the process until you have 16 pastry parcels. Place them on a buttered baking tray and cook in the preheated oven for 15–20 minutes, until the pastry is lightly browned. Serve as soon as they are cool enough to handle.

Asparagus and Poached Eggs on Bread

Asparagus is excellent roasted. I like to serve the stalks on thick slices of bread, which mop up the olive-oily juices. To make a more substantial meal, top the asparagus with a poached egg, so that when you eat it the yolk runs down into the bread. This is a comfortably rustic dish which can be turned into a smart starter by the use of only the tips of the asparagus tips, served on small rounds of bread, topped with poached quail's eggs, 2 or 3 per plate. If you are not confident of poaching eggs (and it is a tricky process), you could use eggs baked in well-greased ramekins.

Preparation time: 5 minutes
Cooking time: 20 minutes
Grade: moderate

Suggested accompaniment: none needed

1 bunch of asparagus, preferably small sprues	½ a clove of garlic
3 tablespoons extra virgin olive oil	1 tablespoon white wine vinegar
coarse sea salt	4 large fresh eggs
4 thick slices of good white bread	freshly ground black pepper
	2oz (55g) Parmesan (*optional*)

- Pre-heat the oven to 180°C/350°F/Gas Mark 4. Trim the woody ends of the asparagus and peel the bases if they are thicker than sprues. Place them flat on a baking tray, dribble over the olive oil, sprinkle with coarse salt and roast in the oven. The exact timing will depend on the thickness of the stalks, 5–7 minutes for sprues, 10–14 minutes for thick stalks. Check regularly with a fork. When the asparagus is cooked, remove and allow to cool slightly.

- Meanwhile rub the slices of bread all over with the cut side of the clove of garlic and put one on each plate. Bring a large pan of water to the boil with the vinegar. Carefully break each egg into a cup and when the water is at a rolling boil, slip the egg in. Using two spoons, gather up the trailing white in the water and shape it round the egg yolk and allow to boil for 3 minutes, then remove with a slotted spoon. [Repeat the process with the other 3 eggs],

- Dribble the oil from the roasted asparagus over the bread. Put a pile of sprues on top of each slice, top with a poached egg, and season the egg with black pepper. Finally sprinkle with shavings of Parmesan, if you have some.

ARTICHOKES

The globe artichoke is one of my favourite vegetables for a summer starter, simply boiled for 40 minutes or so in salted water, until the leaves pull easily away so that you can suck the flesh from their base, dipping each in a little sauce of olive oil and lemon juice, preferably flavoured with a touch of garlic and an anchovy fillet or two. But this will not sustain you through an evening. More substantial dishes, such as risotto or *frittata* with artichokes, generally require you to go through elaborate procedures to remove the choke of the vegetable so that you can cook with just the heart. This is not an activity to undertake when you are in a hurry.

So I generally stick to the whole fresh vegetable or bottled or canned artichoke hearts. Mixed with a little cooked rice and dressed with lemon juice and good olive oil, they make a pleasant summer salad, or serve them as part of a selection of antipasti.

AUBERGINES

The substance of aubergine makes it especially suitable for vegetarian main courses. My favourite is the Turkish dish *Imam Bayildi* – whole aubergines stuffed with onions, sultanas and nuts and cooked in olive oil. The Imam swooned due to the richness of the dish and it is not one you will prepare every day, for it is time-consuming as well as indulgent. But there are many ways of preparing aubergines without having to use lashings of oil: for example, they make excellent kebabs. I am also very fond of aubergine curries, and include here a mildly spiced dish from Nepal.

When buying aubergines, look for purply skins with no tints of brown, tautly stretched rather than wrinkled. When you come to cook, allow time to salt the aubergines in advance so that the bitter juices are extracted.

Aubergine Kebabs

One of the nicest ways to prepare aubergines is to grill them, so that the flesh becomes slightly browned and crispy on the outside and tender, almost glutinous on the inside. Preparing the vegetable this way also limits the amount of oil absorbed. You can grill whole slices of aubergine, but I particularly like it cut into chunks and threaded on to kebabs, so that there is a high ratio of skin to flesh. The pieces of aubergine can be interspersed with a wide range of ingredients: cubes of halloumi cheese, lengths of spring onion, small meatballs made of minced lamb. Plain aubergine kebabs are good served with thick Greek yoghurt and a small bowl of fresh herbs such as dill, mint and parsley.

Preparation time: 5 minutes, 15 minutes at least before cooking
Cooking time: 15 minutes
Grade: basic

Suggested accompaniments: yoghurt and pitta bread

2 large aubergines	olive oil
salt and freshly ground black pepper	kebab sticks

- Wash the aubergines and remove the stalks. Slice across at 1in (2.5cm) intervals then cut each slice into 4 pieces. Sprinkle with salt and leave to drain in a colander for 15 minutes or so.
- Pre-heat the grill to maximum.

● Rinse the aubergine well and thread the pieces on to kebab sticks. Dribble a little olive oil (about a teaspoon) over each kebab. Cook for 15–20 minutes as close to the grill as possible, turning regularly and basting with more olive oil as necessary, until browned all over. Season with black pepper and serve.

Nepali Aubergine Curry

Aubergine is as popular in Nepal as it is in neighbouring India. It is prepared in a variety of ways – stuffed, fried, puréed and of course curried. Nepali curries are generally mild, relying on ginger and garlic more than on chilli. Potato, a staple of the hills, is often added to give body, making this an ideal vegetarian main course.

Preparation time: 20 minutes
Cooking time: 40 minutes, 15 of which require the cook's attention
Grade: moderate

Suggested accompaniment: the quantities given here are for a curry for 4 to be accompanied by rice, as would be expected in Nepal

3 medium potatoes (*a waxy rather than a floury variety is best*)	3 tablespoons vegetable oil
	½ teaspoon turmeric
1 large or 2 small aubergines, approx. 12oz (350g)	1 teaspoon whole cumin seeds
	1 teaspoon ground coriander
2 large tomatoes	1 teaspoon coarse salt
1 large onion	1 pint (600ml) water
2 cloves of garlic	½ teaspoon garam masala
1in (2.5cm) piece of fresh ginger	chopped fresh coriander

● Peel the potatoes, chop across in half and then cut each half into 4 pieces. Cut the washed aubergine across at 1in (2.5cm) intervals and then divide each slice in 4. Wash the tomatoes and slice finely. Peel the onion and chop coarsely. Chop the peeled garlic and ginger finely.

● Heat the oil over a medium high heat in a heavy frying-pan large enough to take all the ingredients. Add the onion, garlic and ginger and fry, stirring regularly, for 10 minutes until browned all over. Now add the sliced tomatoes, turmeric, cumin, and ground coriander. Fry for another couple of minutes, still stirring, then add the aubergine, potatoes and salt. Fry for 2 minutes more, then pour in the water. Bring to the boil, turn down the heat to medium, and leave to cook, uncovered, for 25 minutes. Stir once or twice during this time.

● When the potatoes are soft and there is a little thick liquid left, the dish is ready. You may need to add a drop more water during cooking, or alternatively boil a little liquid off at the end – this will depend on the type of potatoes. To finish, stir in the garam masala and sprinkle over the chopped coriander.

Stir-fried Aubergine with Bacon

In China, aubergine is stir-fried with small pieces of pork or even pork mince, but I prefer to use bacon, which gives a slightly smoky taste to the soft strips of vegetable. It is important to blanch the bacon first to reduce the saltiness. This is a rich dish which I serve in small quantities on egg noodles, almost as if it were a sauce for pasta.

Preparation time: 15 minutes
Cooking time: 10 minutes
Grade: easy

Suggested accompaniment: Chinese egg noodles

1 large aubergine, approx. 10–12oz (280–350g)	2 tablespoons vegetable oil
4 spring onions	2 tablespoons dry sherry
4 rashers smoked streaky bacon	2 tablespoons light soy sauce
2 teaspoons black peppercorns	2 teaspoons sugar

- Wash the aubergine and cut it into long, thin strips, no more than ¼in (5mm) wide. Roughly chop the spring onions. Finely chop the bacon, including the fat. Roughly crush the peppercorns.
- Bring a pan of water to the boil, plunge in the bacon pieces for 30 seconds and drain.
- In a wok or large frying-pan, heat the oil. When it is nearly spitting, add the onions and peppercorns and fry for 1 minute, stirring continuously. Add the strips of aubergine and the bacon and stir-fry for another couple of minutes, until the aubergine begins to wilt. Now turn the heat down to low, cover the pan and leave for 3 minutes, so that the aubergine releases the oil it has taken up. Take off the lid, turn the heat back up and add the remaining ingredients. Cook over a high heat for a further 2 minutes, stirring continuously, and serve.

BEANS

Tins of ready-cooked beans should always be given space in the store-cupboard, for they provide an instant vegetable which is bulky enough to eliminate the need for further carbohydrate. Cook lamb chops or leg steaks on flageolet beans with a scrap of garlic and a knob of butter and you have a meal in itself; mix tinned tuna with white haricot beans and slivers of red onion, and dress with lemon juice and olive oil for a substantial salad, or use smoked salmon instead of tuna for an elegant lunch dish. And beans can stand quite on their own in powerfully flavoured soups and stews.

Warm Haricot Bean Salad

Beans straight from the tin can be a little soulless. Warmed through with olive oil, onion and garlic, coloured with tomato paste, sharpened with lemon juice and sprinkled with spices they rapidly acquire character. This is a basic recipe which can be adapted in many ways: flavour the olive oil with rosemary as well as garlic for an Italian touch, stir in quartered tomatoes, or slices of cooked sausage, sprinkle in parsley or coriander, use cinnamon and cayenne rather than paprika. Whatever variant you decide on, do not leave out the finishing touch of fresh lemon juice and extra virgin olive oil.

Preparation time: 5 minutes
Cooking time: 10 minutes
Grade: basic

Suggested accompaniment: plenty of good bread and perhaps a few spicy sausages

2 white onions	1 dessertspoon tomato paste
3 cloves of garlic	salt and freshly ground black pepper
4 tablespoons olive oil	juice of 1 lemon
2 x 14oz (400g) tins white haricot beans	extra virgin olive oil

● Chop the onions into fine slivers and finely chop the garlic. Gently heat the olive oil in a casserole dish, or an earthenware dish which can go over the heat, if you have one. Add the sliced onion and garlic and sweat gently for 5 minutes. Now add the beans, together with half of the liquid from the tin, and carefully stir in the tomato paste. Season well, and continue to cook over a low heat for a further 5 minutes. Remove from the heat, season with lemon juice and extra virgin olive oil, sprinkle over the paprika and serve.

Spicy Creole Bean Stew

As with many bean dishes, this one derives from a poverty-stricken culture where the beans were kept simmering long and slow on the stove to provide cheap filling nourishment, enriched with a slice of fatty salt pork and flavoured with the local chilli. If only for its rapidity of preparation this is a traduced version of a poor man's dish, but it retains its comfort level.

Preparation time: 15 minutes
Cooking time: 30 minutes
Grade: easy

Suggested accompaniments: quantities here are for a main course, which could be served with rice or baked potatoes; this also makes a good side dish for grilled or roast pork

8 rashers of smoked streaky bacon	salt and freshly ground black pepper
2 large Spanish onions	1 tablespoon tomato purée
1in (2.5cm) piece of fresh ginger	2 teaspoons sweet chilli sauce
4 cloves of garlic	2 x 16oz (450g) tins red kidney beans
2 fresh red chillies	
2 tablespoons vegetable oil	1 lemon
1 teaspoon sugar	

- Dice the bacon, removing the rind. Peel the onions and slice them into very fine half-moons. Peel the ginger and garlic and chop both finely; deseed the chillies and chop them finely too.
- In a large heavy-based casserole, heat the oil over a medium heat. Add the ginger and fry for 2 minutes, then add the onions. Fry, stirring, for 5 minutes, then sprinkle in the garlic and chillies, together with the sugar and seasoning. Fry for a further 5 minutes, until the onions are lightly browned.
- Stir in the tomato purée and chilli sauce, then pour in the contents of the tins of beans, including the juice. Turn the heat down to low, cover, and leave to cook for 20 minutes. Stir once or twice during the process, to make sure that the beans are not sticking.
- By the end of cooking, the mixture should be fairly dry, the sauce almost glutinous. Add lemon juice to taste and serve. Any left-overs reheat well.

Quick Tuscan Bean Soup

This is another cheat's version of a peasant classic; but whether you are using dried or tinned beans, the important feature is the enriching of the soup, just before it is served, with thick green olive oil scented with garlic and herbs. Italians would serve the soup as a starter but it is sufficiently substantial for a comforting supper.

Preparation time: none
Cooking time: 30 minutes
Grade: easy

Suggested accompaniment: none needed

3 cloves of garlic	1½ pints (850ml) beef or chicken
2 x 14oz (400g) tins cannellini	stock
beans	1 sprig of rosemary
6 tablespoons extra virgin olive	4 slices of ciabatta or other
oil	country bread
freshly ground black pepper	3oz (85g) grated Parmesan

- Finely chop 2 of the garlic cloves. Drain the beans and reserve the liquid. In a large heavy-based pan, heat 2 tablespoons of the oil with the chopped garlic. Fry for a couple of minutes then add the beans and stir to coat with the oil. Season with plenty of pepper and cook over a gentle heat for 5 minutes. Now add the stock and the bean liquid and bring to the boil. Simmer for 15 minutes. Meanwhile heat the rest of the oil with the remaining clove of garlic, halved, and the rosemary – when the garlic starts to sizzle, take the oil off the heat and leave it to stand.
- Fish out 3 ladlefuls of beans and purée them. Stir the purée back into the soup and cook for a further 5 minutes. Toast the bread and put a slice in the base of each bowl. Taste the soup to see if any salt is needed (it probably won't be if you have used stock cubes). Spoon the soup into the bowls, pour some of the flavoured hot oil into each bowl, sprinkle with Parmesan and more black pepper, and serve.
- See also smoked salmon and bean salad (page 199) and lamb and flageolets (page 67).

BEETROOT

Vacuum-packed boiled beetroot in salted water is now available from supermarkets, a pleasant development from the vinegar-soused variety which used to be our lot. If I have a little time, I like to roast beetroot in its skin (an hour or so in a medium oven), but more often than not I use them ready-prepared. Beetroot makes a good salad with herring and potatoes (see herring, beetroot and potato salad on page 142), particularly when combined with a sour cream or yoghurt dressing. Cooked beetroot briefly boiled in meat stock, perhaps with a few cooked potatoes, and then puréed, produces a substantial soup – flavour it with fennel seeds, chestnuts or walnuts.

Beetroot, Garlic and Fennel Sauce for Sausages

Beetroot blended with stock produces a sauce of bright colour and intense flavour, which needs the edge taken off with a little *crème fraîche*. Flavoured with juniper berries instead of fennel seeds, this sauce goes well with pork chops and venison steaks as well as with sausages.

Preparation time: 5 minutes
Cooking time: 20 minutes
Grade: easy

Suggested accompaniments: good-quality pork sausages and mashed potato

2 cloves of garlic	salt and freshly ground black
12oz (350g) cooked beetroot (not	pepper
in vinegar)	10fl oz (300ml) beef or chicken
1oz (30g) butter	stock
1 teaspoon fennel seeds	2 tablespoons *crème fraîche*

● Peel the garlic and chop finely. Roughly dice the beetroot. Melt the butter over a gentle heat and fry the garlic for 5 minutes. Now add the diced beetroot and the fennel seeds and fry for a further 5 minutes. Season well with plenty of pepper but go easy on the salt, especially if you are using a stock cube. Add the stock and allow to bubble for 5 minutes. Liquidize and return to the pan. Stir in the *crème fraîche* and simmer for a few moments before serving with grilled pork sausages.

BROCCOLI

Broccoli makes a good substitute for cauliflower in many dishes – indeed, it is sometimes known as the *choufleur d'hiver* or winter cauliflower. When buying broccoli look for tightly-packed heads – be careful to avoid any that look as if they have gone to seed, with tinges of yellow colouring and a dry bobbly feel to the head. Avoid any where the leaves are heavily wilted, and look out for the delicious purple sprouting broccoli.

When preparing broccoli for cooking, it is a good idea to remove a thin outer layer from the stalk, using a potato peeler. This will help to ensure that the head is not cooked before the stalk. Even if it is subsequently to be fried or baked, broccoli should first be briefly boiled or steamed.

Stir-fried Broccoli with Ham

Stir-frying is one of the best ways to cook broccoli, which should first be briefly parboiled. The strips of ham serve to make this dish more substantial, but they can be left out if you are cooking for vegetarians.

Preparation time: 15 minutes
Cooking time: 10 minutes
Grade: easy

Suggested accompaniment: boiled rice

1½ lb (675g) broccoli	vegetable stock
4 slices of ham	2 tablespoons groundnut or
4 cloves of garlic	vegetable oil
2in (5cm) piece of fresh ginger	1 teaspoon sugar
1 teaspoon cornflour	2 tablespoons light soy sauce
4 tablespoons chicken or	

- Slice the broccoli into small florets, discarding any large stalks. Cut the ham into strips. Peel the garlic and ginger and chop both finely. Mix together the cornflour and stock, beating to eliminate any lumps.
- Bring a large pan of salted water to the boil and cook the broccoli florets for 2 minutes then drain them well.
- Heat the oil in a wok or large frying-pan and when it is very hot add the ginger and garlic. Stir-fry for 30 seconds then add the broccoli. Stir-fry for 3 minutes then throw in the ham. After 1 more minute add the sugar and soy sauce, allow to bubble for a few seconds, then pour in the stock and cornflour mixture. Turn the contents of the pan over a few times and then serve.

Broccoli, Potato and Anchovy Salad

Broccoli for a salad should always be dressed when hot, even if the salad is to be served cold. This mixture is one I first tried in southern Italy – you could add other sharp ingredients such as Parmesan and capers.

Preparation time: 5 minutes
Cooking time: 30 minutes
Grade: easy

Suggested accompaniment: none needed

1lb (450g) waxy salad potatoes	4 tablespoons extra virgin olive oil
1¼ lb (550g) broccoli	freshly ground black pepper
2 cloves of garlic	juice of 1 lemon
1 small dried red chilli	
2oz (55g) tin anchovy fillets	

- Scrub the potatoes and boil or steam them until tender, 15–20 minutes. Allow the potatoes to cool slightly, then chop them roughly.
- Cut the broccoli into small florets and again boil or steam until just this side of tender (al dente). This will take about 5 minutes.
- Peel the garlic and slice finely. Roughly chop the chilli. Remove the anchovy fillets from their oil and roughly chop them.
- Gently heat the oil with the garlic, chilli and anchovy and cook for 5 minutes, stirring to dissolve the anchovy. Now add the cooked broccoli and potatoes and stir to coat in the oil. Cook gently for another few minutes then take off the heat. Add plenty of pepper and a squeeze of lemon juice to taste. Serve warm or cold.

CABBAGE

So you hate cabbage? Are you sure? Have you tried it lightly steamed and finished with lemon juice, a pinch of sugar and plenty of freshly ground black pepper? Or perhaps stir-fried with oyster sauce? Or even cooked in mustard oil with little black mustard seeds to pop sweetly between your teeth, as they prepare it in Gujerat?

The almost white Dutch cabbage and the wrinkled dark green Savoy both take well to such rapid methods, although they are also happy with long slow cooking, which is the only way to treat the purple red cabbage, preferably with a clove or two, some wine, vinegar or beer and a little sugar.

Portuguese-style Cabbage and Potato Soup

The Portuguese classic, *caldo verde*, does not at first sound very appetizing – after all, it is essentially cabbage and potato soup. But the difference comes from the olive oil, the garlic and the cabbage itself, which in Portugal is a dark green, sometimes almost black vegetable, with a sugary juiciness. It may be difficult to get hold of such cabbages in Britain, but whatever type you use (Savoy is best), make sure it is lightly cooked to keep its crunch. This is my rapid version of the dish.

Preparation time: 10 minutes
Cooking time: 25–30 minutes
Grade: basic

Suggested accompaniment: good bread

1lb (450g) potatoes	salt and freshly ground black
2 shallots, or ¼ of an onion	pepper
3 fat cloves of garlic	1lb (450g) green cabbage,
2 tablespoons olive oil	preferably Savoy (*approx. ½ a*
1 pint (600ml) chicken stock	*medium-sized head*)
1 pint (600ml) water	extra virgin olive oil

● Peel and dice the potatoes and put them into a large pan. Finely chop the peeled shallots or onion and the garlic, and add them to the potatoes. Pour in the olive oil, stock and water and add seasoning to taste (be careful with the salt if using stock cubes). Bring to the boil and simmer for 15 minutes, until the potatoes are soft. Now liquidize the mixture.

● While the potatoes are cooking, remove any coarse outer leaves from the cabbage, then cut out the core. Shred the remainder very finely (this is easy with a food processor).

● Add the shredded cabbage to the liquidized mixture and return to a gentle heat for 10–15 minutes, until the cabbage wilts but still retains some crunch. Check the seasoning and pour a little extra virgin oil over each portion of soup – or leave a bottle on the table for diners to help themselves.

Cabbage and Tomato Curry

The key to this dish is the use of plenty of mustard oil, giving the slightly hot, spicy taste which is a constant feature of Bengali cooking. Mustard oil is available in ethnic shops as well as some supermarkets, but if you can't get hold of any you can cheat by stirring mustard powder into vegetable oil – not quite the same effect but near enough. Do not however leave out the mustard seeds, which add sweetness and crunch.

Preparation time: 10 minutes
Cooking time: 15 minutes
Grade: easy

Suggested accompaniments: boiled Basmati rice and poppadums

1lb (450g) white cabbage (approx. ½ a small head)	2 teaspoons black mustard seeds
4 large, firm tomatoes	¼ teaspoon cayenne pepper
4 tablespoons mustard oil (*or, failing that, 4 tablespoons vegetable oil and 1 teaspoon mustard powder*)	1 teaspoon salt
	1 teaspoon sugar
	juice of 1 lemon

● Remove the core of the cabbage. Now cut the cabbage into 1in (2.5cm) squares. Peel the tomatoes by dipping them in boiling water, and cut them into quarters.

● Heat the mustard oil in a large frying-pan with a lid and when it is very hot add the mustard seeds. As soon as they start to pop (which will take about 30 seconds) add the quartered tomatoes, the squares of cabbage, the cayenne pepper, salt, sugar and lemon juice. Stir everything together, cover the pan, and leave over a medium heat.

● After 10 minutes taste the cabbage – it should be wilted but still with a little crunch and may need a few more minutes, depending on the vegetable's freshness. Before serving, check the balance of sweet and sour and add a little more lemon juice or sugar as necessary.

Cabbage and Bacon Cooked in Beer with Caraway Seeds

The cabbage has always been an important element of northern European peasant cookery, served fresh in the summer, pickled in the winter. As the autumn drew in, the last of the fresh cabbage would be specially prepared with bacon fat and a little beer and seasoned with caraway and dill.

Preparation time: 10 minutes
Cooking time: 20 minutes
Grade: easy

Suggested accompaniments: the cabbage goes well with sausages, or can be served on its own with baked potatoes

---

1 large white cabbage, approx. 2½lb (1.1kg)
8oz (225g) smoked streaky bacon
2 teaspoons caraway seeds
pinch of sugar
coarse sea salt and freshly ground black pepper
6fl oz (175ml) lager
1 tablespoon chopped fresh dill

- Shred the cabbage coarsely, discarding the core. Remove the rind from the bacon but leave the fat. Cut the bacon into small dice.
- In a wide lidded pan into which all the cabbage will fit, gently heat the bacon until the fat runs – this will take 8–10 minutes. Now add the shredded cabbage and turn in the fat. Sprinkle with the caraway seeds, add the sugar, season well and turn again. Pour over the lager, allow to bubble for 1 minute then turn down the heat to medium low, cover and leave to cook for 10 minutes, until the cabbage is wilted but retains crunch. Rapidly boil off any excess liquid, stir in the dill and serve.

CARROTS

The carrot is a versatile vegetable. It can be boiled, braised, stir-fried, steamed, roasted; served in matchsticks, in rounds, as a purée, grated or whole; used in salads or in puddings. It is a friend to spices and herbs, dried fruits and nuts and it caramelizes obediently when it meets butter and sugar. It is happy to take centre stage, whether in a savoury or sweet role, but just as willing to play a bit part, albeit a vital one, as the base for sauces and soups. And of course it can be eaten raw, preferably grated very finely and mixed with shallots, lemon juice and olive oil, as well as made into excellent juice. Altogether, the carrot is very well brought up.

But its behaviour does reflect its age. Baby young carrots are ideal for steaming or braising whole, but they are not the thing to accompany the roast. If you are grating carrots for salads or puddings, you want adolescents, half-grown but still retaining a certain sweetness, whereas the large solid adults need longer treatment, in soups or stews, to bring out their full character. Whatever age of carrot, try to remove as little of the skin as possible, as the most of the nutrients are near the surface. And never buy carrots which look in any way wrinkled – the skin should be taut, and the root should ooze juice when broken in two. Carrots with their green tops attached tend to keep better.

Carrot and Cashew Pilav

Cracked wheat or burghul is often used in Anatolia and Armenia as the basic ingredient for the pilav, rather than rice. You can make the traditional burghul pilav with nothing more than fried onions, oil or butter and water, but extra vegetables, dried fruit and nuts and some spices liven up the dish and turn it into a vegetarian main course rather than an accompaniment to meat.

I am fond of both this carrot and cashew version and the red pepper pilav (see page 273); in each case the inherent sweetness of the vegetables suits the dish well.

Preparation time: 10 minutes, if you have a food processor
Cooking time: 20 minutes, 10–15 minutes before serving
Grade: moderate

Suggested accompaniment: none necessary, but if you are feeding non-vegetarians you might like to add a few *merguez* or other type of spicy sausage

1¼ lb (550g) medium-sized carrots	salt and freshly ground black pepper
1in (2.5cm) piece of fresh ginger	4oz (115g) cashew nuts
10oz (280g) burghul wheat	4oz (115g) raisins
1 pint (600ml) water	1 teaspoon ground cumin
1 onion	1 teaspoon ground coriander
2¾ oz (75g) butter	1 teaspoon sweet paprika

- Peel the carrots and grate them finely (this is easiest in a food processor). Peel and grate the ginger. Rinse the burghul wheat very thoroughly under cold running water. Bring the water to the boil. Finely chop the onion.
- In a lidded pan large enough to take all the ingredients, melt 1½oz (40g) of the butter. Add the onion and ginger and fry over a gentle heat for 5 minutes. Now stir in the carrots and season well. Fry for another 2 minutes then add the burghul, cashew nuts, raisins and spices. Mix well. Pour over the boiling water, bring back to the boil for 2 minutes, then turn the heat down to low, cover the pan and leave to cook for 10 minutes. Take the pan off the heat, remove the lid and cover the pilav with a clean teatowel. Leave for 10–15 minutes before serving. When you are ready to eat, dot the pilav with the remaining butter and fluff it up with a fork.

Carrots with Dates and Walnuts

The sweetness of carrots makes them the ideal partner for dried fruits and nuts. In the Middle East dates and walnuts are cooked with carrots and a few spices in plenty of butter, creating a rich dish which can stand alone or precede a roast bird.

Preparation time: 5 minutes
Cooking time: 25 minutes
Grade: easy

Suggested accompaniments: a bowl of yoghurt, a dish of fresh herbs such as parsley, dill, coriander and mint, and flat Middle Eastern bread

2lb (900g) large carrots	1 teaspoon ground cumin
1 clove of garlic	½ teaspoon ground cinnamon
2oz (55g) butter	½ teaspoon paprika
4oz (115g) stoned chopped dates	¼ teaspoon salt
2oz (55g) chopped walnuts	½ a lemon

- Scrub the carrots and peel the clove of garlic. Bring a large pan of water to the boil with the garlic and boil the whole carrots for 10–15 minutes, until just tender. Drain and discard the garlic. As soon as the carrots are cool enough to handle, slice them diagonally across at ¼ in (5mm) intervals, so that you have oval shapes.
- Melt the butter in a large frying-pan over a gentle heat. Add the cooked sliced carrots and the remaining ingredients except the lemon, and stew gently, stirring occasionally, for 10 minutes. Finish with a squeeze of lemon juice.

CAULIFLOWER

In too many people's taste memories the word cauliflower produces images of soggy, waterlogged florets coated in a sauce liberally dotted with lumps of flour. Properly made cauliflower cheese, in other words crispy pieces of the vegetable coated in a smooth, rich cheesy sauce and browned in the oven, is in fact a very good dish, but it is quite hard work to prepare. The gratin recipe opposite is altogether easier. And don't think cauliflower cheese is the only way to use this versatile vegetable: it makes good salads, and an excellent curry.

When buying cauliflower, look for firm heads with no flecks of black or green on the creamy white surface.

Cauliflower Salad

Cauliflower intended for a salad should be only briefly cooked so that the florets still retain a little toughness to the bite. It is important to dress the cauliflower as soon as it has been drained or has finished steaming, even if the salad is to be served cold, so that the vegetable absorbs some of the oil and vinegar. Cauliflower is not a vegetable typically associated with the South of France, but that is the source of my favourite recipe, the Provençal touch being in the use of anchovies and capers. The salad can be served hot, warm or cold.

Preparation time: 5 minutes
Cooking time: 5 minutes
Grade: basic

Suggested accompaniment: you can serve the salad just on its own with bread as a light supper, or as part of a selection of salads

1 large cauliflower	4 tablespoons extra virgin olive oil
2oz (55g) tin anchovies, drained	1 tablespoon white wine vinegar
salt and freshly ground black pepper	2 tablespoons capers, drained

- Remove the stalk from the cauliflower and cut into small florets. Chop the drained anchovies into small pieces.
- Bring a large pan of salted water to the boil. When the water is boiling, add the cauliflower florets and allow to boil hard, uncovered for 5 minutes, by which time they should be al dente. Drain them well. (Alternatively, steam the florets for 3–4 minutes). Immediately season and dress with the olive oil and vinegar. Stir in the chopped anchovies and the capers.

Cauliflower Gratin

This is the Mediterranean version of our own cauliflower cheese. It is a lot quicker to prepare – no fiddling around with a bèchamel sauce, you simply pour over the oil, sprinkle on the cheese, add some breadcrumbs for crunch and put it all in the oven. The result is more to my taste as well. This approach also works well with broccoli.

Preparation time: 5 minutes
Cooking time: 15 minutes
Grade: basic

Suggested accompaniment: hot, crusty bread

---

1 large cauliflower
salt and freshly ground black pepper
4 tablespoons extra virgin olive oil

4oz (115g) grated Parmesan (you could also use Gruyère)
5 tablespoons fresh breadcrumbs

- Put a large pan of salted water on to boil and pre-heat the oven to 200°C/400°F/Gas Mark 6. Meanwhile break the cauliflower into florets about 1in (2.5cm) across, discarding the central stalk. When the water is boiling, add the cauliflower and boil hard for 5 minutes – the cauliflower should be al dente. Drain well.
- Lay the cauliflower in an earthenware gratin dish. Season well, evenly pour over 3 tablespoons of the olive oil, sprinkle over the Parmesan and finally scatter the breadcrumbs over. Dribble over the remaining tablespoon of oil. Put in the oven for 10 minutes, until the top is nicely browned, and serve very hot.

Cauliflower and Potato Curry

The first time I drove from Dum Dum airport into central Calcutta, I was surprised to find the road lined with piles of cauliflowers for sale. This was not a vegetable I associated with the exotic subcontinent, but apparently January was cauliflower season and business was good. This curry was later prepared by our host's cook, using the mustard oil which is typical of Bengali cooking. Variants on the dish are found throughout northern and eastern India, often to provide a filling lunch to go in the tiffin carriers. You might like to try altering the spices yourself – for example, mustard seeds go well.

Preparation time: 15 minutes
Cooking time: 20 minutes
Grade: moderate

Suggested accompaniments: none needed, although in India the curry would be served with rice or breads and fresh chutneys or pickles

1 large cauliflower, approx. 2lb (900g)	1 teaspoon ground coriander
3 medium-sized potatoes	½ teaspoon turmeric
3 small dried red chillies	1 teaspoon salt
4 tablespoons mustard or vegetable oil	½ teaspoon freshly ground black pepper
1 teaspoon whole cumin seeds	4 tablespoons water
1 teaspoon whole fennel seeds	¾ teaspoon garam masala
½ teaspoon fenugreek seeds	juice of ½ a lemon

● Remove the leaves and stalk from the cauliflower and cut into florets. Now cut each floret into quarters, so that you have pieces approximately ½ x 2in (1 x 5cm). Peel the potatoes and cut into ½in (1cm) dice. Finely chop the chillies.

● In a large lidded frying-pan, heat the oil over a high heat. Add the cumin, fennel and fenugreek seeds and the chillies and fry, stirring, for 1 minute, until they start to brown. Turn the heat down to medium and add the cauliflower, potatoes, coriander, turmeric, salt and pepper. Stir well to make sure the vegetables are well coated with the spices and continue to fry over a medium heat for 5 minutes, stirring regularly. Now turn the heat down as low as it will go, add the water, cover and leave to cook for 10 minutes.

● By this time the vegetables will be tender. Sprinkle over the garam masala and the lemon juice and serve either immediately, or just warm.

CELERIAC

The root of celeriac, with its brown skin and knobbly appendages, may be an unappetizing sight, but it is one of the most delicious of winter vegetables. Grate the flesh coarsely, blanch it and mix it with a mustardy mayonnaise for a starter; boil the cubed vegetable with potatoes before mashing with plenty of butter; cook it with tomatoes as a gratin; make celeriac chips, particularly good with game. When buying celeriac, look for roots heavy for their size; older roots will become porous as they dry out.

Celeriac and Tomato Gratin

Celeriac is briefly fried in olive oil before being cooked with tinned plum tomatoes, with the gratin being given the characteristic topping of cheese and breadcrumbs towards the end of cooking. This is a good vegetarian main course for a winter's day, but will also make a side dish for a roast of meat – it goes especially well with venison.

Preparation time: 10 minutes
Cooking time: 40 minutes
Grade: easy

Suggested accompaniments: plenty of bread and a salad

2lb (900g) celeriac, unpeeled weight	2oz (55g) grated Parmesan
2 tablespoons olive oil	4 tablespoons fresh white breadcrumbs
salt and freshly ground black pepper	good pinch of nutmeg
14oz (400g) tin tomatoes	1 tablespoon extra virgin olive oil

- Pre-heat the oven to 200°C/400°F/Gas Mark 6 and put a shallow earthenware gratin dish in to warm up.
- Peel the celeriac and cut into ¾in (2cm) cubes. Heat the oil in a large frying-pan over a high heat and fry the celeriac cubes for 5 minutes, stirring, until lightly browned. Season well. Chop the tomatoes up in the tin and pour them over the celeriac. Bubble for 5 minutes until the juice is substantially reduced, then transfer the contents of the pan to the warmed gratin dish.
- Cook uncovered in the pre-heated oven for 20 minutes. Meanwhile mix together the Parmesan, breadcrumbs and nutmeg, add black pepper to taste, and when ready spread the mixture over the celeriac. Dribble over the extra virgin olive oil and cook for another 10 minutes, until the top is lightly browned. Serve piping hot.

Celeriac and Potato Mash

Although this really needs the accompaniment of, say, sausages or a few good slices of ham to satisfy as a main course, this simple dish is so good that I cannot fail to include it. On a cold winter's day it is far more gratifying than straight mashed potato.

Preparation time: 10 minutes
Cooking time: 30 minutes
Grade: basic

Suggested accompaniments: sausages, ham

1½lb (675g) celeriac	salt and freshly ground black
1½lb (675g) potatoes	pepper
3oz (85g) butter	clove of garlic

- Peel the celeriac and potatoes and cut it into 1in (2.5cm) pieces. Put them in a pan, add 2oz (55g) of the butter and plenty of seasoning, and just cover with boiling water. Bring to the boil and boil hard, uncovered, for 15 minutes, until there is little liquid left and the vegetables are very soft. Mash the contents of the pan – the mixture should be slightly sloppy.
- Pre-heat the oven to 200°C/400°F/Gas Mark 6. Rub an earthenware dish with the cut side of a clove of garlic and fill with the mash. Dot the surface with the remaining butter and a good grind of pepper. Bake for 15 minutes, until the surface is lightly browned.

CELERY

Most people eat celery raw, but it is even better cooked. Fry it briefly in olive oil and then braise it in stock for a side dish for roasts or grilled meats, or grill it, stuffed with goat's cheese (but never boil it). If you are using it raw in salads or as a crunchy accessory to Stilton, look out for the celery hearts now stocked in supermarkets.

Celery should be white and green; avoid any stalks that are tinged with brown. The stalks should break cleanly, not leaving behind strands of outer flesh. If you are lucky, you may find celery with its leaves still attached, as it is sold in France, Spain and Italy, where they understand that chopped celery leaves add vital flavour to the mixture of onions, garlic and carrots fried in oil which forms the base to so many dishes. This is a lesson which most of our retailers have yet to learn.

Grilled Celery Filled with Goat's Cheese

The familiar British cocktail snack of celery stuffed with cream cheese takes a new and rather nicer turn if the celery is grilled and finished with goat's cheese melted under the heat.

Preparation time: 5 minutes
Cooking time: 15–20 minutes
Grade: easy

Suggested accompaniment: crusty brown bread

8 thick stalks of celery olive oil 8oz (225g) goat's cheese	freshly ground black pepper walnuts (*optional*)

- Pre-heat the grill to maximum.
- Wash the celery well and remove the tightly curled green end, leaving the wider, flatter base. Turn the celery rounded side up and brush with oil. Grill for 10 minutes, until lightly browned on the surface. Now turn the celery over and spread goat's cheese into the concave surface. Season with plenty of pepper and return to the grill. Cook for another 5–10 minutes, until the cheese is melted and lightly browned on the surface. Sprinkle with pieces of walnut if you have them, and serve.

Celery Heart and New Potato Salad

This salad of warm soft potatoes and cold crunchy celery dressed in double cream is very simple and rather luxurious. It needs a slice or two of ham to turn it into a main meal.

Preparation time: 5 minutes to assemble the salad
Cooking time: as long as it takes the potatoes to cook
Grade: basic

Suggested accompaniment: a few slices of good ham

1lb (450g) small new potatoes, preferably a waxy salad variety
2 large celery hearts
4fl oz (125ml) double cream
1 teaspoon Dijon mustard

salt and freshly ground black pepper
1 tablespoon white wine vinegar

- Scrub the potatoes and boil them in salted water until tender. Meanwhile finely chop the washed celery. As soon as the potatoes are cool enough to handle, slice them roughly and mix them with the celery.
- Whip the cream with the mustard and seasoning. Mix in the vinegar and pour over the salad.

CHICKPEAS

Although dried chickpeas soaked and cooked at home may have a better texture, their preparation is a time-consuming process and nine times out of ten no one will know yours came out of a tin. Process tinned chickpeas, tahina, olive oil, garlic and plenty of lemon juice and you will have a hoummos much improved on the shop-bought variety. Cook tinned chickpeas with flavouring agents such as garlic and olive oil, ginger and chilli, or tomato paste and rosemary and they will soon lose their tinned characteristics.

The only dishes to beware of when using tinned chickpeas are those in which there is no cooking, and therefore no opportunity for the chickpeas to absorb extra flavourings, such as salads, or where the liquid in which the chickpeas are cooked forms an integral element of the dish, as in the classic vegetable stew to accompany couscous. If you are using tinned chickpeas for salads, heat them with some olive oil, a scrap of garlic and some herbs and allow to cool in the oil, which can then be used for the dressing.

Pasta and Chickpea Soup

This is one of those soups which is so substantial that it is a main dish in itself. Only an Italian would think it a first course, to be followed by a piece of meat or fish. Or, rather, an Italian peasant who had put in a hard morning's work in the fields, and was looking forward to a siesta after lunch. The more sedentary will find this an ideal lunch or supper for a cold winter's day when you have to rely on store-cupboard ingredients. In Italy the pot would have been boiling all morning while the chickpeas cooked, but tinned ones will do well. Don't leave out the authentic touch of a swirl of extra virgin olive oil at the end, which adds fruitiness and depth to the soup. You could also add some freshly grated Parmesan.

Preparation time: 5 minutes
Cooking time: 15–20 minutes
Grade: basic

Suggested accompaniment: a post-prandial siesta

2 fat cloves of garlic	2³/₄ pints (1.5 litres) chicken or vegetable stock
1 large sprig of fresh rosemary, or ¹/₂ teaspoon dried rosemary	2 bay leaves
2 small dried red chillies	8oz (225g) dried pasta (*use a shaped pasta rather than a long thin one*)
1 dessertspoon tomato paste	
3 tablespoons olive oil	salt and freshly ground black pepper
14oz (400g) tin chickpeas	extra virgin olive oil

● Crush the garlic cloves, remove the rosemary needles from the stalk if you have the fresh herb, and chop up the chillies. Dissolve the tomato paste in a little warm water. In a large pan, heat the olive oil over a moderate heat and add the garlic, rosemary and chillies. Cook, stirring, for a couple of minutes, then add the diluted tomato paste. Stir well together then pour in the contents of the tin of chickpeas and the stock. Add the bay leaves. Turn up the heat and bring to the boil. As soon as the liquid is bubbling add the pasta and cook uncovered until the pasta is ready, 10–15 minutes according to the type of pasta. Taste to check whether the pasta is ready and season (if you add seasoning earlier you may end up with too salty a liquid as the stock reduces). Serve the soup with a bottle of extra virgin olive oil, so that each diner can stir a little into the soup.

Sour Chickpea Curry

My favourite snack in India is sour chickpeas, sold wrapped in twists of paper on just about every street corner. This curry version is more liquid than the snack variety but still has that essential sourness, provided by the last-minute addition of fresh lemon and lime juice, as well as onion, chilli and grated ginger. Despite the fact that it originates from a hot climate, this is a good dish for a cold day. Don't be put off by the long list of ingredients – it is essentially a store-cupboard meal.

Preparation time: 15 minutes
Cooking time: 30 minutes
Grade: easy

Suggested accompaniments: rice and poppadums

4 onions	3 teaspoons ground cumin
4 cloves of garlic	3 teaspoons ground coriander
1in (2.5cm) piece of fresh ginger	1 teaspoon freshly ground black
1 lime	pepper
2 lemons	stick of cinnamon
1 fresh green chilli (*or more to taste*)	$^1/_4$ teaspoon cayenne pepper
$^1/_2$ teaspoon salt	14oz (400g) tin chopped plum
1 teaspoon garam masala	tomatoes
2 tablespoons vegetable oil	2 x 14oz (400g) tins chickpeas

● Chop 3$^1/_2$ onions coarsely and the remaining $^1/_2$ finely. Finely chop the garlic. Peel the ginger and grate the flesh. Squeeze the juice from the lime and lemons. Deseed the chilli and chop the flesh finely.

● Mix together the finely chopped $^1/_2$ onion, the grated ginger, lime and lemon juice, chilli, salt and garam masala. Set aside (this mixture is added at the end of cooking to give the vital sourness).

● Heat the oil in a large pan over a moderately high heat. Fry the onions and garlic, stirring regularly, for 10 minutes until lightly browned. Now add all the spices and stir well. Pour in the contents of the tin of tomatoes and the 2 tins of chickpeas (including their liquid). Stir again, turn the heat down so that the contents of the pan just simmer, cover, and leave to cook for 15 minutes.

● Add the sharpening-up mixture and stir in well, then leave to simmer, uncovered this time, for another 5 minutes. You can serve this dish straight from the heat, but it is also good warm.

CHICORY

Chicory should be white with a touch of green (ignore any that is tinged with brown) and firm to the touch. It should never be boiled or it will become waterlogged. If you plan to serve chicory Belgian-style, wrapped in ham and topped with a cheese sauce, fry it in butter or braise it in a little stock before baking it in the oven. Chicory is excellent for winter salads – look out especially for the red-tinged chicory of Treviso, which is very popular in Italy.

Salad of Chicory, Blue Cheese, Walnuts and Orange

Crisp, slightly bitter chicory can stand quite on its own for a salad, but for a more substantial dish add some salty blue cheese, a few sweet oranges and a handful of walnuts.

Preparation time: 10 minutes
Cooking time: none
Grade: basic

Suggested accompaniment: good bread

4 oranges	2oz (55g) shelled chopped walnuts
4 heads of chicory	freshly ground black pepper
6oz (175g) blue cheese, such as Stilton, Fourme d'Ambert, Bleu de Bresse	walnut or extra virgin olive oil

- Peel the oranges and remove any pith. Slice across into thin rounds, taking care not to lose any juice. Roughly chop the chicory and crumble the cheese.
- To assemble the salad, mix together the rounds of orange, the cheese and the chicory, together with any orange juice. Stir in the walnuts, add plenty of pepper and dribble with your chosen oil.

Braised Chicory

Chicory braised in the oven with orange juice and good stock, until the vegetable is lightly caramelized, makes a good light supper dish, perhaps with a slice of ham, as well as a splendid side dish for roast pork.

Preparation time: 5 minutes
Cooking time: 40–45 minutes
Grade: basic

Suggested accompaniments: bread and ham

4 large heads of chicory	2oz (55g) butter
4fl oz (125ml) reduced beef stock	salt and freshly ground black
juice of 1 orange	pepper

● Pre-heat the oven to 180°C/350°F/Gas Mark 4. Cut the chicory in half lengthways. Arrange it in an earthenware dish in which it will just fit, pour over the stock and orange juice, dot with the butter and add seasoning. Bake uncovered in the oven for 40–45 minutes, turning half-way through, until the chicory is tender and slightly caramelized and the stock and orange juice have reduced to a syrup.

CUCUMBER

Cucumber is usually eaten raw in Britain but it is even better cooked (as it always is in China), provided it has been well salted first to firm it up and that the cooking is brief. When buying cucumber, make sure you give the vegetable a squeeze to ensure it is firm – the slightest hint of sogginess and it should be rejected.

Cucumber with Noodles in Peanut and Sesame Sauce

This Korean-style noodle dish can be served cold as well as hot, but in that case don't add the dressing and the final sprinkling of toasted sesame seeds until just before serving.

Preparation time: 15 minutes
Cooking time: 10 minutes
Grade: moderate

Suggested accompaniment: none needed

1 large cucumber	pinch of sugar
salt	2 tablespoons dark soy sauce
10oz (280g) Chinese egg noodles	cayenne pepper
2 tablespoons sesame seeds	2 cloves of garlic
4 tablespoons sesame oil	1 tablespoon groundnut oil
1 tablespoon white wine vinegar	2 tablespoons peanuts

- Slice the cucumber into thin slices, about 2in (5cm) long. Sprinkle them well with salt and leave them to drain for 10 minutes.
- Cook the noodles according to the instructions on the packet (one of the best ways is to plunge them into fiercely boiling water, take the pan off the heat, and leave them to stand for 4 minutes), and drain.
- Toast the sesame seeds in a dry frying-pan until they start to pop, taking care that they do not burn. Make a dressing with 3 tablespoons of the sesame oil, 1 tablespoon of the toasted sesame seeds, crushed, the vinegar, sugar, soy sauce and cayenne pepper to taste.
- Peel the garlic and chop into fine flakes. Rinse the cucumber and pat dry. Heat the oil over a high heat in a wok and toss the garlic for 1 minute. Now add the strips of cucumber and stir-fry for 2 minutes before adding the peanuts. Cook for 1 more minute then add the noodles. Stir well to warm through then take off the heat.
- Pile the noodles on a serving plate, pour over the dressing, and sprinkle with the remaining sesame seeds and sesame oil.

FENNEL

Sliced fennel in lemon juice makes a nice little salad; lightly fried fennel is good with fish and pork; quartered bulbs slowly cooked in plenty of olive oil until they caramelize are an excellent accompaniment to roast chicken; and fennel is a good vegetable for a gratin. It should never be boiled, however.

When buying fennel, look out for bulbs with some of the feathery fronds still attached – these are a useful herb in their own right and it is a mystery to me why they should be removed. Look for perfectly green and white fennel, with no tinges of brown, and buy only firm bulbs.

Gratin of Fennel with Bacon

Whole chunks of vegetables roasted in an earthenware dish in a hot oven and finished with cheese and breadcrumbs make good supper dishes. Fennel is one of my favourite vegetables for this treatment. Additional flavour and sustenance can be given in the form of ham or bacon wrapped around the fennel bulb; if you are cooking for vegetarians simply leave this stage out and reduce the cooking time by 5 minutes.

Preparation time: 10 minutes
Cooking time: 30 minutes
Grade: easy

Suggested accompaniments: this is a light supper dish to which you need add only a green salad and some bread

---

6 fennel bulbs
freshly ground black pepper
12 rashers of streaky bacon (*it is vital for this recipe that the bacon should be of good quality – insipid bacon which gives off water will ruin the dish*)
3 tablespoons olive oil
2 cloves of garlic

2 dried red chillies
3oz (85g) grated hard cheese (*it is best to use a cheese which has a slightly stringy character when cooked, such as Emmenthal or Gruyère*)
2oz (55g) breadcrumbs from good-quality country bread

12 cocktail sticks

● Preheat the oven to 220°C/425°F/Gas Mark 7 and bring a large pan of salted water to the boil. Meanwhile scrub the fennel bulbs and trim them of their stalks and any discoloured outer leaves (but try to keep this to a minimum to avoid them falling apart). Cut the fennel in half vertically. When the water is boiling add the halved fennel, just bring back to the boil, and then drain. Season with plenty of black pepper.

● Trim the bacon of any rind. Wrap a rasher of bacon around each halved fennel bulb and secure with a cocktail stick. In a flame- and oven- resistant earthenware dish (metal can give an unpleasant taste to the fennel), gently heat the oil for 3 minutes with the whole unpeeled garlic cloves and the chillies. Now add the bacon-wrapped fennel bulbs and transfer the dish to the oven. Bake uncovered for 20 minutes, by which time the fennel bulbs should be fairly tender. Remove the garlic cloves and chillies from the dish and sprinkle the cheese and the breadcrumbs over the fennel. Return the dish to the oven and bake for another 10 minutes, until the cheese is melted and slightly browned and the breadcrumbs are crisp. Serve piping hot.

LEEKS

To appreciate the leek fully cook the sliced vegetable slowly in butter or oil, braise it whole in a little stock, or subject it to a fierce heat, whether sliced in a stir-fry or halved in a gratin. Don't boil it, unless you want a soggy, tasteless result – the exception is if the cooking liquid is to be an integral element of the dish. As well as a being an excellent stand-alone vegetable, the leek is an important element of flavouring for stocks and stews.

Smaller leeks are generally sweeter and less fibrous. If cooking the vegetable whole, make a deep cross at the white end and stand it in water for 20 minutes, to flush out any grit.

Leek and Parsley Strudel

Leeks make the ideal soft filling for the crisp, buttery pastry of a savoury strudel. This makes a good vegetarian main course; alternatively serve one strudel between 4 people as a starter (the quantities given here make 2 long, thin strudels).

Preparation time: 25 minutes
Cooking time: 20–25 minutes, requiring no attention
Grade: easy, if fiddly

Suggested accompaniment: a bowl of plain thick yoghurt

2lb (900g) leeks	4 tablespoons chopped flat-leaved parsley
2 cloves of garlic	salt and freshly ground black pepper
3½oz (100g) butter	
4 tablespoons vermouth or white wine	8 sheets of filo pastry

● Discard the green ends of the leeks and chop the white part into fine rings. Finely chop the garlic. Melt 1oz (30g) of butter in a large pan, add the garlic and leeks and stew gently over a low heat for 5 minutes, until the leeks are softened. Now pour in the vermouth, turn up the heat so that the liquid bubbles and continue to cook, stirring, until the mixture is nearly dry. Take off the heat and stir in the parsley and plenty of seasoning.

● Pre-heat the oven to 180°C/350°F/Gas Mark 4. Melt the remaining butter. Lay out a sheet of filo pastry, keeping the remaining sheets covered with a damp cloth, and brush all over with butter. Lay another sheet on top and repeat the process. Continue until you have used 4 sheets. Now spread half the leek and parsley mixture down one of the narrow ends of the pastry, taking care to leave a gap at each edge so that the mixture does not spill out when you roll the pastry up. Roll carefully from one end, so that you have a long sausage shape. Brush the surface with butter and lay the strudel on a baking sheet, then repeat the whole process with the rest of the ingredients.

● Bake the strudels for 20–25 minutes, until the surface is nicely browned, and serve them very hot.

Leek Gratin

One of the best and easiest of starters is leeks vinaigrette, while a gratin of leeks with Parmesan, olive oil, red wine and a final sprinkling of black olives makes a good supper dish.

Preparation time: 5 minutes
Cooking time: 30–35 minutes
Grade: easy

Suggested accompaniment: crusty brown bread

4 large leeks, 2–2³⁄₄ lb (900–1.25kg)	2oz (55g) stoned black olives
2 tablespoons olive oil	2oz (55g) fresh white breadcrumbs
1 clove of garlic	2oz (55g) grated Parmesan
freshly ground black pepper	extra virgin olive oil
4 tablespoons red wine	

● Trim the leeks of their green ends. Trim the stalk end very carefully, so that the leek still holds together when you slice it in half vertically. Wash the halved leeks.

● Pre-heat the oven to 220°C/425°F/Gas Mark 7. Heat the olive oil in a frying-pan into which all the leeks fit and fry them cut side down for 5 minutes, until lightly browned.

● Halve the garlic and rub the cut side around an earthenware gratin dish into which the leeks fit snugly side by side, then chop the garlic finely. Arrange the leeks rounded side uppermost in the dish and season with plenty of pepper. Pour over the oil from the pan and the red wine. Bake uncovered in the oven for 20 minutes.

● Roughly chop the olives. Mix together the breadcrumbs, chopped olives, chopped garlic and Parmesan. Sprinkle this mixture over the leeks and dribble over some extra virgin olive oil. Return to the oven and cook for 5–10 minutes, until the surface is lightly browned – be careful not to let it burn. Serve very hot.

LENTILS

The key to cooking lentils is fat and flavour. Although they have acquired a reputation as a vegetarian staple, lentils taste best when cooked or at least mixed with bacon, ham, sausage – something porky and slightly fatty. Roast cod on a bed of lentils cooked with bacon is splendid. But lentils don't need to be confined to side dishes – they make good casseroles and warm salads. Always use brown or green lentils, best of all those from Puy, unless the recipe specifies the red variety.

Lentil, Carrot and Bacon Casserole

Lentils, carrots and bacon are a classic combination which can be served warm with a mustardy vinaigrette as a first course, as a side dish for roast meats and sausages, or all on its own as a casserole. This is not, however, a dish for vegetarians, for if you leave out the bacon and meat stock the mixture will lose much of its savour.

Preparation time: 10 minutes
Cooking time: 45 minutes
Grade: basic

Suggested accompaniment: baked potatoes

1½lb (675g) medium-sized carrots	10oz (280g) green lentils
8oz (225g) smoked streaky bacon, preferably in one or two thick slices, or ready-prepared lardons	(*preferably Puy*)
	salt and freshly ground black pepper
2 cloves of garlic	2 bay leaves
2¾ pints (1.5 litres) chicken stock	1 tablespoon of Dijon mustard
1oz (30g) butter	

- Scrub and dice the carrots. Remove the rind, but not the fat, from the bacon and cut the flesh into lardons. Peel the garlic and chop finely. Bring the stock to the boil.
- In a large heavy-based lidded casserole, melt the butter with the bacon and garlic. Cook over a medium heat for 5 minutes, then add the carrots and lentils. Stir well to coat in the fat, season with salt (go easy if you are using stock cubes) and pepper, pour over the boiling stock and tuck in the bay leaves. Regulate the heat so that the liquid is at a fast simmer, cover, and leave to cook for 35 minutes. Remove the lid and take out a ladleful of hot liquid, mix it with the mustard and return to the pan. Bubble hard for 2–3 minutes, check seasoning and serve.

Lentil and Ham Salad in a Roast Garlic and Coriander Dressing

The secret of a good lentil salad is always to dress the lentils when they are hot, even if the salad is to be served cold. This allows the lentils to absorb the flavours and the oil. One of my favourite dressings is made with the pulp from roasted cloves of garlic, mixed with plenty of olive oil, a few spices and lots of coriander.

Preparation time: 5 minutes
Cooking time: 30 minutes, 15 minutes before serving
Grade: basic

Suggested accompaniment: plenty of good bread

12oz (350g) green lentils
  (*preferably Puy*)
1 whole head of garlic
8 tablespoons extra virgin olive
  oil
2 tablespoons sherry vinegar
1 teaspoon paprika

$\frac{1}{2}$ teaspoon cumin
2 tablespoons fresh coriander
salt and freshly ground black
  pepper
4 slices *jamon serrano* or Parma
  ham

- Pick over the lentils and wash them well. Bring a large pan of salted water to the boil and cook the lentils at a fierce boil for 20–25 minutes, until tender.
- Meanwhile, split the head of garlic into individual cloves, but do not peel them. Roast in an oven pre-heated to 180°C/350°F/Gas Mark 4 for 15 minutes, until soft to the touch. To make the dressing, squeeze out the pulp from the papery skins of the garlic. Add the oil, vinegar, paprika, cumin, coriander, and salt and pepper to taste, and purée to a smooth mixture.
- Drain the lentils and pour the dressing over them. Chop the ham into bite-sized pieces and mix in. Leave to stand for 15 minutes or so for the flavours to combine, and serve warm.

MUSHROOMS

Perhaps a campaign similar to that run on behalf of the tomato should be started for the mushroom. Where has the flavour gone? The tiny, perfectly white cultivated mushrooms that are most commonly seen taste of nothing at all – their purpose appears purely decorative. To be fair, the fault may be with the consumer who continues to buy these pretty, insipid little things rather than with the supermarkets, who now stock shaggy field mushrooms with their almost black undersides, brown shiitake and grey-pink oyster mushrooms, all of which have that distinctive woody taste. In the autumn season, we can now even find delicious wild mushrooms such as ceps and chanterelles.

The meaty texture and powerful flavour of good mushrooms make them ideal candidates for vegetarian main courses; non-vegetarians will find a little bacon further enhances the taste. My favourite snack is mushrooms fried in butter and piled on toast.

Nepali Mushroom Curry

Mushrooms are very popular in Nepal in the summer months, when they can be gathered from the hills. One of the books I bought in Kathmandu, *The Joys of Nepalese Cooking* by Indra Majupuria, has the following worrying instructions amongst its excellent recipes: 'The second method of detecting poisonous mushrooms from non-poisonous ones is to use a silver spoon. If the spoon with which the mushroom is turned over gets a black coating on it then the mushroom is poisonous.'

The first method hardly gives more confidence – apparently if the turmeric you have rubbed into your mushrooms turns black after 10 minutes, you should beware.

I ate several mushroom curries in Nepal and never suffered any ill-effects, so presumably the methods work. For the British cook using cultivated mushrooms, the worries disappear.

Preparation time: 20 minutes
Cooking time: 20 minutes
Grade: moderate

Suggested accompaniment: boiled Basmati rice and pickles

1¼lb (550g) mushrooms	*don't have mustard oil, use vegetable oil)*
1½in (4cm) piece of ginger	2 teaspoons fenugreek seeds
3 cloves of garlic	½ teaspoon turmeric
4 small dried red chillies	4 floz (125ml) water
½ teaspoon coarse salt	
2 tablespoons mustard oil (*if you*	

- Wash the mushrooms and slice them across finely. Peel the ginger and garlic. Process the ginger, garlic, chillies and salt to a paste with a tablespoon or so of water – add just enough to produce a smooth paste. If you don't have a processor, use a pestle and mortar, which will take 5 minutes extra.
- Heat the mustard oil over a high heat and add the fenugreek seeds. When they start to pop add the paste – stand well back, as the oil will spit. Cook, stirring, for 1 minute, then add the mushrooms and turmeric. Stir well to make sure all the mushrooms are coated with the spice mixture, pour in the water, and bring to the boil. Now turn the heat down to medium, cover the pan, and cook for 15 minutes.
- Take off the lid and boil hard to reduce the liquid – the curry should be almost dry. Serve very hot.

Baked Field Mushrooms Stuffed with Potatoes, Garlic and Onion

Shaggy brown field mushrooms are ideal for baking, having a firm, meaty texture. For a substantial vegetarian main course, stuff the caps with a garlicky, slightly spicy potato and onion mixture.

Preparation time: 20 minutes
Cooking time: 20–25 minutes
Grade: easy

Suggested accompaniment: none needed

16 large field mushrooms	salt and freshly ground black pepper
4 large firm potatoes	1 teaspoon paprika
2 onions	good pinch of cayenne pepper
4 cloves of garlic	4 tablespoons olive oil

- Wash the mushrooms well. Remove the stalks and chop them coarsely. Peel the potatoes and cut the flesh into small dice. Grate the onions and finely chop the garlic.
- Turn the oven on to heat up to 180°C/350°F/Gas Mark 4. Bring a large pan of salted water to the boil and boil the potato pieces for 5 minutes, adding the grated onion for the last minute. Drain well.
- In a large bowl mix the potatoes and onions with the garlic and chopped mushroom stalks. Season very well and add the paprika and cayenne.
- Lay the mushrooms caps underside up on an oiled baking tray. Pile the potato mixture into the caps and dribble over the oil. Bake in the pre-heated oven for 20–25 minutes, until the caps are tender.

Penne with Mushrooms and Bacon

This is no more than a fricassée of mushrooms, garlic and bacon stirred into pasta, but as with so many Italian dishes the simplicity of its parts combines to a rather special whole – especially if you have wild mushrooms to hand.

Preparation time: 10 minutes
Cooking time: 15 minutes
Grade: easy

Suggested accompaniment: Parmesan

8oz (225g) mushrooms (*you can use slightly less if you have wild mushrooms*)
2 cloves of garlic
4oz (115g) pancetta or smoked streaky bacon

12–16oz (350–450g) penne
4 tablespoons of olive oil
salt and freshly ground black pepper
parsley

- Wipe the mushrooms clean with a damp cloth and slice them thickly. Peel the garlic and chop finely. Remove the rind from the bacon and dice the flesh.
- Bring a large pan of salted water to the boil and cook the penne according to the instructions on the packet.
- Meanwhile gently heat the oil with the bacon in a large frying-pan. After 5 minutes turn up the heat to medium and add the garlic. Toss for 2 minutes then stir in the mushrooms, together with plenty of seasoning. Continue to cook, stirring, for 3 or 4 minutes, until the mushrooms start to wilt.
- Drain the penne and toss with the mushroom mixture. Season with freshly ground black pepper, sprinkle with parsley, and serve with plenty of freshly grated Parmesan.

OKRA

The most important part of cooking okra comes in the shopping – you must be sure that your okra are young, fresh and tender, not dried out and woody. You can tell by squeezing them: the old ones will feel tough and fibrous, younger ones will be more pliable, a brighter green, and may even ooze a little juice. Okra are one of the best vegetables for a main course, for they are very filling. Note that when preparing okra you should always wash them before chopping them up, not afterwards.

Okra and Tomato Stew

Okra are very popular in the Caribbean, from where this recipe originates. Typically they would be served as a side dish but this way of preparing them also makes a good vegetarian main course. If you want an authentically Caribbean flavour, increase the amount of chilli, or use the very hot bell chilli peppers.

Preparation time: 15 minutes
Cooking time: 25–30 minutes
Grade: easy

Suggested accompaniment: plain boiled long-grain rice

2lb (900g) okra
1 large Spanish onion
2 fat cloves of garlic
2 small fresh red chillies (*or more if you like*)
2 tablespoons vegetable oil
4 tablespoons water

2 x 14oz (400g) tins plum tomatoes
good pinch of sugar
$1/2$ teaspoon dried thyme
salt and freshly ground black pepper

- Wash the okra, top and tail them well. Chop the onion coarsely, the garlic finely. Remove the seeds from the chillies and chop the flesh finely.
- Heat the oil in a large deep-sided heavy-based frying-pan. Fry the onion over a medium high heat, stirring, for 5 minutes until it is lightly browned. Now add the okra, garlic and chillies and fry for a further 3 minutes. Pour in the water and the contents of the tins of tomatoes, breaking up the tomatoes with a wooden spoon. Bring to the boil and turn down to a simmer. Add the sugar, thyme and seasoning, cover, and leave to cook for 15–20 minutes, until the okra are very tender. Check the seasoning and serve.

Okra and Lentil Curry

Southern India is the centre of vegetarianism on the subcontinent, and the dishes from the region reflect this experience in their balance of nutrients. Here okra are cooked with lentils and spices and finished with yoghurt to make an all-in-one vegetarian main course.

Preparation time: 15 minutes
Cooking time: 25–30 minutes
Grade: moderate

Suggested accompaniments: boiled Basmati rice and poppadums

1lb (450g) okra	1 teaspoon sugar
1 large onion	½ teaspoon salt
1in (2.5cm) piece of fresh ginger	4 heaped tablespoons green
3 small fresh green chillies	lentils (*you could also use yellow*
4 tablespoons vegetable oil	*Indian split peas*)
2 teaspoons whole cumin seeds	2 pints (1.2 litres) of water
2 teaspoons black mustard seeds	juice of 1 lemon
2 teaspoons ground coriander	4fl oz (125ml) thick plain
1 teaspoon turmeric	yoghurt

- Wash the okra and top and tail them. Cut each one into 2 or 3 pieces, depending on size. Peel the onion and the ginger and chop both finely. Deseed the chillies and chop them finely.
- Heat the oil in a large frying-pan and when it is hot add the spices. Fry them, stirring all the time, for 1 minute then add the chopped onion and ginger. Continue to cook, stirring, over a medium high heat for 5 minutes, then add the chopped okra, the chillies, the sugar and the salt. Stir well, then ladle in the lentils. Pour over the water, add the lemon juice and bring rapidly to the boil. Cook over a medium high heat, uncovered, until all the water has been absorbed, stirring occasionally. Now taste the lentils, if they are not quite soft enough add a little more water and continue to cook until this has been absorbed.
- When the lentils are to your satisfaction, take the dish off the heat and stir in the yoghurt before serving.

ONIONS

The onion is the base flavouring for so many dishes that it is hard to imagine cooking without it. Onions also make excellent stand-alone vegetable dishes. When buying onions, look for unwrinkled skins and squeeze them to make sure they are firm. Store onions in a dark place and discard any which have started to sprout. I usually use the large, mild Spanish onions rather than the fiercer British variety. I also keep red onions for salads.

Onion Soup

This onion soup is somewhat different from the familiar French variety. It is a creamy yellow rather than a caramelized dark brown; the taste has a light hint of Indian spices behind the predominant onion; it is made with water and yoghurt rather than beef stock; and it is topped not with croûtons and stringy cheese but with floating flecks of bright green coriander. I find it surprisingly subtle by comparison.

Preparation time: 10 minutes
Cooking time: 40 minutes
Grade: easy

Suggested accompaniment: nan bread

2lb (900g) large, mild white onions	1 teaspoon salt
3 cloves of garlic	$\frac{1}{2}$ teaspoon turmeric
1in (2.5cm) piece of fresh ginger	2 pints (1.1 litres) water
2 small dried red chillies	10fl oz (300ml) thick Greek
2 tablespoons sunflower oil	yoghurt
2 teaspoons black mustard seeds	fresh coriander

- Peel the onions and chop them into very fine half-moons. Finely chop the garlic, ginger and chillies.
- Heat the oil in a large pan and add the chopped ginger, garlic and chillies. Fry, stirring, for 3 minutes over a medium high heat, then add the mustard seeds, salt and turmeric. Fry for a further minute then add the chopped onions and stir well to coat. Pour in the water and bring to the boil, then turn the heat down so that the mixture is simmering actively. Cover and leave to cook for 30 minutes.
- By the end of the cooking time the onions should be very tender, almost creamy. Take the mixture off the heat and leave to stand, uncovered, for 5 minutes before stirring in the yoghurt (if the yoghurt is stirred in too quickly, it will curdle). Sprinkle in some fresh coriander and serve.

PEAS

Petits pois are one of the few tinned vegetables to find their way into my store-cupboard. I prefer their sweet, slightly soft nature to the frozen variety, which offer the eery combination of unnatural crispness and excessive water.

Pea and Cream Sauce for Pasta

Of course this simple sauce is at its very best when prepared with fresh peas straight from the pod, but few cooks in a hurry are going to shell several pounds of peas. Using tinned petits pois the preparation is rapid and the end result still luxurious. You could if you like add strips of cooked ham to add further flavour, but in this case I would leave out the basil. Parmesan sprinkled over the dish before serving is vital.

Preparation time: 5 minutes
Cooking time: 15 minutes
Grade: easy

Suggested accompaniment: none needed

---

1 Spanish onion	5fl oz (150ml) double cream
1oz (30g) butter	salt and freshly ground black
1 tablespoon olive oil	pepper
tagliatelle (allow 3–4oz (85–115g) per person)	a handful of fresh basil
	freshly grated Parmesan
14oz (400g) tin petits pois	

- Peel and finely chop the onion. Melt the butter over a gentle heat in a heavy based pan and add the oil. Sweat the onion for 10 minutes, until tender. Meanwhile bring the salted water for the pasta to the boil.
- Put the pasta on to cook. Drain the peas and rinse well. Add them to the butter and onion mixture and stir well to make sure all the peas are coated. Cook for a couple of minutes then pour in the cream. Season to taste, stir well, and allow the cream to bubble for a couple of minutes. Shred the basil leaves with your fingers and add to the sauce just before serving with plenty of Parmesan.

Pea Curry

The pea may not be the first vegetable that comes to mind when you think of Indian cooking, but in fact it is very much a part of the repertoire of at least the north of the subcontinent. The classic dish is *muttar paneer*, peas cooked with cottage cheese Indian-style. You can buy paneer in some large supermarkets and specialist shops, but if I happen to have some mozzarella lying around I add chunks to this dish as a substitute. Even without the cheese this mild curry is a rich dish.

Preparation time: 10 minutes
Cooking time: 10 minutes
Grade: easy

Suggested accompaniment: boiled Basmati rice

---

1 large onion
2 tablespoons ghee (*you could also use vegetable oil*)
2 x 14oz (400g) tins petit pois
2 cloves of garlic
2 small fresh green chillies (*or more to taste*)
½ teaspoon turmeric
1 teaspoon ground coriander
¼ teaspoon coarse salt
1 teaspoon garam masala
4fl oz (125ml) double cream
4fl oz (125ml) Greek yoghurt
2 tablespoons chopped fresh coriander

- Peel and chop the onion into very thin half-rings. Heat the ghee or oil over a high heat and fry the onion rapidly, until it is crisp and brown. Remove with a slotted spoon and set aside. Pour off most of the oil and discard.
- Drain the peas. Finely chop the garlic and the deseeded chillies and cook in the remaining oil for 2 minutes over a moderate heat, until the garlic is just starting to change colour. Now add the turmeric, coriander and salt and stir well. Pour in the peas, stir in the garam masala and the cream and allow to simmer for 3 minutes. Finally add the yoghurt and just warm through (be careful – although Indian yoghurt cooks well, those available here have a tendency to curdle). Take the pan off the heat, sprinkle over the coriander and the crispy onions and serve.

PEPPERS

Capsicum peppers, green, orange and red according to their ripeness, have in recent years experienced an increase in popularity in this country. This coincided with the realization that peppers are rather nicer cooked, and especially roasted, than raw, when they tend to be bitter and watery. We were a little slow to catch on to a fact that the Mediterranean nations have known for centuries, but now we have got the message, there seems to be no stopping us. It is rare to see a menu without peppers somewhere on it.

Their shape makes peppers the ideal vehicle for stuffing, usually with a rice and meat mixture, but this is a time-consuming process. For rapid suppers, combine peppers with bulky items such as burghul wheat or pasta.

Red Pepper Pilav

I prefer the texture of burghul wheat to rice in many pilavs (see carrot and cashew pilav, page 244). In this lightly spiced version the red of the peppers contrasts with the brown burghul, flecked with green parsley, making an attractive dish which is ideal for a vegetarian main course.

Preparation time: 5 minutes
Cooking time: 30 minutes, 15 minutes before serving
Grade: easy

Suggested accompaniment: this makes an excellent vegetarian main course; you can also serve it with lamb – grilled chops, for example – in which case the quantities will be sufficient for 6 people

2 onions	1 teaspoon allspice
4 red peppers	½ teaspoon ground cinnamon
2 cloves of garlic	½ teaspoon freshly ground black
2 tablespoons olive oil	pepper
10oz (280g) large-grain burghul wheat	1 teaspoon coarse salt
1 pint (600ml) water	3oz (85g) sultanas
1 teaspoon ground cumin	2 tablespoons finely chopped flat-leaved parsley

- Peel the onions and remove the core of the peppers. Coarsely chop both, and finely chop the garlic.
- In a large lidded frying-pan, heat the oil over a medium heat and fry the peppers and onions for 5 minutes. Add the garlic and continue to cook for another 5 minutes, stirring regularly. Meanwhile put the

burghul in a small-holed colander and rinse well under cold running water. Bring the water to the boil in the kettle.

- Add the rinsed burghul, the spices and the salt to the pan and cook over a medium heat for 2–3 minutes, stirring all the time. Add the sultanas, then pour the boiling water into the pan. Allow to bubble for 3 minutes then turn down to a simmer and leave to cook for 10 minutes, stirring once or twice during this time.
- After 10 minutes all the liquid should have been absorbed – if it has not, turn the heat up again for a minute or two to bubble off. Turn off the heat, cover the pan with a clean teatowel and put the lid on top. Leave to rest for 15 minutes.
- Just before serving, fluff up the pilav with a fork and stir in the parsley.

Fusilli with Roasted Red Peppers, Cumin and Pinenuts

This is a variant of a Sicilian dish, the cumin seeds betraying the island's Arab heritage. It can be served hot or cold, making a gaily coloured salad. The type of pasta is important – the crunchy cumin seeds, the pungent slivers of garlic and chilli, the fruity olive oil all become trapped in the spirals of the fusilli. Try this sauce with a smooth pasta, however, and you will end up with a pool of oil at the bottom of the serving dish.

Preparation time: none
Cooking time: 25 minutes
Grade: moderate

Suggested accompaniment: none needed

2 large red peppers	3oz (85g) Parmesan in one piece
12oz (350g) fusilli	4 tablespoons extra virgin olive oil
2 tablespoons pinenuts	grated zest of ½ a lemon, preferably unwaxed
1 dessertspoon whole cumin seeds	2 tablespoons chopped fresh flat-leaved parsley
2 fat cloves of garlic	freshly ground black pepper
2 small dried red chilli peppers	

- Pre-heat the grill to maximum and put a large pan of well-salted water on a high heat. Cut the peppers vertically into quarters and remove the core. Grill them skin side uppermost, close to the heat, until the skin is blackened (this should take about 10 minutes). Cover with a clean teatowel for 5 minutes.

- When the water is boiling, add the pasta. You can make the sauce while it is cooking. Heat a large heavy-based frying-pan over a moderate heat and when it is fairly hot add the pinenuts. Toast for 1 minute, stirring, then add the cumin seeds. Toast both together for another minute, being careful to keep stirring, then remove from the frying-pan.
- Peel the blackened skin off the peppers and cut the flesh into thin strips. Roughly chop the garlic and chilli and make thin shavings of the Parmesan. Gently heat the oil in the frying-pan and when it is hot add the garlic and chilli. Cook for 2 minutes then add the pinenuts, cumin, peppers and lemon zest. Cook for another minute to warm through.
- When the pasta is cooked (taste to check), drain it and stir in the contents of the frying-pan. Add the chopped parsley, shavings of Parmesan and plenty of black pepper and the dish is ready. If serving cold make sure you still add the sauce (but not the parsley or Parmesan) while the pasta is hot, so that it has a chance to absorb the flavours.

Green Peppers with Chilli and Scrambled Eggs

The most famous recipe for peppers and eggs may be the Basque *piperrada*, but there are similar dishes from all around the Mediterranean. Most include tomatoes in the mixture, but I find they give a slightly mushy consistency and prefer this very simple version from Turkey. Traditionally it is made with slightly hot, long green peppers – the same effect is achieved with a combination of fresh green chillies and green capsicum peppers.

Preparation time: 5 minutes
Cooking time: 15 minutes
Grade: easy

Suggested accompaniment: pitta bread

2 green peppers	2 tablespoons olive oil
2 fresh green chillies	salt
4 large eggs	

- Remove the seeds from the peppers and cut the flesh into long strips. Do the same for the chillies. Lightly beat the eggs.
- Heat the oil in a large, heavy based frying-pan over a medium heat. When it is hot, add the strips of pepper and chillies and cook, stirring, for 10 minutes, until the skin of the peppers is lightly browned and the flesh soft. Salt well, turn down the heat to low, and add the eggs. Keep stirring until the eggs are almost set and serve very hot.

POTATOES

The potato is such an everyday item that we tend to forget that it comes in so many different forms. We all know that the potato was brought to our island by Sir Walter Raleigh, but how many of us realise that he carried to his Queen the sweet potato, a quite different variety from that which was to become infamous in Irish history? Waxy salad potatoes, floury fat potatoes, taut-skinned kidney-shaped flukes from Jersey and long pinky-red sweet potatoes from warmer climates require different approaches and accompany different dishes. Whole books have been written on the subject.

For the confused, supermarkets now provide a brief description of which potato is best suited to which treatment (baking, boiling, roasting and salad potatoes being the starting point). Where necessary in my recipes, I have distinguished between the use of waxy and floury varieties. Whatever type you choose, look for potatoes which have unwrinkled skins, no brown patches and an earthy but in no way mouldy smell. Discard any that appear to be sweating and store them loose in a dark place rather than in a plastic bag. Use new potatoes as quickly as possible; if stored potatoes start to sprout, they should be rejected.

As a rule, potatoes provide the bulk to a dish and are especially good when cooked with other ingredients, for they absorb flavours wonderfully. But they are not incapable of standing alone. Baked in their jackets and topped with cheese, mashed (after being boiled in their skins) with butter, cooked in a gratin dish with cream, they are a luxury.

New Potatoes with Ham

Instead of boiling new potatoes in plain water and then adding butter or oil and flavourings, try cooking all the ingredients together, so that the potatoes have a chance to absorb the fat and the spice and the water boils down to a syrupy glaze. This is a popular way of cooking slices of old potatoes in Spain and translates well to smaller new ones. To make a more substantial country dish, small pieces of ham are added at the end of cooking – for a luxurious version, use air-dried *jamon serrano*.

Preparation time: 10 minutes
Cooking time: 20 minutes
Grade: basic

Suggested accompaniments: serve as a light supper with a green salad, or reduce the amount of ham (even leave it out altogether) and serve as a vegetable dish with a roast chicken

1½ lb (675g) small new potatoes	1 teaspoon ground cumin
1 large Spanish onion	3 tablespoons olive oil
4 slices ham	1 tablespoon chopped fresh
½ teaspoon coarse salt	coriander (*optional*)
2 teaspoons sweet paprika	freshly ground black pepper

- Scrub the potatoes and cut any large ones in half. Peel the onion and dice finely. Chop the ham coarsely.
- Put the potatoes in a heavy-based casserole (preferably earthenware) in which they will just fit in one layer. Mix together the salt, paprika, cumin and oil and pour this mixture over the potatoes. Add sufficient water just to cover.
- Bring the contents of the pan to the boil over a high heat and then turn down the heat so that the liquid simmers actively. Cook for 20 minutes, stirring occasionally, until the potatoes are tender and almost all the liquid has been absorbed. Stir in the chopped ham and the coriander, grind over some black pepper, and serve.

Kashmiri Stuffed Potatoes

Kashmiri cuisine is famous for its use of dried fruits and nuts but, in Britain at least, these are more usually associated with rich meat dishes than with the potato. Yet potatoes are one of the staples of Kashmir, and the princely cooking methods translate to it happily. This recipe is rather more complicated than many included here, as it involves several stages, but it is worth the trouble. In India the potatoes would be cooked in a mixture of yoghurt and water, but the yoghurt available here curdles if boiled, and so should be stirred in at the end of the cooking time.

Preparation time: 25 minutes
Cooking time: 20–30 minutes
Grade: moderate

Suggested accompaniment: steamed or boiled peas

8 small to medium-sized old potatoes (*use a waxy, firm variety such as Desirée*)	1 tablespoon vegetable oil
	3 tablespoons sultanas or currants
	2 tablespoons flaked almonds
1 large onion	2 heaped teaspoons garam masala
2 cloves of garlic	1 teaspoon turmeric
1in (2.5cm) piece of fresh ginger	½ teaspoon salt
1 or 2 small green chillies	1 tablespoon tomato paste
2 tablespoons chopped fresh coriander	1 pint (600ml) water
	14oz (400g) thick Greek yoghurt

- Peel the potatoes and with an apple corer make a central hole through the narrow end to within ½in (1cm) of the opposite end. Bring a large pan of water to the boil and parboil the potatoes for 3 minutes. Chop the onion, garlic, ginger, chillies and coriander very finely, reserving a few leaves of the coriander for a garnish.

- Heat the oil in a frying-pan over a medium high heat and fry the onion, ginger, garlic and chillies together for 5 minutes until lightly browned. Now add the sultanas, almonds, chopped coriander and garam masala and fry for a further minute. With a teaspoon stuff this mixture into the cavities in the potatoes, using the handle end of the spoon to pack the mixture down. Reserve any remaining stuffing.

- Mix together the turmeric, salt and tomato paste with the water. Pack the potatoes in a heavy-based pan into which they will just fit and pour over the water mixture.

- Over a high heat bring the pan to the boil, and then turn down to a steady simmer. Leave to simmer uncovered until the potatoes are tender but not falling apart – this will take between 20 and 30 minutes depending on the size of the potatoes. Make sure you turn the potatoes over half-way through, to ensure they cook evenly.

- Remove the potatoes and put to keep warm. Bring the sauce to the boil and reduce hard, until you have a slightly thick liquid. Take off the heat and stir in the yoghurt. Reheat gently for a few minutes but on no account allow to boil or the yoghurt will curdle. Serve the potatoes whole with the yoghurty sauce, sprinkled with a few leaves of coriander. The potatoes are good warm as well as piping hot.

PUMPKINS AND OTⁿ
SQUASHES

The best-known squash is the pumpkin, which can grow to
though it is at its sweetest when small. It is a vegetable es___ ___y well
understood in Italy, where it is used to make thick country soups, silky
risottos and unusual stuffings for pasta. Other squashes are now increasingly
available – look out especially for the butternut squash.

Pumpkin Risotto

A pumpkin risotto is a most sensuous
dish. The fat, juicy grains of rice, each
perfectly separate and glistening with
a coating of stock and butter, mix with
strands of yellow pumpkin flesh,
almost imperceptible individually,
which combine together to give
golden colour and sweetness to the
whole. Only an Italian could devise a
recipe which transforms such basic
ingredients to this satisfying, warming,
generally pleasing end.

Preparation time: 5 minutes provided
you have a food processor with a
grater attachment
Cooking time: 35 minutes
Grade: moderate

Suggested accompaniment: none
needed

1lb (450g) pumpkin	3oz (85g) unsalted butter
1 small onion	10oz (280g) arborio rice
2³/₄ pints (1.5 litres) chicken or vegetable stock	pinch of saffron
	3oz (85g) Parmesan cheese

● Remove the rind and seeds from the pumpkin and grate the flesh
finely (this is best achieved using a food processor). Bring a large pan
of water to the boil and blanch the pumpkin for 1 minute then drain.
Finely chop the onion. Heat the stock to just below boiling point.
● In a large heavy-based pan, melt half the butter. Gently fry the onion
for 5 minutes, until translucent. Add the rice and the grated blanched
pumpkin and stir well. Add a ladleful of hot stock and cook, stirring
occasionally, until all the liquid is absorbed. Continue this process
until the rice is plump and tender, but still with bite and all the liquid
absorbed – about 25 minutes in all, but you will have to taste to
check. Dissolve the saffron in a little hot water and stir the saffron

...d into the risotto, together with the rest of the butter. Season to taste (be careful with the salt, especially if using stock cubes), stir in the Parmesan and serve.

Pumpkin, Bacon and Tomato Sauce for Pasta

Pumpkin and pasta is a good combination – the flesh of the squash mashed with cream and nutmeg is one of my favourite fillings for ravioli. I also use pumpkin as the main ingredient of a bulky, filling pasta sauce.

Preparation time: 10 minutes
Cooking time: 30 minutes
Grade: easy

Suggested accompaniments: penne or rigatoni are good pasta to use; you should also have plenty of Parmesan

---

1lb (450g) pumpkin
6oz (175g) pancetta or smoked
  streaky bacon
1 small onion
1 clove of garlic
1 small dried red chilli

2 tablespoons olive oil
14oz (400g) tin plum tomatoes
4fl oz (125ml) red wine
salt and freshly ground black
  pepper

● Remove any rind and seeds from the pumpkin and cut the flesh into ³⁄₄in (2cm) cubes. Remove the rind from the bacon and dice the flesh. Peel the onion and garlic and chop both finely. Chop the dried chilli.
● Heat the oil in a casserole large enough to take all the ingredients. Fry the bacon, onion, garlic and chilli for 5 minutes over a medium heat, until the fat runs from the bacon and the onion is soft. Now add the cubed pumpkin and turn it in the oil for 1 minute. Pour in the contents of the tin of tomatoes, breaking up the tomatoes with a wooden spoon. Finally add the red wine and seasoning.
● Bring to the boil then simmer covered for 20–25 minutes, until the pumpkin is tender. Serve with pasta and plenty of Parmesan.

Pumpkin Soup

Pumpkin makes an exquisite velvety soup. Mixed with cream as it is prepared in France, it is an elegant starter, but this rough and ready country version from Italy is sufficiently substantial for supper.

Preparation time: 10 minutes
Cooking time: 40 minutes
Grade: basic

Suggested accompaniment: none needed

2lb (900g) pumpkin	pinch of nutmeg
1 large onion	2 $^3/_4$ pints (1.5 litres) vegetable or
3 sticks of celery, including leaves	chicken stock
if possible	4 slices of ciabatta or other
3 cloves of garlic	country bread
4 tablespoons olive oil	extra virgin olive oil
salt and freshly ground black	freshly grated Parmesan
pepper	fresh basil

- Remove the rind from the pumpkin and chop the flesh coarsely. Roughly chop the onion, the celery including the leaves and 2 cloves of garlic. Heat the oil over a gentle heat in a large heavy-based lidded casserole, and add the chopped onion, celery and garlic. Stew gently for 10 minutes, then add the chopped pumpkin and season with plenty of pepper (leave the salt until later, to adjust for the stock) and the nutmeg. Turn the pumpkin in the oil, then pour in the stock. Bring to the boil, turn down to a fast simmer, cover and leave to cook for 30 minutes or until the pumpkin is very tender. Liquidize and add salt as necessary.
- Toast the slices of bread. Cut the remaining garlic clove in half, and rub the bread with the cut side. Put a slice of bread in the bottom of each bowl, pour in the soup, dribble in a little extra virgin oil and sprinkle with Parmesan and a few shreds of basil before serving very hot.

SPINACH

Spinach should be bright green, with no yellow leaves. If packed in cellophane, make sure there is no slime around the edges of the pack and take it out of the plastic as soon as you get home. You should always buy far more spinach than you think you need, because as it wilts it reduces substantially in quantity. Before cooking pick over the leaves carefully, removing any that are discoloured, and wash very well – there is nothing worse than gritty spinach.

I prefer to cook spinach in its own juice rather than boiling it, as in this way it retains all its flavour without becoming watery. Spinach also makes good salads, but only the smallest, tenderest leaves should be used for this purpose.

Spinach and Chickpea Casserole

This is a popular dish in Spain, where small quantities of the mixture are served in little earthenware dishes as tapas. It also makes an excellent vegetarian main course. It is important that you use fresh rather than frozen spinach, as the latter gives off too much liquid during cooking.

Preparation time: 10 minutes
Cooking time: 20 minutes at least 15 minutes before serving
Grade: basic

Suggested accompaniment: the quantities given here are sufficient for a vegetarian main course, which could be served with boiled potatoes or plain rice; smaller quantities make a good spring starter, which can be served cold as well as lukewarm

3lb (1.3kg) fresh spinach	pepper
1 large Spanish onion	4 tablespoons olive oil
2 x 14oz (400g) tins chickpeas	juice of 1 lemon
salt and freshly ground black	extra virgin olive oil

- Wash the spinach very thoroughly and remove the stalks. Peel the onion, slice in half and then into very thin half-moons. Drain the chickpeas, reserving the liquid.
- In a large heavy lidded casserole, put a layer of spinach, covered with a layer of the sliced onion followed by some chickpeas. Season well. Continue the layers until all the spinach, chickpeas and onion are used up, seasoning each layer as you go and making sure you finish with spinach. Pour the reserved liquid from the chickpeas and the

olive oil into the casserole and cook, covered, for 20 minutes over a medium low heat, until the spinach and the onion are tender. Check occasionally that there is sufficient liquid and if necessary add a tablespoon or so of water. If there is any liquid remaining at the end of cooking, boil it off.

● Add lemon juice and extra virgin olive oil to taste and serve lukewarm.

Spinach and Eggs

The Florentines taught us that eggs and spinach were a good combination, but theirs is not the only way of making the dish. This version comes from the South of France. The gratin can also be served as a side dish for meat, in which case leave out the topping of eggs and increase the number stirred into the spinach.

Preparation time: 10 minutes
Cooking time: 25 minutes
Grade: easy

Suggested accompaniment: warm, crusty bread

3lb (1.3kg) fresh spinach	salt and freshly ground black
4 tablespoons olive oil	pepper
2 cloves of garlic	6 large eggs

● Wash the spinach very well and cut into strips ½in (1cm) thick, discarding the stalks. Peel the garlic and chop finely. Put the oven on to heat up to 220°C/425°F/Gas Mark 7.

● In a large heavy pan or casserole into which you can fit all the spinach, gently heat 3 tablespoons of the oil. Add the garlic and cook, stirring, until it is just beginning to colour (a minute or two). Now add the spinach and plenty of seasoning. Turn the heat up to medium and cook, stirring all the time, for 10 minutes. The spinach will first give off lots of liquid, which should be bubbled off.

● Once the spinach is dry, transfer it to a large gratin dish, preferably earthenware. Beat two of the eggs together and stir into the spinach. Break the remaining eggs over the spinach and dribble the remaining spoon of olive oil over the top. Cook in the pre-heated oven for 10 minutes, until the eggs are set.

Spicy Spinach and Potatoes

Spinach is a common vegetable in India and is cooked in many different ways with a wide selection of spices. In this dish it is bulked up with potatoes and flavoured with garlic, chilli and mustard seeds, with powerful and filling results. Frozen spinach does well here, as the liquid it gives off helps to cook the cubed potatoes.

Preparation time: 10 minutes
Cooking time: 35 minutes
Grade: easy

Suggested accompaniments: boiled Basmati rice and plain yoghurt

1½lb (675g) frozen chopped spinach	4 small dried red chillies
6 medium-sized potatoes	pinch of sugar
4 cloves of garlic	½ teaspoon coarse sea salt
4 tablespoons vegetable oil	1 tablespoon water
2 teaspoons black mustard seeds	½ a lemon

- Bring a large pan of water to the boil, plunge in the frozen spinach and drain immediately. Peel the potatoes and cut into ½in (1cm) cubes. Peel the garlic and chop finely.
- Heat the oil in a large pan and when it is very hot add the mustard seeds. As soon as they pop, add the garlic, whole chillies and potatoes and fry for 2 minutes, until the garlic is just starting to colour. Now add the spinach, sugar and salt and stir well. Finally add the water. Cover and turn down the heat to low. Cook for 30 minutes, stirring once or twice during the process and adding more liquid if necessary, until the potatoes are tender. Finish with a squeeze of lemon and serve very hot.

SWEETCORN

Rather than boiling sweetcorn, try roasting it whole or grilling it, still wrapped in its leaves, until they blacken and burn. Serve it with olive oil and coarse salt, rather than smothered in butter. Tinned sweetcorn is not a favourite of mine, being too sweet and too squidgy. It takes no time at all to scrape fresh cobs with a potato peeler for soup; the kernels do not have to be kept whole.

Sweetcorn Soup

Sweetcorn or maize, the staple of Central and South America, was particularly warmly welcomed in Spain, when the conquistadores brought it home. Much of the crop is turned into maize flour but fresh corn is popular roasted or made into soup. This rich man's version uses saffron and sherry, enriched with olive oil. To make it more substantial, add a little cooked rice.

Preparation time: 10 minutes
Cooking time: 30 minutes
Grade: basic

Suggested accompaniment: bread

---

2 tablespoons olive oil
4 sweetcorn cobs
$\frac{1}{2}$ teaspoon saffron strands
$\frac{1}{4}$ teaspoon cayenne pepper
good pinch of mace or nutmeg

$\frac{1}{2}$ teaspoon ground cinnamon
salt and freshly ground black pepper
$1\frac{1}{2}$ pints (850ml) full fat milk
1 pint (600ml) chicken stock or water
1 glass of dry sherry

● Put the olive oil in a heavy casserole over a gentle heat. Remove the outer leaves and the hairy strands from the corn and with a potato peeler scrape the kernels straight into the pan. Add the spices and plenty of seasoning and fry gently for 5 minutes. Now pour in the milk, stock or water and sherry, bring to the boil and leave to simmer actively for 25 minutes or so, until the corn is very tender. Liquidize thoroughly, return to the heat, and boil uncovered for a few minutes to reduce. Check seasoning and serve with a jug of oil for everyone to pour a little into their bowl of soup.

TOMATOES

At last we seem to be getting somewhere in the search for flavoursome tomatoes, which has been a constant gripe of British food writers for decades. Supermarkets now stock Italian plum tomatoes for cooking, and are encouraging some growers to return to the old-fashioned varieties which may not be such good croppers but have that all-important taste. They are worth the extra expense.

Tomatoes Stuffed with Tuna, Anchovy and Egg

This recipe for cold stuffed tomatoes comes from Nice and uses two of that city's favourite ingredients, preserved tuna and anchovies. You will be rewarded if you buy these two store-cupboard items with care: anchovies preserved in salt are better than those in oil and are now available in some supermarkets as well as in Italian delicatessens; tuna should be preserved in good-quality oil rather than in brine. In this recipe, soft-boiled eggs are used to bind the tuna and anchovy into a paste. You could also mix the two fish with cooked rice, if you happen to have some available.

Preparation time: 15 minutes
Cooking time: none
Grade: basic

Suggested accompaniment: serve with bread as a light meal, or as part of a selection of salads

6 large, firm tomatoes	3 eggs
7oz (200g) tin tuna in oil	1 lemon
2oz (55g) tin anchovies	freshly ground black pepper

- Cut the tomatoes in half horizontally, scoop out the flesh and discard. Strain the oil from the tuna and the anchovies, or rinse them under cold running water if they have been preserved in salt.
- Boil the eggs for 3 minutes. Run the boiled eggs under the cold tap and peel. Reserve one anchovy fillet and process the remainder in a food processor (or use a pestle and mortar with the tuna and the soft-boiled eggs, to give a slightly chunky consistency. Add lemon juice and black pepper to taste, and stuff the tomato shells with the mixture. Decorate each stuffed tomato with a little piece of the remaining anchovy.

Tomatoes Stuffed with Chickpeas

In this Middle Eastern version of stuffed tomatoes the use of whole rather than powdered spices gives crunch to the stuffing, and the chickpeas provide substance.

Topped off with herby yoghurt, this dish is a favourite vegetarian main course, especially good in summer, but you could also serve one tomato per person for a starter.

Preparation time: 10 minutes
Cooking time: 8 minutes frying plus 20–25 minutes in the oven
Grade: easy

Suggested accompaniment: flat middle Eastern bread or boiled Basmati rice into which you have stirred a few sultanas, a handful of herbs and a dribble of extra virgin olive oil

---

6 large, firm beef tomatoes
1 very large or 2 medium-sized onions
2 fat cloves of garlic
2 tablespoons olive oil
4 teaspoons whole cumin seeds
2 teaspoons whole fennel seeds
2 teaspoons tomato paste

14oz (400g) tin chickpeas
a pinch of sugar
salt and freshly ground black pepper
a handful of fresh herbs (*chives, coriander or flat-leaved parsley*)
7oz (200g) thick Greek yoghurt

- Pre-heat the oven to 180°C/350°F/Gas Mark 4. Halve the tomatoes horizontally, with a teaspoon scoop out the centres and reserve them. Finely chop the onion(s) and garlic.
- Heat the oil over a medium high flame and fry the onion for 5 minutes, stirring occasionally, until lightly browned. Now add the chopped garlic and the whole spices and fry, stirring, for a further minute or two before adding the tomato paste, the drained chickpeas and the reserved centres of the tomatoes. Stir well, take off the heat and add the sugar. Season with salt and black pepper.
- Lay the tomatoes hollowed side up on an ovenproof dish and pile the stuffing into the centres. Bake in the pre-heated oven for 20–25 minutes, until the tomatoes are soft.
- Stir the chopped herbs into the yoghurt, together with seasoning to taste. Put the herb and yoghurt mix on the table, for diners to spoon over their tomatoes.

Chinese Stewed Tomatoes

This peasant recipe from China brings out the all too elusive taste of tomato from the meaty beef varieties in our shops. The secret is the use of dripping or poultry fat, which emulsifies with the soy sauce and tomato juice to form a thick sauce (the Chinese would use lard, but I am not a fan of our commercially produced varieties). The result is surprisingly substantial.

Preparation time: 10 minutes
Cooking time: 5 minutes
Grade: easy

Suggested accompaniment: boiled rice

6 large firm beef tomatoes	1 tablespoon white sugar
6 spring onions	3 tablespoons soy sauce
2 tablespoons of beef dripping, or duck or goose fat	1 teaspoon coarse salt

- Skin the tomatoes by pouring boiling water over them. Chop each peeled tomato into quarters, or 6 sections if they are very large. Roughly chop the spring onions, including the green ends.
- Melt the fat in a pan large enough to take all the tomatoes flat. When the fat is very hot, add the chopped spring onions and turn to coat. Immediately afterwards put in the tomatoes and again turn to coat in the fat. Now add the remaining ingredients and continue to fry over a medium high heat for 2–3 minutes, until the tomatoes have just started to go soft on the outside and there is plenty of juice. Serve very hot.